Solihull Sixth Form College	The Learning Cer	
Return by the last date stamped	Don't forget!	
28 JUN 2002	25 JUN 2000	
27 SEP 2002		
11. NOV. 2002		
-7. FEB. 2003		
-1. MAY 2003		
26. JUN. 2003		
-9. OCT. 2003		
16. JUN. 2004		
15. OCT. 2004		
26/11/04.		
-3. MAY 2005		
24 JUN 2005		
29/6/07		
Ask to renew, by phone 0121 704 2581	Or by bringing your id to the reception desk	Don't forget!

D1491968

CHECKED   JUN 2008

CHECKED -- AUG 2002

CHILDREN'S VIEWS ABOUT TELEVISION

Children's Views About Television

BARRIE GUNTER
Independent Television Commission

JILL McALEER
Royal Borough of Kensington and Chelsea

BRIAN CLIFFORD
Polytechnic of East London

Ashgate

Aldershot • Brookfield USA • Singapore • Sydney

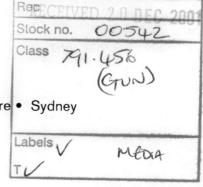

© Barrie Gunter, Jill McAleer, Brian Clifford 1991

Published by
Ashgate Publishing Limited
Gower House
Croft Road
Aldershot
Hants GU11 3HR
England

Ashgate Publishing Company
Old Post Road
Brookfield
Vermont 05036
USA

Reprinted 1998

A CIP catalogue record for this book is available from the British Library and the US Library of Congress.

ISBN 1 85628 069 1

Printed in Great Britain by Biddles Ltd
Guildford and King's Lynn

Contents

Preface

Children's Views About Television explores the things children themselves have to say about the television programmes they watch. For all that has been written about young viewers' responses to television, and there is a great deal of published and unpublished material on this subject, there have been few studies of children's opinions about the full range of programmes typically on offer on the major television channels each day of the week. More often, the focus of attention has tended to be on specific issues or types of programme content.

This book is not about the effects that television may have on children. Instead it concentrates on children's impressions and opinions about what they have watched. In taking this approach, intriguing insights are revealed concerning children's involvement with and understanding of television programmes, and indeed, in a broader sense, the role of television in their lives.

It is clear that children watch television for many different reasons. They recognise different qualities and attributes across different types of programmes. Even within a particular programme type, however, children, even at primary school, can articulate varying tastes, interests and preferences.

The research is almost entirely qualitative and is built upon the nature of the quotes and comments children themselves supplied, rather than upon quantitative measures of levels of agreement with specific points of view. The work reported here represents part of a project funded by the Independent Broadcasting Authority and carried out under the direction of Brian Clifford at the Polytechnic of East London.

BG, JM, BC

1 Television viewing and children

A great deal has been written, from learned academic texts to sensationalist newspaper articles, about the role of television in children's lives and various, supposed effects it may have on their social attitudes and behaviour. The concerns that children may watch too much television or be exposed to programmes which show things likely to upset or harm them have been discussed far and wide. There is a pervading, largely middle-class parental view that television is bad for children. The violence shown in popular television series is believed to play a significant part in encouraging children to adopt aggressive tendencies from their early years and contributes in later life to delinquency.

Television is seen as being intellectually limiting. Watching is perceived to be a passive activity and that passivity then extends to other areas of the child's life. Television stops children reading, learning to play a musical instrument, or simply talking among themselves and hence developing important conversation skills. But have its critics always been fair to television? Are the accusations frequently levelled against the world's most popular mass medium justified?

The answer to such questions we believe is that television has not always been treated fairly. Criticisms of its impact on children are one-sided and often exhibit a poor understanding of how children actually watch and respond to programmes. Looked at thoroughly, it soon becomes clear that television can have positive as well as negative effects on viewers - young and old. Television watching does not invariably or inevitably turn children into passive zombies; it can stimulate and entertain them. Furthermore, simply because children enjoy watching television does not mean that they don't spend time on other things such as reading or other hobbies and active

1

pursuits. Indeed, television can actively encourage children to read or take up other pursuits, especially if such things have been covered on television. In the end, much depends on how television is used by children. As we will see, children, as they grow older, become quite sophisticated viewers, who have well-formed viewing tastes and opinions about programmes.

No one, who makes a proper study of the viewing figures, could deny that children do spend a sizeable portion of their waking lives watching television. Television is readily available in nearly every family household, and many families have two or three or even more sets scattered throughout the home, both upstairs and downstairs. But not all children are heavy viewers. Some children watch television only sparingly, while many others watch only moderate amounts. It is true that the average child up to the age of 15 watches around 23 hours a week, or more than three hours each day. But this needs to be considered in a wider context.

Up to the age of 10, children do most of their viewing between 4 pm and 6 pm - the time, after school, when children have their own programmes on both BBC and ITV. Teenagers tend to switch their viewing from children's programmes to family and adult entertainment and this means that much of their viewing takes place after 6 pm. However, this age-group watches less television in general than younger children anyway.

Thus, the picture which emerges is not one of viewing inertia or passive watching for hours on end among all children. Patterns of viewing change with age, as both programme preferences and time allotted to watching the box alter. That children are not irretrievably hooked on the tube is corroborated further by the seasonal fluctuations in viewing. Children watch far less television when the weather is fine. The child audience drops by around a fifth in July compared to December. Adult audiences drop in the summer as well, but not quite so much.

Concerns about the effects of television on children have likewise concentrated on the negative side of the story. The focus on the supposed harms of television has distracted attention away from the good that television brings into the lives of children. Sadly lacking from critiques of television is a thorough analysis of children's responses to the rich variety of programmes which typically characterize their normal viewing diets.

To worry about the possible harmful effects of a single programme ignores the fact that children usually watch several programmes during a single session of television watching, which between them may provide a variety of forms of entertainment, drama and edification. The extent to which a single episode or portrayal within an episode will have any lasting effects on the child viewer, once it has been diluted by the surrounding programme material is rarely, if ever, considered.

This is not to make excuses for television - there *are* times when a child may be exposed to something which it finds upsetting. But it is important when analysing the impact of television to reflect on the way in which children normally watch programmes.

Children's attitudes towards television and their motives for watching it are important factors underlying their reactions to programmes. Children often treat television as a friendly presence in their lives. It is a convenient source of pleasure and amusement, a time-filler, and something from which they can learn. It brings companionship through inviting young viewers' vicarious involvement in the lives and problems of television characters. It can take them to places and introduce them to areas of life they might never experience directly themselves.

Television's near universality makes it an area of life which nearly all children have in common. It thus provides a common talking point. Far from inhibiting conversation, television provides something to talk about. What happened on television last night is a source of today's conversation in school. Television creates its own subculture of conversation. To be unable to discuss what happened in last night's episode of *Neighbours* or *Moonlighting* means being excluded from the in-crowd. This is not to say that children's lives revolve around the world of television; they don't. Other areas of experience are important too. Life's priorities change dramatically through primary and secondary school years. The latter developments are reflected in changing viewing patterns, tastes and preferences as children grow older.

Nevertheless, while programme favourites vary with maturity, television remains a central reference point to which children and teenagers return in search of a variety of enduring and transient gratifications.

Children don't simply watch television impassively. One critical view of the box, as we have noted already, is that it breeds physical and mental passivity in young viewers. While overindulgence in watching cannot be construed as a good thing, neither does it represent the norm. Young people generally watch television for a reason and not just simply to kill time. Television can serve a number of important needs. It provides entertainment and a source of distraction or temporary respite from the problems of everyday life. But it also has a range of other positive functions. Television's fictional enactments can offer insights into ways of coping (or not coping) with personal problems with family, friends, emotions and the pressures of life. Magazine programmes give advice and information about health and medical matters, consumer affairs, holidays, gardening and other practical subjects. Documentaries inform about the latest developments in science and technology. News programmes provide regular updates on the latest international, national and local happenings.

When we take a considered look at children's use of television, we begin to see that it is a far more varied and complex process than often assumed. Not only does viewing behaviour vary quite a lot among children, but also what children have to say about programmes can reveal insights and opinions which become ever-more mature as they grow up.

It is seldom that children's views about television are examined in any detail. Yet, with increasing age, children become more articulate about television and demonstrate through their own remarks that they know when to take programmes seriously or not.

Scope of the Study

This book then, makes some attempt to redress the balance by critically examining a range of comments made by children themselves about the kinds of programmes they like to watch. These comments were obtained from a series of discussions carried out with groups of children aged 7-16 in the

3

latter half of 1988. The children who took part (384 in total) were all attending schools in an outer London suburb, which contained a wide ethnic and social mix. This figure of 384 includes 48 youngsters who were asked for their views about television advertising; the findings from these discussions are not reported in this book. They were interviewed in groups of six, three girls and three boys in each group, by an experienced interviewer who was also a qualified teacher and therefore used to talking to children. Each group ran for approximately one hour and was audio-taped throughout.

Although some children initially were wary of having their opinions recorded, much of their nervousness disappeared after the first few minutes. Two factors appeared to contribute to the relaxed atmosphere that developed for much of the discussion time. First, the children were interviewed in their school environment so that they would be in familiar surroundings; they were also with their own classmates with whom they had a long established rapport. Secondly, all the discussions followed a similar structure in that initially each child was asked about the kinds of viewing equipment to which they had access, i.e. the number of videos and TVs in their own household and which rooms they were situated in. In addition to this, they were also questioned about the number of hours they spent watching television and which member of the household tended to have control of the set and therefore was responsible for deciding which programme the family was likely to view. Not only did this line of questioning provide interesting background material as to children's viewing behaviour, it also acted as an "ice-breaker". These initial questions were all ones that even the youngest children were capable of answering, so that by the time the discussion moved on to specific programme areas, they had begun to open up and relax and were less reticent about saying what they thought. In fact, by the end of each discussion, many children spontaneously expressed regret that it was all over and clamoured to continue.

Use of TV Set
As can be seen from the following table, watching television is an important part of children's lives, with the majority of the youngsters we spoke to maintaining that they viewed for approximately 4 hours a day. This was slightly higher than the national average of 3-3½ hours a day[1]. In many households there was more than one television set and the older children in particular, often claimed to have four of five sets at home.

In all, 202 out of the total 384 claimed to have a personal set in their own bedroom. This ownership of a personal set tended to apply to boys more than girls. In fact, many of the girls we spoke to stated that their brothers had their own televisions whereas they were not so fortunate, although very few of them seemed perturbed by this obvious sexual discrimination. However, the majority of those with their own sets still preferred to view the main television with the rest of the household, regarding the activity as an integral part of family life. These children stated that they used their own sets for late night viewing in bed or when there was something on that they were particularly interested in, but that no-one else wanted to watch, although there was the odd isolated individual (notably within the younger teen groups) who claimed to view on their own every night. Only 30 children had no video, but in contrast to this some households (once again, this was more often claimed among older children) had more than one. This proportion of video recorder ownership (around 92% of the sample) exceeds the national average for households with children (73%)[2].

TABLE 1.1 VIEWING EQUIPMENT AND VIEWING HOURS

	Primary School Children				Secondary School Children			
	7-8s	8-9s	9-10s	10-11s	11-12s	12-13s	13-14s	14-15s
Claimed amount of viewing (hrs/day)								
0 - 2	6	3	3	3	5	6	6	6
2 - 4	13	12	30	21	23	48	29	15
4 - 6	12	15	9	13	21	21	27	8
6+	0	0	0	1	4	3	11	7
Number of TV sets in household								
1	5	3	12	4	4	3	0	0
2	16	14	17	21	21	27	21	5
3+	9	13	13	18	35	48	50	31
Location of TV sets								
Living room	30	30	42	42	60	84	60	36
Parents bedroom	9	16	9	15	26	28	33	19
Own bedroom	7	14	13	20	30	45	48	25
Kitchen	5	3	5	10	20	27	10	5
Possession of videorecorder	26	27	39	38	56	73	61	34

Control Over Viewing

There were also some interesting responses in terms of who had control of the set. In the majority of households our children admitted that it was their parents who decided what programme should be on, with fathers regarded as the people who had ultimate control. A few youngsters maintained that it tended to be a joint decision although there were others who insisted they always got their own way and that everyone else fitted in with them. A few children complained that it was their brothers or sisters who made the

5

decision and that this was usually achieved in an unjust way. If the siblings were older they tended to assert themselves physically and if younger throwing a tantrum usually proved fairly successful. Some children still watched programmes selected by other family members even if they had no real interest in them, but the majority at this point tended to leave the room and watch an alternative programme elsewhere in the house or find something else to do (although this latter choice was less likely).

TABLE 1.2   WHO CONTROLS HOUSEHOLD VIEWING

	Primary School Children				Secondary School Children			
	7-8s	8-9s	9-10s	10-11s	11-12s	12-13s	13-14s	14-15s
Males								
Father	3	7	8	10	7	8	10	4
Mother	4	5	4	1	5	7	10	3
Both parents	4	2	2	6	12	7	3	3
Brother	2	0	0	1	0	2	3	3
Sister	1	0	3	0	1	1	0	0
Self	1	1	3	0	4	6	3	0
All	0	0	1	3	1	5	4	4
Females								
Father	7	6	7	7	6	13	13	4
Mother	2	4	5	4	5	5	6	1
Both parents	4	3	1	3	12	5	4	5
Brother	0	0	2	2	1	3	4	1
Sister	2	2	0	2	1	1	1	0
Self	0	0	4	3	1	8	4	4
All	0	0	2	0	3	3	1	4

Programme Preferences

Having elicited general information about children's viewing habits, our discussion moved on to concentrate on specific programme areas. Each group was questioned about their likes and dislikes of a pre-selected programme type, for example, Sport, Soap Opera, Situation Comedy and so on, as well as their likelihood to watch them and why. Once children's general attitudes towards a specific programme area had been probed, they were shown clips from a range of relevant programmes and encouraged to discuss these in more detail.

In the case of narrative texts, i.e. Situation Comedy, Soap Opera, Drama, questions were raised about characters, story-lines and to what extent different examples of programming could be perceived as realistic and of relevance to their own lives. Clips from information programmes such as Science or News broadcasts gave rise to questions about television's ability to put information across to a child audience and the extent to which differences in programmes style could hinder or enhance this element. Questions on entertainment programmes such as Chat shows, Variety and Cartoons concentrated on the appeal of different types of programming for different age groups both in terms of content and presentation, a similar kind of questioning was adopted for Sports programmes.

Initially, our sample of 384 children were interviewed on a total of 12 different programme areas (plus advertising), although as can be seen from the following table, some of these areas have since been amalgamated for the purpose of this book. For example, extra children were recruited for the "Light Entertainment" chapter so that a full range of programmes could be discussed, but it was realised at the analysis stage that some of their opinions on certain types of programming, for example, Chat and Variety Shows, tended to be limited and therefore did not seem to justify a separate chapter. There was a similar result with Science and Information programmes, hence the reason for a larger number of children being interviewed on these areas.

TABLE 1.3   NUMBERS OF CHILDREN INTERVIEWED ABOUT EACH PROGRAMME

Programme Areas	Primary School Children				Secondary School Children			
	7-8s	8-9s	9-10s	10-11s	11-12s	12-13s	13-14s	14-15s
Popular drama series	6	6	6	6	6	6	-	6
Serialized drama serials	6	-	6	-	6	6	12	-
Situation comedies	-	-	6	6	6	12	6	-
Quizzes and game shows	-	6	-	6	6	12	6	-
Light entertainment*	6	6	6	6	12	12	-	-
Sport	-	-	6	6	6	6	6	6
Science and information	6	6	6	6	6	18	18	6
News and current affairs	-	-	-	-	6	6	6	12

Note: There were equal numbers of males and females per age group for each programme area
*   Including music, variety and chat

The first programmes we investigated were those that featured a dramatic narrative; these then, are the first reported on in the chapters that follow and from the children's point of view, the ones they were most keen to talk about.

References

1. Gunter, B and McAleer, J. *Children and Television: The One-Eyed Monster?* Television in the Lives of Children. London: Routledge 1990.

2. Svennevig, M. *Attitudes to Television in 1988*. London: Independent Broadcasting Authority 1989, January.

2 Popular drama series

Introduction

The linchpin upon which the success of popular television schedules most commonly hangs is the strength of its drama programming. Drama is the most expensive type of programme to make and broadcasters often place their major drama productions in the most competitive slots in the schedule in the hope that big-investment television series will win the biggest audiences.

Good drama can evoke in audiences a range of emotions as well as providing intellectual stimulation and even a source of learning. The popularity of the genre and its ability to arouse feelings and involve viewers has also led to a great deal of interest in its longer-term effects on viewers. In some instances, curiosity about the impact of television fiction has turned into anxiety, especially where children are concerned.

Widespread debate has been conducted over the years, involving at various times governments, television producers, broadcast policy-makers, researchers, lawyers, educationalists and other informed (and sometimes not so well-informed) lobbyists, about the possibly undesirable side-effects of watching some forms of television fiction.

There has been most concern about the impact on young viewers of television's crime drama or any programmes which feature portrayals or vivid depictions of violence.[1] One argument is that televised violence may enhance the development of aggressive dispositions among individual child viewers and in broader terms contributes towards levels of crime and violence in society. Although the case for television's effects - harmful or otherwise - has not been conclusively demonstrated, critics have been vociferous and the issue has grabbed the headlines over many years. [2]

It is not only the possible behavioural effects of television's drama programmes that have come under scrutiny. Another question is whether television affects our values and beliefs about the world around us. One view is that producers of popular television programmes may select and dramatise certain values rather than others. Television series, it has been claimed, may thus misrepresent society or at least certain aspects of it. For example, some social and demographic groups get to appear numerically more often than others, and some appear more often as central characters in the most significant or attractive roles. [3]

One American writer, Nathan D Heffner has aptly argued that television series may appropriately be viewed as "subtle persuaders". As he put it, "Television, the newest and far more prevalent form of fiction is even more profoundly influential in our lives - not in terms of the stories it tells - but more importantly, the values it portrays." [4]

The influences of television drama upon public perception are mediated by its idiosyncratic style of telling a story, with the nature of leading characters' personalities being a central ingredient here. In addition to this, viewers form their own impressions about television series based upon their knowledge about the world and their experiences in life, including their past viewing experiences. Thus, one central feature in this mediational mix is the perceived degree of familiarity and similarity of the settings and characters in television series with situations and people known to viewers in their own lives. Viewers' reactions to television drama hang to a significant extent on the nature of these comparisons between the world of television and the world they live in. [5]

Thus, television fiction portrayals, even the most serious ones, are not invariably and unquestioningly accepted by viewers. This observation probably applies more to adults than to children. But as we will see, even young viewers can (and do) question and re-define television's serious fiction. In this chapter, we examine what children, in their own words, have to say about popular television drama series. The research 'data' are children's own prompted and unprompted comments.

In all, seven groups of children, covering the ages from 7 to 15, were interviewed about television drama series. With six children in each group this meant that a total of 42 children provided detailed opinions about this category of programming. The questions focused on what children understand a drama programme to be, which examples of such programmes they claimed to like, and their perceptions of the realism of characters, settings and storylines in such programmes. They were also asked if they felt they learned anything from television drama and whether they would like to have the same jobs or lifestyles as the characters in those programmes.

To help the children focus their attention on what the researcher meant by a drama programme, all groups were shown two clips from different television series. All groups saw clips from *One-by-One*, a BBC series

10

about a vet working for a private zoo in the north of England. In addition, secondary school children, aged 11-15, saw a clip from ITV's *The Bill*, while primary school children, aged 7-11 saw a clip from BBC's *Grange Hill*.

What is a Drama Programme?
Programme classification has never been an easy business. Even professional broadcasters and television audience researchers have trouble with it. Typologies vary, sometimes quite a lot. For the sake of our research under the heading of "popular drama series", we were interested in programmes with a dramatic, fictional narrative which had limited seasonal runs. In this type of programme, although the leading characters and settings remained the same, each episode consists of a different story each time, which usually runs its full course through to a final resolution within a single episode. Occasionally, a story might spread across two episodes. This format is to be distinguished from serialised drama, which typifies "soap operas" (which are dealt with in the next chapter) in which there is a continuing storyline across episodes.

Many of the children we interviewed were unclear about this distinction, until it was spelled out to them. When asked to explain what a drama programme is, they thought first of all of soap operas. The soaps were the programmes which most often sprung spontaneously to mind. In saying this they weren't exactly incorrect. Soap operas are a kind of drama - and clearly for children, the most salient kind on television.

Here is an example of opinions from a group of 12-to-13 year olds:

Interviewer:	"What do you think a drama programme or series is?"
Mark (12):	"Like Dallas?"
Int:	"It's one type of drama - any others?"
Julie (13):	"It's like a play."
Mark:	"They just keep making you want to see the next programme."
Int:	"Is it always a serial?"
All:	"No."

When the interviewer offered the same group a sample definition of a drama as "people acting out a story - like a serial or series" and the children were then asked which programmes they could think of, they mentioned *The Bill*, *One-by-One*, *Juliet Bravo*, *Neighbours*, *EastEnders*, *Sons and Daughters* and *The Singing Detective*. Clearly then, teenagers have a grasp of the range of programming which can be subsumed under *drama*.

Perhaps the most amusing, all-encompassing definition was offered by Damien, aged 15.
"It's when everyone sits in front of the TV and goes, 'Oh - I wonder what's going to happen next?"
Younger children tended to be less clear about how to identify a drama programme. A few made a stab at it, however.

Victoria (10):	"Drama's when people act it out, isn't it?"
Int:	"Which ones can you name?"
Stephanie (10):	"*EastEnders, Neighbours.*"
Int:	"Any others that you can think of - ones when you just

	get a few of them and then they stop - not like *EastEnders* that goes on and on and on and on?"
George (10):	"*Playschool.*"
Int:	"Do the rest of you think that's a drama programme or not?"
Mark (10):	"No."
George (10):	"Yes, I do."
Int:	"Why do you think it is?"
Stephanie (10):	"Well they sort of act things and when they tell a story, they act it out."

Others were unable to offer any description of what a drama programme is when asked without specific prompting. When given a description of what sort of programme we had in mind, the oldest primary schoolers (10-11s) were able to name a few - *Murder, Mystery and Suspense*, and *Agatha Christie's "Murder She Wrote"*.

Which Drama Programmes Do Children Like?

Children seem to enjoy a variety of drama series. In particular, they enjoyed a number of police and detective series. Asked to give examples they mentioned: *Cagney and Lacey, Columbo, Dempsey and Makepeace, T.J. Hooker, The Bill, Kojak, Juliet Bravo, Rockcliffe's Babies*, and *The Equalizer*.

Their reasons for liking these programmes were not only associated with action and pace. Contemporary dramas were liked for their realism too.

Int:	"Out of those you've named, which of those do you like"?
Robbie (11):	"*Rockcliffe's Babies* - I watch it every time."
Int:	"Why do you like that?"
Antonella (12):	"It's just so brilliant - there's so much action - everything's like so real - I like it - it's just good - it's so real."
Robbie (11):	"Because it's like what happens in the streets now ... they show like riots or something and they show you what - er - their positions and what they do."

In addition to police and detective series, we asked children if they could think of any dramas associated with other occupations. The most common professions which feature in television drama tend to be legal and medical. This was reflected in other programmes the children mentioned. Teenagers liked *St. Elsewhere, Jimmy's*, and *L.A. Law*. Younger children also mentioned *Casualty*.

Primary age children had mixed opinions about series based around hospitals, such as *Casualty*. Some seemed to appreciate the reality of this sort of programme and felt lessons could be learned from it. Others found that the style of this type of drama was not to their taste.

Barbara (9):	"I don't like ones in hospital."
Emma (9):	"... I think it makes you think about it - to be careful and that, because usually ... like, there was this man at a party and there was smashed glass on the floor and he fell over and cut his wrist and all the blood started

12

	pouring out, and that could really happen in real life."
Int:	(turning to Barbara) "Why didn't you like it (*Casualty*)?"
Barbara:	"Because when you're in hospital, everybody is rushing around and you can hardly hear a word of what everyone says."
Int:	"So it's difficult to work out what's going on?"
Barbara:	"Yeah, it keeps going from scene to scene in a flash."
Int:	"But is that like what happens in a real hospital?"
Majority:	"Yes"
Barbara:	"It's more like that but you don't usually hear doctors saying things like 'Oh I'm going to get married next week.'"
Anna (9):	"That's because it shows you their life and the hospital life, doesn't it?"

Having got the children to talk freely about the television dramas they watch and like, we turned our attention next to their perceptions of the degree of realism which characterises different elements of these programmes. We focused on three principal areas of realism, relating to their characters, settings and storylines.

Realism of Characters
The extent to which viewers perceive television dramas as realistic has a significant bearing on how much they believe what they see in such programmes and how much they may be influenced by them. With maturity, viewers become increasingly able to distinguish the real from the unreal on television. As a result, viewers learn to dismiss a great deal of television's dramatic, fictional material as removed from everyday reality.

There is special concern reserved for children whose understanding of life and of television is not as well developed as it is among most adults. If children are therefore less likely to distinguish television drama from real life, they may also be more susceptible to having their beliefs and behaviours shaped by what they see in these programmes. But just how vulnerable are children? Is their comprehension of television so crude and simple? Or can and do they learn fairly quickly to make sophisticated assessments of television dramas and the characters and settings these programmes contain?

In order to find out answers to these questions we asked children to give their impressions of the *realism* of television drama series. To focus their attention, we concentrated on selected television series known to the children and after showing a video clip taken from a single illustrative episode in each case, we asked a set of probing questions about each one.

Secondary-school children turned out to have plenty to say about *The Bill*, while primary-school children had well-formed views about *Grange Hill*. Despite the fact that it was the only programme excerpted for both age-ranges, *One-by-One* elicited the least comment all round. Both pre-teens and teens generally found the latter series pleasant enough, but did not seem to get deeply involved with the stories or identify strongly with the characters. While they had little enough to say about the realism of the

13

characters in *One-by-One*, neither the younger nor the older children had any worthwhile opinions to articulate about the realism of the setting or storylines of this series. As we will therefore see, our discussion centres for the most part on children's views about *The Bill* (in the case of secondary schoolers) and *Grange Hill* (in the case of primary schoolers).

The Bill. Among secondary school children, aged 11 to 15 years, the first clip was taken from *The Bill.* Just how realistic were the character portrayals in this series? How like real police officers were the ones portrayed in *The Bill*? The general impression among the children we interviewed was that the way police in *The Bill* got on together made them seem more unreal than real.

One feeling was that the police portrayed in *The Bill* were too casual when it came to chasing crooks. Portrayals of bravado on the part of the police in *The Bill* didn't impress the children as being realistic either.

Robbie (11):	"There's one of them - and that was the one who was sitting there - they was all putting their helmets on in there and he said 'I hope it doesn't come to that' and the other one - the fat bloke - he's like that because when they had a raid the other week he's saying 'here we go, here we go, here we go'" (sings this bit as imitation and the others join in).
Antonella (12):	"Yes - he couldn't wait to do it."
Int:	"And do you think that's like real policemen?"
Robbie:	"No (laughs) - but he just plays the part well."
Int:	"Why isn't he like a real policeman? What do you think a real policeman would be like?"
Robbie:	"Well, the police wouldn't start singing, would they?"

The realism of the character portrayals was further undermined to some extent by the lack of seriousness they showed in doing their job as police officers.

Int:	"The main characters - are they like real policemen - like the ones you see out in the street, for example?"
Damien (15):	"I don't know - because like most of them - they all seem to like a laugh - but you get ones, like you get straight ones - but in that, in *The Bill*, they're all a laugh."
Int:	"So you don't think that's very realistic?"
Damien (15):	"No - it'd be better if they only had one or two that was a laugh - the others should be straight."

There were some elements in the series, however, which children perceived to be more realistic. The policewomen, for example, were thought to be fairly true to life by some of the children.

Robbie (11):	"... if you see a policewoman in the street - if anyone like, don't know where they're going or something - they help them out - and so does the WPC (in *The Bill*)."
Antonella (12):	"Yes, and say there's a drunk on the street, she would go 'Oh come on - I'll take you down the station'."

Another element of realism which caught the attention of some children was the way the characters agreed with each other a lot, though this opinion was by no means universal.

Honor (12):	"They tend to agree a lot."
Julie (13):	"Yes - they always agree."

Int:	"Is the way they agree realistic - would it happen like that in real life?"
Melanie (13):	"Yes - like if you're in a difficult situation and you're trying to get someone, then you'd get tense."
Int:	"Do you think the main characters are like real policemen?"
Honor (12):	"I think they're all realistic."
Satinder (13):	"They portray the characters well - but as policemen they seem a bit over dramatic."

One-by-One. The second clip shown to the older children was taken from *One-by-One*. This is one of two popular peak-time television series in which the storyline revolves around the life and exploits of a vet (the other one being *All Creatures Great and Small*). The setting in *One-by-One* is contemporary, while *All Creatures Great and Small* is set between the two world wars.

What impression do children have of the way television vets are portrayed? Do they compare with the real thing? It turned out that most of the children we interviewed had had no direct contact with a vet and so had little other experience against which to compare these television characterisations.

Int:	"How many of you have been to a real vet?"
Joseph (12):	"Yes - but most of them just want money - vets are after your money, you know? One of them - like after a while might say 'this sort of thing's happened - that'll be £5 please', you know - all of a sudden, he'll stop and start talking about money."

In continuing this conversation, Robbie contrasted this cynical view of vets in real life held by Joseph with the character portrayed in *One by One*.

Robbie (11):	"There was one programme when he had to fix an eagle and he didn't want nothing for doing it, because if he didn't do it, it would have - probably got killed - but he saved it, and it started flying and they go 'We've got to repay you somehow' - and he goes - 'Oh, don't worry - I don't want money.'"
Int:	"And you think that's very realistic?"
Robbie:	"That is very realistic - because they don't usually want money - vets! They just want to save the animals - and suddenly, he looks around and they go - 'There's your thing for doing it', and there's a Land Rover there."
Int:	"So how real do you think that is?"
Robbie:	"I don't think that's real at all."

One of the unusual features of *One-by-One* is the fact that the vet works in a zoo where he often has to treat exotic, foreign animals. This was not an aspect of a vet's work which had previously occurred to many children. They associated vets with the treatment of animals you might find on a farm (horses, cows) or which people would normally keep as pets (dogs, cats).

Did the children think that *One-by One* could help them realise what it's like to be a vet? The general impression was that it could, though the series showed more of what it is like to be a vet in a zoo than one whom you would take your own pets to see.

Honor (12):	"Sometimes - yes - but not a domestic vet only - like a tropical or zoo vet."
Int:	"Has it given you a wider perspective on vets - did you always think it was just cats and dogs, or did you think there was more to it?"
Honor:	"Well, I knew there was other animals that needed to be treated but I didn't think an ordinary domestic vet could do it."

Grange Hill. Primary school-age children (7 to 11s) were shown a clip from the children's series *Grange Hill.* This programme is set in an urban school with the storyline centred on the lives and problems of the pupils. The main characters are teenagers and may be thought of as providing potential role-models for primary age children who have yet to experience secondary school for themselves.

The series has been the source of some public controversy and criticism for its supposedly realistic portrayals of antisocial behaviour among teenagers, both inside and outside the school setting. Certain personal and social problems teenagers themselves might experience in real life have been acted out in *Grange Hill*, with occasionally dramatic illustrations of consequences and resolutions.

One sub-plot dealt with teenage shop-lifting. Was this a good thing or a bad thing to show? Nine- and ten-year-olds held mixed opinions.

Victoria (10):	"It's encouraging people to get up to things"
Stephanie(10):	"And it also shows you what happens when you shop-lift - so it's teaching you how to do it and it also shows you what trouble you get into when you shop-lift."
Int:	"The fact that it shows you that you get into trouble for doing it - do you think it still encourages it or not?"
Stephanie:	"Yes - because she was trying to prove to her mates that she wasn't just a boffin, that she could do something and they dared her to do it - these girls done dares and one girl had a tattoo on her arm and she got into serious trouble - because then she found out that you could have tattoos that you could take off and she had one that you couldn't."

Primary-school children felt there were other times when *Grange Hill* showed things that provided bad examples for children.

In addition, portrayals of domestic accidents caused by carelessness or negligence on the part of characters were felt to be potentially upsetting to viewers, especially if it might have reminded them of similar things that had happened to them.

Int:	"Is there anything else you can think of that's happened in it - that you think encourages people to do wrong things?"
Stephanie (10):	When they were on a school bus - um - on an outing and a boy had left the gas on - I think that's bad because people have left the gas and they've blown up and then they watch it and then it just reminds them what happened and then they just feel upset about it."

Another theme covered by *Grange Hill* was drug-taking. While this was perceived to add an element of realism to the series, children felt that it was potentially a dangerous subject to cover because it might encourage imitation among young children. For that reason there was a strong current of negative opinion about it.

Victoria (10):	"It's just encouraging people to take drugs"
The rest agreed.	

Even though the series showed the drug-taker being sent away and trying to get over his drug problem, the children still felt it encouraged young people to take drugs. They believed that the programme should have showed you how to stop taking drugs as well.

George (10):	"Well - I think it encourages people because I know they're trying to tell you what happens, but as they're doing it, it's teaching people how to take drugs - like those who do want to take drugs."

Some children did feel that there were lessons to be learned from this episode in the series, however. They were put off themselves by the way the boy (a character called Zammo) looked after taking drugs - all white and ill. They felt that this could probably deter young children from wanting to take drugs, if they thought they would end up looking like that. In particular, the girls were put off drugs by the whole episode.

Emma (9);	"Well, I don't really think it's real - but I like it. But they take drugs and stuff and - um - it's not like a real school at all - it makes you frightened when you go up to senior school - that's what it does. It makes you think 'Oh God, they all take drugs here, they're going to make me start taking drugs' - and things like that. I don't think it's a good idea to show it - I like it -but I don't think its a good idea."
Int:	"Does it make senior school look frightening then?"
Emma:	"Yeah but when you go there, you know it's nothing the same as it, so the first day you go to senior school there's no drugs or nothing."
Angela (9):	"It can teach people how to do drugs and everything - when they go to senior's and that."

Here we can see that even quite young children make sophisticated judgements about plots dealing with sensitive or controversial subjects. It is also apparent that there sometimes develops a tension between conflicting judgements. Emma is trying to discount the realism of *Grange Hill* and contrasts events such as drug-taking, that are shown in the television school, with what she expects things to be like in real secondary schools. However, there is still a lingering and worrying doubt in her mind that maybe secondary school is like *Grange Hill*. She *hopes* rather than knows that it is not.

Despite these apprehensions we found some evidence that primary children perceived valuable social lessons in the portrayals of drug-taking featured in *Grange Hill*. The series depicted that the harm of drugs clearly outweighed their pleasures in the end. This was not necessarily a good reason for showing drug-taking, however. Some children still felt that such television portrayals could implant the wrong ideas in susceptible young viewers.

Int: "Does *Grange Hill* show that it's clever to take drugs then?"

Mixed response of yesses and noes.

Barbara (9): "No because all the teachers are telling the people off who take drugs; the people who take drugs are taken to things like detention centres and it warns you not to take drugs or anything."

Int: "Do you think then that showing people taking drugs and what happens to them is a good thing or a bad thing?"

Barbara: "I think it's a good thing because you can be aware of what can happen to you if you take drugs."

Int: "But some of the rest of you think it can encourage you to take drugs?"

Anna (9): "I don't think so - because it shows what happens afterwards, what happens if you do do it and it shows how terrible it can be afterwards."

Angela (9): "Yeah, but it would be fun while you're doing it."

Anna: "But then they might realise what eventually would happen and then they'd think it's a stupid idea and they wouldn't do it."

Another girl was concerned that even though the consequences of drugs were shown, portrayals of drug-taking could still put the idea into people's heads. The teachers in the programme did not act responsibly as real life teachers were thought likely to do.

Other themes salient in the minds of this young group were smoking, drinking and stealing. One of the male characters in *Grange Hill* was remembered as being guilty of stealing - his TV father was a thief and the boy was trying to emulate his dad. In another instance, a girl was depicted shop-lifting. Once again there was some concern about showing stealing because it could encourage others to copy it.

Karl (9): "Well, because this girl - she went into this shop because she thought she needed some money and then she started shop-lifting and so then they caught her doing it but they didn't say nothing because then they know that when she walked through the door the alarm would go off and when she walked through the door, the alarm went off and they took her to the police

	station and they started questioning her and her mum came and all her mum done was told her off and that ...."
Int:	"So you think more than that would have happened in real life?"
Karl:	"Yes"
Emma (9):	"You know, as Karl said with the girl, it was because these two other girls made it look easy, they'd stolen a lipstick which hasn't got a tag on it for when you go through the door and - um - I don't think it does teach them to steal because at the end that girl got caught out."
Karl:	"And - um - when these people are lining up to go to the cinema, this man dropped his wallet and she took - um - well she kept it and she spent the money."

In broadening the discussion of television drama, some primary school children drew comparisons between *Grange Hill* and an American counterpart series, *De Grassi Junior High*. Compared with *De Grassi Junior High*, the 9-year-olds, by and large, preferred *Grange Hill* - because they felt they could learn things from it.

There was a feeling that *De Grassi Junior High* would set bad examples.

Karl (9):	"It does encourage things, because this boy went to school on his skate-board and he made out, like, that these vitamin C capsules were drugs and he sold them to these girls for five dollars each, so then they thought they were real and they were laughing because they had gone nutty; but they hadn't, they were giggling - so then, they kept wanting more and they told their friends and they told this - um - I think he was paralysed - um - this disabled boy and he even wanted to take them."
Anna (9):	"The other thing wrong with *De Grassi Junior High* is they say about stealing one time and drugs another, but the first one they did, the next time you thought they were going to go on with it, but they didn't - it was though it had never happened - it went from drugs to stealing."

One of the major differences between the two programmes lay in the way plots unfolded and are resolved. *Grange Hill* was serialised and resolved problems over time. *De Grassi Junior High* was perceived to jump from issue to issue, and sometimes in the latter there isn't even any resolution.

Anna:	"Like somebody [in *Grange Hill*] gets into trouble at the end and then it finished (Karl agrees) but it starts again on the next one, but in *De Grassi Junior High* some things are at the end and then they don't show you what happens."

Opinions about the teachers that were featured in *Grange Hill* revealed that they were seen in different instances as being silly, strict, and understanding. Some teachers were seen as being not really strict enough

- and that was why they were shown being given a hard time by their pupils. The headmistress, Miss McClusky was held in mixed esteem. The majority did not feel she was strict enough, others thought she was realistic.

Stephanie (10):   "She's an understanding sort of person."
Emily (10):   "She's a bit silly."
Mark (10):   "She's too kind to people when they do things. She just says 'Don't do it again' when some people are punching and bullying for nothing ... she just says 'Don't do it again.'"

The majority felt that when they go to secondary school, the teachers wouldn't be as soft. They would in fact be much harder than the ones on *Grange Hill*.

Emily (10):   "And you'll get much more work lessons than you do on the telly - you'll get much more education."

Realism of Settings

Quite apart from the characters who populate television drama series, what do children think about the realism of the settings? Past research has indicated that the extent to which viewers perceive television settings as similar to ones in the real world affects their reactions to programmes.[6] Children are known to be able to distinguish the realism of the news from the make-believe of television's fictional offerings. Even fictional genres can vary significantly in how much their settings resemble the familiar, contemporary world of the young viewer.[7] How subtle and perceptive are children's impressions about the realism of popular television drama settings? For instance, is the police station in *The Bill* like a real police station?

Carol (12):   "Yes, because there's all people running around and everything."
Antonella (12):   "And you see loads of calls coming in."

Juliet Bravo, on the other hand, was not seen as being very real because it was usually so quiet in the police station there. The children did not seem to realise that the latter was set in a small town where generally life is quieter than in a large city.

The police station in *The Bill* was also regarded as realistic because it looked like a real police station.

Alex (13):   "The desk and where the complaints department is - it's got the backyard out where the vans park and everything"
Julie (13):   "And it's really busy - there's always lots of things going on."

Grange Hill was generally perceived by primary age children to give an inaccurate and unrealistic impression of secondary or comprehensive school life. In particular, they had problems accepting the authenticity of classrooms and the numbers of pupils in a class.

Int: "What about the way the classrooms are set out? And how they carry on in the classrooms when they show you their lessons?"

Emily (10):   "Well, they're much bigger and the lessons are much different. I mean you wouldn't have - um - I don't know the teacher's name but he's so soft on the children - he's literally scared of all of them."

Story Realism

Are the storylines and events in television series realistic or far-fetched? In police and detective series, do crimes always get solved to the same extent as in real life? The answer is, of course, that success rates are far higher on television. Children were, interestingly, aware of such discrepancies. Furthermore, they realised that some television series were more realistic than others because they reflected real world statistics more accurately. While children noted that crimes were generally solved in *The Bill* (making it less like real life), in *Rockcliffe's Babies*, the story was different.

John (12):   "... in *Rockcliffe's Babies*, when it used to be on - what happened is - it's so realistic - I even said this to my mum - I said I really like *Rockcliffe's Babies* because this kid, he went missing, and next day they were searching for him and then they found his teddy bear under a bush and they looked for him and he was lying there dead - and that's probably the thing that would happen - not like *The Bill* - they just like to shoot someone or something and then suddenly, they break in and shoot them."

The Bill was seen to be less predictable than some American police series. In the latter the story formula was seen as being quite repetitive. *The Bill* was thought to be characterized by nice neat endings, however. Only occasionally was there a departure from this norm, with the crooks getting away. Do the police really manage to solve crimes most of the time?

Damian (15):   "No - but they're not going to show us the ones that aren't solved, are they?"

Int: "Why not?"

Damian: "Because they're just showing you what they think people want - like if they put on things like murders, she and he were away to another country, then it's not a good ending is it?"

Sharon (15):   "Yeah, I mean, it's not really what the public want - they want to see a proper story and that."

And what about the types of crimes television police have to deal with? Were the crimes which police on *The Bill* were shown having to solve the same as those real police, such as ones who work in the children's own locality, might have to deal with?

John (12):   "Not every day in London - may be once a year or something."

Int: "So do you think the types of crimes they have are exaggerated or what?"

John: "Sometimes, yes."

Robbie (12)   "No, because on *The Bill*, they showed a riot, and a riot really happens."

Int:	"Do you think a real police station would have to deal with that many types of crime or problems each week?"
John:	"I don't think it would in one day."
Carol (12):	"I don't think they would have to deal with drugs and that, that much."

Many of the children, however, were unable to say whether *The Bill's* handling of different types of crime was realistic or not. This was apparently a difficult question for many of them to answer. There was a perception that *The Bill* depicts lots of different crimes each week many of which were small or minor offences.

Teenage viewers recognised that the story in *The Bill* does vary from week to week. The storyline in each episode was seen to be complete - there was no carry-over or serialisation. They felt, however, that when crimes were usually solved in each programme, this was where the series departed from real life.

What about the sorts of crimes police in *The Bill* have to deal with. Are these realistic or not?

Int:	"What about the crimes themselves - are they like the crimes a real policeman would have to solve?"
Honor (12):	"Some of these are a bit over the top - but I think it's pretty realistic."
Julie (13):	"They have the sort of things that really do go on."
Satrinder (13):	"It's like every single police station in Britain squashed into one."
Alex (13):	"If they had normal crimes, it would be boring - there wouldn't be any action in it."

The Dramatic Value of Action

All agreed that the series has to have a lot of licence to dramatise crimes in order to make good entertainment. The children recognised that there are lots of different crimes dealt with by the series. This leads to variety and makes the programmes more appealing to the audience. It is unlikely that a real police station would have to deal with as many crimes.

There was no overwhelming support for the idea of showing you more of the lives of the characters at home - their private lives rather than their work lives. These 15-year-olds felt that there probably wasn't room in the series to cover both aspects thoroughly. They also felt that there were already enough characters in *The Bill* - any more would probably make the show difficult to follow.

Although they were not shown clips from such programmes, primary age children, while being questioned about watching other police and detective series, did volunteer opinions and perspectives about the realism of certain aspects of these television dramas.

As well as being interesting in themselves, their other remarks reveal the extent to which even young children are aware of production techniques and make contrasts between the stylised action typical of American crime-drama series and the slower, more domestic atmosphere of *The Bill*.

One boy, Karl, aged 9, felt that *Starsky and Hutch* lacked realism. When asked why, he answered:

Karl (9): "Because they go in cars and they jump over things and they jump over ... and things like that - it's just not real."

Some of these children showed an advanced degree of television literacy which was evidenced, for instance, in their awareness of the tricks and special effects as used in television drama.

Angela (9): "*Murder She Wrote* is good, because I think the blood is like tomato ketchup or something."

Peter (9): "They have this little bag under their things and you shoot it with a little dart and it bursts and there's all blood like ..."

(The rest agree)

Barbara (9): "I saw a programme on special effects."

Anna (9): "Well, I thought they had - um - like - um - a bag inside there somewhere, like a bag of tomato ketchup and then where somebody shoots something at them, it pierces the bag ..."

Barbara: "No, what happens is, they have an electric charge there and when they make the bang, then this goes sssh - and all the blood comes out - that's why there's so much blood."

Karl (9): "I think it's not like a real bullet, but it's something like a bullet and you have a bullet-proof vest on and it - um - there's some dye stuff put in a little bag and you stick it to your bullet-proof vest and when someone shoots it with a pretend dart, it hurts it and then it explodes."

Anna: "But that's what I just said."

Int: "So are you saying, you like watching all the action and the violence, but really you know it's not real?"

All: "Yes."

Emma (9): "That's why it doesn't give me nightmares - because when I was little *The Incredible Hulk* used to give me nightmares."

What these remarks seem to show is that, although children may be upset by certain programmes during their very early years, once they learn to recognise the fictional or fantasy character of television drama, they develop their own immunity to such effects. Among some, perhaps most, children, this would appear to happen by the time they are in their mid-primary school years.

Does TV Show What it is Like to be a Police Officer?

Television has been criticised in the past for over-representing and glamorising some jobs and occupations at the expense of many others. If it has any influence at all, according to some writers on the subject, it may be to narrow the range of job options children and teenagers find attractive or believe to be available to them when they grow up. [8] There is some evidence that television portrayals may offer ideas for or about employment to young viewers, and that these portrayals may cultivate a distorted impression of what it is like to work in particular jobs.

In this vein, we asked children to say how much they believed that programmes like *The Bill* give you an idea of what if would be like in the police force? Teenagers were sceptical about this, believing that what was shown on camera in *The Bill* would necessarily be different from real life.

Generally, they did not believe that *The Bill* gave a good idea of what life in the police would be like. One admitted that although he may have been inclined to believe the series when younger, he saw it differently now.

Int:	"Do you think it [*The Bill*] gives a real impression of what it would be like to be a policeman?"
Julie (13):	"I think it does give a very good impression."
Satrinder (13):	"It gives an impression of the situation but it doesn't actually give you what the other people would be like - you'd know the situation, what types of crimes there are going to be but you don't get a very - um - like - the way to handle the problem."
Julie:	"I think it could put you off - it wouldn't make me want to be a policewoman."

Is a Policewoman's Job Different to a Policeman's?
And what about policewomen? Do they do the same work in real life as policeman? In general, the girls said 'no', the boys said 'yes'.

Mark (13):	"Well, not if it's a really dangerous thing - like they've got to go to fight - like there's going to be a big fight or something, they'd probably send a man; they might send a girl as well, but she wouldn't actually go in if there was going to be a big fight."

One of the girls, Honor (12) disagreed with this point of view totally and felt that all officers, male and female should be doing the same thing.

Int:	"Does *The Bill* make being a policeman look like it would be exciting or dangerous or interesting or boring or what?"
Julie (11):	"Dangerous and exciting."
Robbie (11):	"It makes the policeman look like it's pretty good work, but then you see them suddenly with a pile of paperwork - about that big!".

This unglamorous element was perceived to smack of realism. Policewomen were thought to be less likely to get involved in the more dangerous aspects of police work. Thus, chasing after armed criminals and using firearms were restricted to male police officers, while female officers tended to be deployed in dealing with victims and the bereaved.

Robbie (11):	"Sometimes it is [dangerous] - because if they - like - have to use firearms, the lady's just ready to go in there because there's a kid and they'll say 'Are you all right' and say what's going to happen - but the men just go and get their firearms and get ready to shoot."
John (12):	"Yeah, because the ladies don't do a lot of violence."
Carol (12):	"Yeah, they don't go on the roofs and things."

John:	"But they help."
Antonella:	"They'd like to".
Robbie:	"Like on *The Bill* the other day - they had a lady standing on a window thing and she was going to jump and if a man had gone out there, I reckon she would have jumped but the lady went out and she started talking to her."
Jackie (15):	"They don't get hit on the head or sent to riots and things like that - they get breaking bad news to people - they get sort of sheltered by the male police."

This was a fairly common impression of *The Bill*. Occasionally though WPCs were seen to get in on the action - and this was seen as likely to happen in real life too, by a few children.

Would Children Like To Become Police Officers?

On the evidence of television portrayals, to what extent would children like to join the police force as a career? In general, not many children held that ambition. One of the main reasons for this was the perception that a police officer's job can be dangerous. These danger elements, far from making the job seem exciting, turned a lot of children right off. In general, police work was perceived to be more dangerous than exciting.

Robbie (11):	"... it's pretty dangerous because if you go on a raid or something, you can easily get shot, it's a bit dangerous job so I think I'll stick to something else."

As a career prospect, however, it was also seen to depend on the type of police officer you were and where you worked.

Jackie (15):	"I think it depends on where you are and whether you're just ordinary and on the beat and that, but if you're sort of higher up - and in the CID or something ....." (pauses)
Int:	"What sort of things might happen to you - you said you thought it would be dangerous - would it always be like that?"
Sharon (15):	(interrupts) "Sometimes it could be like exciting - say if there was a child being beaten or something and you could go and get this child out of the house or wherever it was - it could be exciting to put the child into safety."

What are perceived characteristics of a police officer?

Carol (12):	"You'd have to be patient."
Antonella (12):	"And training."
John (12):	"You've got to be quick."
Carol:	"You have to be very agile."
John (12):	"You have to be fit."
Robbie (11):	"You have to be ready - you have to be ready for anything and you have to be patient because if you go on a raid, you have to wait for someone to come out."
Int:	"What other things do you think they have to do?"
Robbie:	"You have to learn how to use firearms."

| Antonella: | "They have to be sober all the time." |
| John: | "Yeah - they can't drink on duty - or smoke." |

Conclusion

In this chapter, we began our investigation of children's opinions about different genres of television programming by examining their comments about television drama. In addition to asking the children we interviewed to express, in their own words, their thoughts and feelings about drama programmes in general, we showed them episodes from some popular series that were being televised at the time of the study. This procedure was designed to focus their minds on specific examples and to give them something concrete to talk about.

Despite the concerns that some contemporary dramas may depict behaviour unsuitable for young viewers and provide bad examples of social conduct which could lead them astray, we found a refreshingly open, though occasionally critical, attitude towards one of television's major programme genres.

Drama programmes as a class undoubtedly have popular appeal. This appeal derives from a number of sources and is manifest through a variety of functions it performs for viewers. Television drama can teach lessons about life. It can impart knowledge about the world. It can offer new ways of looking at old problems[9]. A major factor in drama's appeal to viewers lies in its capacity to involve members of the audience vicariously in the action it portrays. With drama, viewers can also eavesdrop on the private lives of television characters in a way they would love to be able to do with neighbours and friends.

Children enjoy television drama programmes as much as do their parents, and for many of the same reasons. Young viewers' abilities to follow dramatic storylines is limited at first, but it quickly matures. By the end of primary school, children are already able to comment on the realism of television dramas and can critically appraise the medium's degree of social responsibility in showing some of the things it does in these programmes.

By their early teens, young viewers are able to express more sophisticated opinions about different kinds of realism in drama programmes. Important distinctions are made in terms of the realism of characters, settings and storylines. We can take *The Bill* as one case example. While secondary schoolchildren found certain aspects of police station life as shown in the series to be realistic, they were not always as convinced by the portrayals of police officers.

On some occasions, the children were able to relate their perceptions of the series back to their own, real-life experiences. Clearly, children's opinions of television fictional portrayals are mediated by what they already know. Where television portrayals and real life do not match, the former may be seriously questioned.

There are times when children's questioning of the veracity of television drama is based on more speculative or 'hearsay' knowledge. The latter may have been gleaned second-hand from friends or other sources. Alternatively, we observed instances in which children had seen something on television which worried them, when they would try to 'wish away' the reality of what television depicted. We noticed this on one particular occasion with a primary school girl in respect of portrayals of drug-taking in *Grange Hill*. While accepting, on the one hand, that the series seemed in many ways to provide a convincingly realistic look at life in a secondary school, this girl could not believe that the secondary school she would eventually end up going to would be the sort of place where this sort of behaviour took place. She tried to convince herself therefore that this particular storyline in *Grange Hill* showed something out of the ordinary. Nevertheless, seeds of doubt were sown in her mind.

Other children commented that *Grange Hill* was, on balance, right to show such things, because it could teach important lessons to other young children who might be thinking of experimenting with drugs. Young viewers felt that this was, however, a highly sensitive issue which needed to be handled by television with care.

In general, the children we interviewed seemed to appreciate realistic, contemporary, television dramas. This preference may in part reflect the fact that children adopt more adult viewing tastes with age (or wish to be seen doing so) and increasingly eschew programmes which are perceived to be made for children younger than themselves.

The development of more adult-like tastes are accompanied by more adult-like perceptions of programmes. Children are not easily taken in by television fiction, no matter how contemporary and realistic it tries to be. Indeed, the more realistic television producers try to make their programmes, the more critical an eye children cast over the behaviour of characters and the settings in which the action occurs. This would suggest that more obvious fictional programmes can get away with a great deal more than those which purport to mirror reality because as far as young viewers are concerned the former have the licence to do so. Once a programme labels itself as depicting contemporary realism, this immediately places it under the microscope. Children, expect 'true-to-life' television drama to be just that in every respect. Children through primary and early secondary school years, quickly learn to distinguish between different kinds of dramatic television entertainment and know what to expect from each type of programe.

References

1. Gunter, B. Plenty of evidence, very little proof. *The Listener,* 1986a, January, 28. 7-9.

2. Gunter, B. 1986a, *op. cit.*

3. Gunter, B. *Television and Sex-Role Stereotyping. London: John Libbey and Company, 1987.*

4. Heffner, R.D. Televisision: The subtle persuader. *TV GUIDE, 1973 (September 18) 21, 25-26.*

5. Gunter, B. 1987, *op. cit.*

6. Gunter, B. *Dimensions of Television Violence.* Aldershot, England, Gower Publishing Company, 1985.

7. Van der Voort, T.H.A. Television Violence: *A Child's Eye View.* Amsterdam, Holland: Elsevier Science Publishing, 1986.

8. Signorelli, N. The demography of the television world. In G. Melischek, K.E. Rosengren and J. Stappers (Eds). *Cultural Indicators: An International Symposium,* Vienna, Austria, Austrian Academy of Sciences, 1984.

9. Johnson, J. and Ettema, J.S. *Positive Images,* Beverly Hills, CA: Sage, 1982.

   Williams, F., La Rose, R. and Frost, F. *Children's Television and Sex-Role Stereotyping.* New York: Praeger, 1981.

3 Soap operas

Some definitions:

Interviewer: "What is a soap opera?"

Victoria (14):   "Something that goes on and on .... It's usually something that you can relate with."

Kirsten (14):   "I think it's something to escape to."

William (10):   "A soap opera's a thing which either happens weekly or daily and it's about real life."

These were some of the responses given by children when asked to define a soap opera. But how right were they? Just what is a soap opera?

Soap opera as a term appears to have originated in the US entertainment press of the 1930s as a way of describing the genre of the 'daytime dramatic serial'. These serials were regarded by soap manufacturers such as Proctor and Gamble and Lever Brothers as ideal sponsorship vehicles for attracting large audiences of potential consumers (i.e. housewives) to listen to daytime radio. With the advent of television, the unparalleled success of radio soaps invited their transfer to the screen. However, unlike a traditional dramatic serial, soap operas have no end; in fact, they rarely have a recognisable beginning , only a continuously expanding middle of interweaving narratives and overlapping resolutions. As Victoria (14) rightly said it's "something that goes on and on".

What else is it about soap operas that make them such a unique form of entertainment - to what extent do they reflect 'real life'? Viewers have come to demand certain things of soap operas; time should reflect 'real' time, characters should behave like 'real' people and although some exaggeration of events is expected, they must remain within the realms of possibility.

Traditionally, soaps have focused on the everyday lives of a small community or family, with a tendency to highlight female characters and women's concerns. As the genre has grown in popularity, changes have occurred and modern soaps can be categorised in two ways. For example, some of the US soaps, notably *Dallas* and *Dynasty*, are not only screened at peak-viewing times, they are also expensive, glossy and above all melodramatic with character and events consistently portrayed as larger than life. In contrast to these, the British and Australian soaps feature working and lower-middle-class characters, whose problems reflect those of the viewers themselves. Their preoccupation with everyday human concerns are made evident by the way problems are personalised; socio-political issues are only reflected according to the extent to which they affect the individual.

Soap characters tend to be stereotypical although not obviously so, which is a necessary feature if they are to be recognised by the viewer as representative of the real world. Characters become known for their individual personality traits and are expected to respond to specific situations accordingly, thereby fulfilling viewers' expectations. But because of the nature of the genre, character behaviour and interaction is still contrived. For example, the major part of all soaps is given over to conversation, much of which is repetitive. This allows viewers to obtain different characters' viewpoints on a specific happening, as well as to catch up on events if they have missed episodes.

Settings are also important; characters need a reason to keep meeting each other. Hence the tendency to feature 'Streets' or 'Squares' as a backdrop e.g. *Coronation Street, Brookside, EastEnders* where most of the characters are either neighbours or relatives with a high propensity for popping into each other's houses or the local pub.

But what is the fascination of peering in on a fictitious group of people's lives on such a long term basis? Is it because their problems are our problems or is it pure escapism? - And where do children fit in with all of this?

From the children we spoke to, we attempted to ascertain not only the extent to which they understood and followed the various soap plots and character action, but the reasons why they appreciated them so much. The two they seemed to want to talk about most were *Neighbours* and *EastEnders*; the other British and American soaps eliciting more limited responses. *Neighbours*, a comparatively recent Australian import, is set in the attractive suburban environment of Ramsey Street, where every house reflects a comfortable lower-middle-class life-style. The series focuses on a small group of its inhabitants and seeks to promote the old-fashioned values of good neighbourliness. The UK soap, *EastEnders*, is more usual in that it is the first soap designed to meet viewers' needs; needs that were identified by extensive market research beforehand. *EastEnders* is set in a run-down London square, whose inhabitants are more concerned with their own survival than being good neighbours, and whose problems reflect those found in many of today's inner-city areas.

In our discussion groups, *Neighbours* proved to be the most popular, which is also reflected in BARB viewing figures, where it seems to have achieved something of a cult status amongst the younger age groups.

TABLE 3.1   YOUNGSTERS' CHART TOPPERS

Position	Programme	% watching
1	Neighbours (Wed)	42.0
2	Neighbours (Tues)	41.4
3	Neighbours (Thurs)	38.9
4	Neighbours (Mon)	38.3
5	Neighbours (Fri)	37.9
6	Grange Hill (Tues)	37.2
7	Only Fools and Horses (Sun)	33.1
8	Grange Hill (Fri)	32.4
8	Tom's Midnight Garden (Wed)	32.4
10	Blue Peter (Mon)	29.9

As reproduced in THE OBSERVER: 26.2.89

As Richard Brooks in the same edition of THE OBSERVER points out:
"The most popular programme for children aged between four and fifteen is the BBC's Australian soap "Neighbours".   It is also the second most popular programme for youngsters, as well as the third, fourth and fifth.   In fact, the 5.35 pm edition of "Neighbours" is watched by nearly half of all four- to fifteen-year-olds".
Out of the 36 children we spoke to about soap operas, 31 watched *Neighbours* every day (23 watching it more than once, if possible), four at least once or twice a week with only one boy (Christian, aged 12) stating that he never watched it.   Our first concern then, was to try and establish just what it was about *Neighbours* that attracted children and young people in the first place and discover why they were so keen to keep watching.

Neighbours
Why They Watch
Initially we concentrated on unprompted responses;   it was only as the discussions progressed that specific questions concerning individual characters and narrative events arising from 'clips' were pursued.   The first interesting point to emerge was the similarities in opinions expressed by 8-year-olds and the oldest age group of 14+ when talking about *why* they watched *Neighbours*.   Each group, without fail, cited the exciting 'cliff-hangers' as being their main reason, closely followed by the realism of the characters which was attributed to good acting.

Michelle (8):   "It's really exciting - because when it gets to the end, it always stops at an exciting bit and you keep wondering at the end ....."

Joanne (8): [interrupts] "You want to watch more and more."

Sarah (12):   "The way it ended;   you just had to watch the next one, because you wanted to know what happened."

31

Andrew (11):[agrees] "Especially on Fridays, because it's always good and you have to wait until Mondays."

Natalie (13): "At the end of each one, there's a cliff-hanger and you have to see what's next [She explains further] ..... they build it up - the part where something goes wrong or something happens."

But Victoria (14) is more critical; although she found the cliff-hangers exciting and feels they encourage her to keep watching, she believed that sometimes they detracted from the realism, citing a recent episode as an example.

Victoria (14): "Yes, but it's really exciting - like the other day when Shane got hit and then you see the next day's episode when they shown it again and then he bounces up and he's still the hard man!"

Victoria's view was that if someone got hit as Shane did, it was unlikely that he/she would be able to "bounce up" again as though nothing had happened. She continues:

Victoria: "You're really interested and you want to know what happens but then it's really silly!"

And what about their views on the characters and the way in which they are portrayed? - the second reason they gave as to why they like *Neighbours* so much.

Kelly (8): "They act like proper people, don't they? They argue or quarrel or fight and that ... it's just like life!"

Denise (10): (who is not only appreciative of the acting but is also aware of the possible presence of cue cards and scripts); "I like the characters in it - and they act so naturally - it's not like - um - they're stuck every sentence for what they're going to say or like they have to look at what's behind the camera - but with *Neighbours*, it's like ... (she pauses) ... they act naturally. It's as if it was happening in real life - as if there was no script or anything like that."

Carrie (12): "It's the people in it - I think they're good actors - and it's a bit like everyday life but it's stretched out a bit."

Perhaps a comment made by James (14) sums up the general feeling best of all:

James: "Well, there's everyone in it that you know".

And then there was Christian (12) who maintained that he never watched *Neighbours*. Despite having made this statement, however, at times he gave the impression that he knew far more about *Neighbours* than he was prepared to admit, perhaps because having scorned the programme at the outset, he was reluctant to lose face in front of his peers. In fact, on one occasion, when he felt compelled to contradict another group member who had re-told part of the narrative incorrectly, he maintained that he only knew about it because he had "happened to be passing the screen when his sister was watching". However, his reasons for non-viewing highlighted the way in which character behaviour is seen as realistic.

Christian (12):   "Well, it's so much like other things that I've seen or that happens around your family, that you get a bit bored with it after a while. I mean I even found that the same topic of conversation turned up at the dinner table (He is referring to his own dinner table) as turned up in *Neighbours*. It really gets incredibly boring after a while!"

As each discussion group got under way, more probing questions were raised in terms of individual character behaviour and plot structure. Many children maintained that some characters were more like "real people" than others, although this did not necessarily mean that they liked them any more. Certain events were also perceived as being more realistic than others; this they were more critical of - it seemed quite acceptable for characters to be 'over the top' but not events.

It was whilst discussing the nature of individual characters that the personalities in *Neighbours* appeared to become people in their own right. In each group, the children referred to Charlene, Madge, Shane and so on as though they were people that they knew intimately. The fact that they were actors playing a part was soon forgotten, although the children themselves realised that this was how they spoke about them.

Roisin (13):   "You talk about the people as though you know them."

There was also more of a difference between the ways in which boys and girls and younger and older children responded to the characters and the ways they behaved.

The Characters In *Neighbours*

Initially children were asked to name the characters who lived in Ramsey Street and define their relationships; even the 8-year-olds had no difficulty with this, being fully aware of all aspects of both family and romantic involvements. Spontaneous comments about current events and the behaviour of individual characters arose naturally from this kind of questioning. One group of 13/14 year-olds became quite animated over the 'teen' relationships and their recent behaviour, revealing a strong sense of moral values. The discussion, at this point, centred around an incident when Mike (one of the 'teen' boys) who has been going out with Jane, kisses another girl (Nicky) in front of Jane; sexual differences in group attitudes were also apparent.

Int: "Did he (Mike) really want to do it or is he trying to make Jane jealous?"

Roisin (13):   "He's trying to be horrible to Jane and that's not fair on Nicky though."

(The boys see Mike's behaviour as justified).

Sean (14):   "Jane's being horrible to him!"

(The girls disagree and Sean argues back).

Sean (14):   "Yes, she is - because Mike tried to apologise and she wouldn't accept his apology."

Roisin (13):   "No, she didn't"!

Daniel (14):   "But it's out of order - she went on the motor-bike with Shane and she was supposed to be back at 5.00

for a meeting or something because they was trying to get a mortgage with Madge for something and she didn't come back till next day - they didn't, did they?"

(Daniel appeals to the rest of the group for support and Sean agrees with him, but Roisin remains unconvinced).

Roisin (13):   "Yeah - but Mike said he went over to apologise but he didn't go over to apologise at all - he went over to be horrible to her again. (She refers to a friend who was with her when she watched this particular episode). Like - umn - we were watching it and he (Mike) said "I came over to apologise" - then he went and had an argument with her and my friend said to me, "I thought he went over to apologise!" So I don't think he was completely sorry about it at all or that he'd forgiven her for anything."

And so it went on. Later, this same group took sides over Shane's attitude to women, with the boys maintaining that he was a "womaniser" and the girls springing to Shane's defence, although it was the boys who had identified with the male character of Mike earlier. Mike, however, was younger than Shane and had less of a 'macho' image, so perhaps this made him a more empathic character in the eyes of 14-year-old boys still struggling to gain their own self-confidence, and who have not yet reached the stage where to be regarded as a 'womaniser' might seem attractive. The girls' defence of Shane was also interesting; the tones of their voices as well as the comments they made, highlighting the way they appeared to be sexually drawn towards his particular personality.

Roisin (13) [reacting to the boys' charge that "Shane is a womaniser!"]:
                 "No, he's not! I don't think he'd force himself on any of the girls - he'd respect them."

Caroline (14) [supports her]: "I don't think he's a womaniser!"

Roisin (13):   "They make out - all the people - they're trying to make him sound bad really - but he's not that bad."

The boys still disagreed and after some thought Daniel managed to think of an example of Shane's 'womanising':

Daniel (14):   "What about that woman who came along on Shane's motor-bike?"

Sean (14) [remembering]: "Oh, yeah!"

Daniel (14):   "He had her in his caravan before you could say - umn ..." [He stops in embarrassment].

Int: "What happened?"

Sean explained, revealing a good understanding of the intricacies of the plot as well as the sexual implications:

Sean (14):   "Well, she came along - right? - and she went in to the caravan and he was living there as well, but they didn't know each other was living there. Then the next thing you knew, they was out for dinner and back in the caravan and - umn - umn - ..."

Sean tailed off in embarrassment but the point has been made and the girls make no further attempt to refute the criticisms of Shane.

It was only with the older children that sexual attitudes and behaviour were discussed; the younger children apparently failing to appreciate the implications in these kinds of situations. However, some of the 9-year-olds did refer glibly to characters having "affairs" but seemed to think this was an acceptable way to describe modern boy/girl relationships. It seems doubtful that they understood the true meaning of the word, as unlike the 14-year-olds, they showed no signs of embarrassment.

To find out what the children thought of individual characters and events, we tried two different approaches. First, each group was presented with a hypothetical situation and then asked how they thought specific characters would respond to the problem. Many of the children, particularly the younger ones, found this line of questioning quite difficult and tended to limit their answers to whether the character under discussion would stop an imaginary fight for not. The situation offered to them was of a group of older teenagers bullying a younger child. The most interesting responses were concerned with Clive (a local doctor) and Mrs Mangel (Jane's grandmother) who were both seen as exaggerated figures.

All groups maintained, irrespective of age or sex, that Clive would try to alleviate the situation by treating it as a joke; they appeared to believe that this was his usual response no matter what the circumstances. Sean (14) took this view of Clive even further, stating "He's just an eccentric!"; this opinion is also re-iterated by some of the younger children.

Emma (10):   "He's a bit silly sometimes."
Darren (9):   "He's not real-like!"

But Paul (13) appreciated Clive's eccentricity:

Paul (13):   "Clive? He's the funniest one in it. It gets boring, then he comes on. He's just different. All the rest are just ordinary people, but he isn't. He goes around kind of being a personality, kind of funny and all that."

And what about Mrs Mangel? How did the children expect her to respond to the hypothetical situation? As far as many of them were concerned, she was the most exaggerated figure in the series, almost a caricature. She was the one they were all most likely to imitate, screwing up their faces and wagging their fingers in the air, obviously feeling that words were not enough to explain the 'awfulness' of Mrs Mangel as they tried to describe her essential characteristics.

Caroline (11):   "She'd be bossing them about."
Natalie (13):   "She'd start shouting at them and nagging."
Sean (14):   "She'd call somebody. She'd go up to them and say, "Stop them! Stop them!"."
Roisin (13):   "Yes - she'd have to stick her nose in, wouldn't she?"

The caricature effect created by Mrs Mangel was made even more apparent when we probed deeper into the children's understanding of character traits and questioned them in terms of character realism. They were asked whether certain characters were more realistic than others, or whether any of them were like people that they knew themselves. As far as the older children were concerned, Mrs Mangel seemed like the archetypal 'old lady', but bore little resemblance to any of *their* grandmothers. However, they still felt that her role was an essential part of the narrative and added to the programme's appeal.

Int: "Is Mrs Mangel true-to-life? Is she like your nan or other old ladies that you know?"

Roisin (13): "No, she's not like mine, but I suppose there's people like her - but she is a bit - umn - over ..."

Sean (14):[interrupting] "She's over the top!"

Victoria (14) [responding to the same question]: "Yeah - but she's more nosey than anyone would be."

Sandra (14): "Well, my grandmother ain't like that - she don't care what I do. But my *great*-grandmother's like that - she's a bit stuck up!"

Victoria (14): "But she's got a bit of all your nans. One minute they're all down to earth and lovely and then they start the major nag. [She mimics an old lady's voice and wags her finger] "Look at the state of your bedroom! I'm going to tell your mother of you!". It's just that little bit out of all them."

Mark (14): "I think they need her in a programme to give it that boost, but she's not like most grandmas. They just need her in a programme."

Some of the younger children also perceived Mrs Mangel to be a necessary part of the programme; a typical 'old lady' character to be found in other soaps as well.

William (10): "You always get one or two like that."

Rhonds (10): "And they're always chattering and telling everyone."

Int: "One or two like what?"

Denise (10): "There's always one person in any street in the whole world that's like Mrs Mangel!"

Daniel (10):[agrees] "Like in *EastEnders* - like it's got Dot Cotton."

However, the 8-year-olds made no attempt to contrast Mrs Mangel with their grandmothers, but they still viewed her as "unreal" by comparing her to a more traditional image of a grandmother, presumably the little white-haired old ladies depicted in story books who sit in their rocking chairs beside the fire.

Joanne (8): "Old ladies aren't usually like that, are they?"

Ian (8): "No, they're not so bossy and they're not usually running around."

Int: "She's not so bossy?"

Ian (8): "Well, she's like a witch and she speaks like it."

Joanne (8): "She's an old bossy boots!"

Anthony (8): "And she works in a cafe!" [In Anthony's eyes, this was a totally unrealistic way for old ladies to behave.]

Joanne: "She pokes her nose into everything, don't she?"

One other character who received a lot of criticism, particularly in terms of her realism, was Lucy, the youngest person in the programme; a character whom younger children in particular would be expected to identify with. However, that was not the case with the children we spoke to.

Rhonda (10): "She's a 10-year-old but ..."

Daniel (10) [Interrupting]: "But she's never in school!"

Rhonda (10) [continuing]: "She's never pleased. She's always - umn - like - [she imitates Lucy in a whining voice] 'Oh, but that's never fair - because - umn -'".

Denise (10): "Because Lucy isn't like us - because the way she talks to people, she talks like an adult. I think she's like a teenager really."

But if Clive and Mrs Mangel were not viewed as being very realistic, who did children perceive as being more like people they knew - one of the reasons they gave for liking the programme in the first place?

The character who received praise for being the most realistic was Madge (Charlene's mother). It seemed to be the mother/ daughter relationship that was most appreciated, particularly by the older girls, who invariably made comparisons with their own mother/daughter relationships.

Roisin (13): "Madge is a bit like my mum; she really reminds me of her. My sister says she's not really like my mum but my mum's not as 'naggy' as she is - but she's very like her, I think."

Carrie (12): "Charlene's mum, Madge - she's just like my mum." "She says the same kind of things to me."

Denise (10): "Well, it's the way she controls Charlene makes her like a real person ... the way she handles Charlene when Charlene does it wrong or when Charlene got in that fight - I think that's very real."

Charlene, herself, was also viewed as realistic and her "prettiness" was admired by all; in fact, the physical appearance of female characters seemed to be a deciding factor amongst the younger age-groups when they were asked the question as to whom they would most like to be like in *Neighbours*.

Sarah (12): "Charlene ... she's always doing things; she's pretty and I like her hair."

Catherine (11): "I like Jane ... she's nice to everyone and she's brainy and pretty; she's pretty."

"Being nice" as well as pretty was an important consideration for the girls in the older age-group too, but they were also concerned with characters' life-styles when deciding whom they would most like to be like. However, it was the traditional female life-style of husband and home that the majority appeared to want for themselves, all of which seemed to be encapsulated in the character of Daphne. Daphne was the young and attractive wife of the local bank manager (Des), and at the time of our interviews, expecting her first baby; this was also viewed as an enviable position to be in by some of our sample.

Roisin (13): "I like Daphne. I think Daphne's really nice."

Int: "In what way?"

Roisin (13): "People go up to her and talk to her; she's very understanding - very nice - she just is. We've talked about this before with our friends; we say 'If you were one of them, who would you like to be?' - and most people say Daphne!"

Natalie (13):   "I'd like to be like Daphne - she's got a nice husband, a nice job and that - and she's happy."

It is frequently argued that characters in soaps and other television dramas can reinforce sexual stereotyping[1] and from the way that some of our four groups responded to the personality traits of the different characters, this may well be true. Girls on the whole wanted to be seen as "pretty" and "nice"; "nice" in their view equated with being helpful, friendly and supportive. Presumably this could be regarded as seeking to perpetuate a subservient role in the eyes of feminists' movements. However, soap characters are also expected to reflect the real world, and as far as our children were concerned, the ones they particularly admired were seen as realistic despite their traditional roles. Although sexual equality in the real world has made great strides, men still hold a dominant role in western society, and it seems that in spite of the current push towards equality, the children we spoke to still tended to aspire to the more traditional 'nuclear' family. However, although emphasis was placed on being "pretty" and "nice", Jane was still admired for being "brainy" and Daphne's "good job" was also seen as an important feature, perhaps revealing a slight change in attitudes and priorities to that of a previous generation.

Buckman[2] argues that: "Only when the liberated woman has become a stereotype herself will she be able to take her place in soap opera". *Neighbours* has made some attempt to redress the balance by highlighting Charlene's aspirations to become a motor mechanic. Many of the girls in our groups saw this as a reflection of Charlene's independent spirit, although not all of them believed it to be an admirable character trait and none of them admitted to similar aspirations themselves.

Michaela (13) [on Charlene]:   "Well - she's really - umn - she's her own person - like - she wants to be a mechanic and - like - girls often aren't mechanics but she knows what she wants and she wants to really get it and she doesn't care about anyone else."

Kirsten (13) [interpreting Charlene's behaviour differently]: "She's selfish - she wants her own way too much."

And what about the boys - who were the characters they admired for their realism and whom did they want to be like? The boys seemed more reluctant to answer this kind of question than the girls; they appeared afraid that their choice might be ridiculed by the rest of the group. Finally, a few decided that Clive's humour (even though they had criticised this earlier) and his ability to work hard were admirable characteristics. Others selected Shane as a role model, but their main reason for this particular choice appeared to be his possession of a motor-bike which was greatly envied by all.

The one situation that the boys did identify with was the sibling relationship between Paul and Scott Robinson. They obviously empathised with Scott, whom they saw as being unfairly dominated by his older brother, Paul, who in a recent storyline had been forced to adopt a paternal role.

Sean (14):   "Well, Jim (Scott and Paul's father) has gone to America and Paul's left in charge and Paul's being a right fool - umn - he's making him wash all the dishes

	and clean out the garage and that. So he (Scott) got this picture (of Paul) and drew a moustache on it and put HITLER on the top and stuck it on the wall and Paul came down and told him to take it off, so they started having an argument and Scott swung at him."
Int:	"Why was that good?"
Sean (14):	"Because Paul deserved it."
Daniel (14):	"Because Paul was really being horrible for about two or three weeks before and you really did want him to get hurt - you knew it was going to happen really."

Having explored children's attitudes towards and perceptions of the different characters in *Neighbours*, we turned our attention to the social problems and issues frequently featured in soaps and the extent to which it enabled children to resolve their own problems. The question we asked was: "Do you think you can learn from programmes like *Neighbours*?".

Learning From *Neighbours*

According to Allen,[3] the situations and problems in soap operas are seen as reflective of today's society; issues discussed in soaps frequently parallel discussions in viewers' own lives and it is often argued that contemplating problems in soaps can assist viewers to come to terms with their own problems, or alternatively escape from them. Max Wylie (a US soap writer)[4] maintains that:

"Women of the daytime audiences are having physical and psychic problems that they themselves cannot understand, that they cannot solve ... (Soap opera) takes them into their own problems or problems even worse than their own (which is the same thing, only better). Or it takes them away from their problems. It gives listeners two constant and frequently simultaneous choices - participation or escape. Both work."

Television is also regarded as a learning medium. Not only can viewers absorb information from news programmes and documentaries; they also have the opportunity to view alternative life-styles and opinions through dramatic narratives. From a child's point-of-view, soap opera families can reflect their own families and perhaps give them insight into some of the ways of dealing with problems in their own lives. But are children themselves aware of this? Do they believe that they can learn anything from soap operas as opposed to alternative forms of programming? How are they watching them - is it for "participation" or "escape"?

When asked to consider the extent to which they might learn from a programme like *Neighbours*, many of the children, particularly those in the younger age-groups, found it a difficult concept to deal with. It had obviously never occurred to them that it was possible to learn from entertainment or drama programmes; as far as they were concerned that was the purpose of documentaries and/or educational television.

Int:	"Do you think you can learn anything from watching programmes like *Neighbours*?"
Emma (10) [misinterpreting the question]:	"Sometimes - some documentary programmes, you can."

| Int: | "Well - no - from *Neighbours*, can you learn from that?" |
| William (10): | "Well, Clive's a doctor ... [He tapers off]." |

After further probing, the younger children finally understood the aim of the question; however, it might well be that their responses by this point were those they believed the interviewer wanted to hear. Furthermore, they were obviously aware that the programme emphasised the nature of family and neighbour relationships, but they were then critical of the portrayal of some of these relationships, believing that they were not always shown examples of good behaviour.

Rhonda (10):	"It can show you that most of them - most of the time, they're always friends - but like - really - some people, they always argue; some people argue."
Emma (10):	"It shows you how you can keep relationships together - but sometimes it doesn't."
William (10):	"Sometimes they push it a bit too far with friendship."

Joanne (8), believed it could help you to learn "not to be so bossy" and Kelly (8), in the same group, thought it taught people not to be "bullies". But when asked more directly as to whether it could teach them how to talk to or get on with people, they thought not and cited instances of arguments and disagreements that had occurred in recent episodes.

The older children thought that a recent storyline that had dealt with the problems of teenage drinking might possibly warn people of the dangers of alcohol. This group also cited a recent episode that had given hints on how to cope with exam pressure; the only direct reference made by any of the groups to the actual influence of a television narrative.

Michaela (13):	"... not to panic so much and not to try and cheat because you can get into more trouble." [The programme had depicted Scott getting into trouble having cheated in an exam.]
Jim (13):	"Yeah - because we had a maths test then."
Kirsten (13):	"Yeah - it was really good because everybody - like - was doing that - they was pressing their thumbs together (she demonstrates) in the classroom."
Int:	"Why were you doing that?"
Kirsten (13):	"Well, Clive was doing it, and you have to press your thumbs together and everybody in the class was doing it."

Further probing revealed that the aim of the exercise had been to reduce tension created by exam pressure, but they were unsure as to how successful it had been.

When the fourteen-year-olds were faced with a similar line of questioning, their responses were more mixed; although they appreciated that social problems and family relationships were being explored within the context of *Neighbours*, they were aware that for the sake of narrative interest and continuity, some of the resolutions to these problems were contrived. Victoria (14) decided that perhaps it could help you to learn "a little bit".

| Int: | "In what way?" |
| Victoria (14): | "Like - how to handle your parents - I do anyway." |

Roisin (13)	"Though it might offer some insight into family situations."
Int:	"What do you mean?"
Roisin (13):	"Well - things that happen in family households - if you've got a bad family, you can see what it's like."

But on the whole, most of the children remained unconvinced of the learning potential of a programme like *Neighbours* and as has been demonstrated by their responses, thought of it in that way only if it seemed to have some direct relevance to their own lives. Although adults, particularly women (traditionally, the audience at whom soaps are principally targeted) might well use the discussion of problems in soap opera to make sense of their own lives, the same does not appear to be true of children. The children we spoke to articulated their own reasons as to why this might be so.

Roisin (13):	"... It's not put on really so that you can learn stuff."
Samantha (14) [agreeing]:	"It's just for enjoyment."

Perhaps Darren (9) sums it up best of all:

Darren (9):	"No - because all the problems they get over, we never have - because most of them are older than us and they get different problems."

The Ramsey Street Environment

Finally, we tried to discover how viewing a soap opera like *Neighbours* fitted in with the children's perceptions of Australia itself and to what extent they themselves would like to live in somewhere like Ramsey Street. Again, the younger children found it difficult to respond to what was a hypothetical situation as far as they were concerned. They already appeared to hold some fairly stereotypical images of Australia but were aware that Ramsey Street was somewhat different and struggled to identify these differences.

Int:	"Is *Neighbours* really like what you thought Australia would be like?"
Joanne (8):	"No - because it's big."
Int:	"What's big?"
Joanne (8):	"Australia ..."
Kelly (8):	"But their town, it's really small."
Joanne (8) [continuing]:	"... and there's lots of land there, isn't there?"
Ian (8):	"But Ramsey Street - that's only about the size of - umn - [He thinks of a local example] - part of New North Road."
Int:	"How do you think Australia is then? You said "It's big?"
Matthew (8):	"It's massive!"
Joanne (8):	"And there's lots of land there and you can get lots of - umn - deserted places - and there's not many houses there either."

The older children had a slightly more realistic view, appreciating the varying nature of the Australian environment; however, they did admit that their superior knowledge had still been gleaned from television.

Roisin (13):	"Sometimes you see a town part - other times they show you deserted parts."
Sandra (14):	"In some programmes, it's all outback - but after seeing a programme like *Whicker's World*, it's not! There's parts where everyone lives and it's like where we live."

So, if in some ways Australia is the same as Britain, how would they feel about living there? This question was taken literally by nearly everybody; they invariably interpreted it as meaning would they like to live in Ramsey Street as opposed to Australia generally. However, it was the way they responded to it that emphasised the way they perceived the *Neighbours'* setting and gave further insight into the attraction that this particular programme has for the youth of today. It offers them the opportunity to escape from their own relatively drab urban environment, where the spirit of neighbourliness seems to them to have vanished forever, to one of sunshine and light where, as in the words of the signature tune, "When you've got neighbours, you've got good friends".

Roisin (13):	"It certainly looks all lovely, doesn't it? ... It would be really nice to live in some of their houses."
Samantha (14):	"All their houses are all spaced out and lovely ... It would be nice to have friends that you could just go to and say "Could you help me with this?"."
Victoria (14):	"Yes - everyone cares for each other and everyone's there to help each other. Where I live, you're lucky if you say "Hello" to the neighbours once a week - because you never see them."

EastEnders

Our next concern was to discover how the children perceived *EastEnders* and other homegrown soaps and identify the kinds of comparisons they made between these and *Neighbours*. The older groups, who were interviewed first, had been encouraged to spend most of their allotted time discussing *Neighbours*, mainly because our initial aim had been to make some attempt to discover why an imported soap opera should be so popular with the younger generation. Inevitably, however, comparisons were made with other soaps and it was because of the nature of these comparisons that it was decided that opinions about other soaps were worth pursuing further. Consequently, in our discussions with primary children, they were encouraged to talk about *EastEnders* in more detail than the older children, with the question structure following similar lines to that of *Neighbours*.

The first important point to emerge was that *EastEnders* was no longer rated by the children as being as good as it used to be. Various reasons were given as to why they felt like this but the main ones concerned changes in characters and lack of excitement.

The lack of excitement:

Roisin (13):	"It's getting stale now. It used to be really good but I don't like it any more."
Int:	"Has it gone down since you've been watching *Neighbours*?"

Roisin (13):	"Yes - in *Neighbours*, you think it's really great but when you think about *EastEnders*, there's nothing really happening in that."
Caroline (14) [agreeing]	"There's the same sort of things happening in it all the time."
Int:	"What kind of things?"
Caroline (14):	"Well - there's Arthur - he's always unemployed."
Sarah (12):	*"EastEnders* is so boring now ... It's always on about Pat and that."
Mark (12):	"They concentrate on one family all the time - at one time they just showed a programme between Dot and Ethel."
Catherine (11):	"Yes - that's so boring - they just nag on all the time."

The character changes:

Ian (8):	"Well - when it first started, I thought it was good - but now it's got boring. The people never do nothing - the talent's gone out of it."
Int:	"What do you mean - the talent's gone out of it?"
Joanne (8):	"Angie and Lofty have gone out of it."
Denise (10):	"I think it's been taken over by Frank and Pat."
Emma (10):	"Because Angie doesn't give it any excitement now she's gone."
Denise (10):	"And Den's going out of it!"
Darren (9):	"Yeah - they've got a lot of new people coming in now."
Denise (10):	"Because Angie and Den - they made it good in the Vic, didn't they? She's [Angie] like part of the scenery."
Darren (9):	"The first time I watched it, there was lots of excitement like *Neighbours* - but now, there's nothing really happening - like in *Neighbours*, they put something on the end to give you like - umn - so you can say, 'Oh, I must see it tomorrow! Oh, what's going to happen?' but in *EastEnders* now ..."
Denise (10):	[interrupting]: "Like *EastEnders*, they used to have the Vic in there and that used to be the star thing with Den and Angie - but now they've the Wine Bar or the Vic or you don't see hardly any of the - umn - what's its name? - umn - the Dagmar. I think they've added too much to it and taken too much away. I think they should have left it as it was before."

Some of the children were also critical of the way in which the storylines were presented, particularly in the treatment of sexual or violent scenes. Although they were aware that *EastEnders* had to be made suitable for family viewing, they seemed to feel that if elements of this nature were introduced, then they should be presented more graphically and felt cheated because of the way the camera cut the action at critical moments.

Darren (9):	"It's like the affair things - I'm not being - umn - but they like - umn - start, but you don't see a thing - I'd

	like it if you saw them going down the alleyway - and you saw this man but then ..."
Denise (10) [interrupting]:	"Yes - that's it! It cuts!"
Darren (9):	"Yes, then it cuts and it like stops - and in the next episode you see the man coming up to her and starting doing things - but you don't see any rude bits or anything."
William (10):	"Yes - you see something happening and then it cuts short and in the episode, then it's already happened and it's afterwards."

This group continued with this line of criticism citing another incident when a character had been injured having been hit by a car, and complaining that explicit portrayals of the accident and subsequent injuries had been excluded from the narrative. They obviously felt that at the age of ten they were mature enough to cope with these kinds of scenes, although in sharp contrast to this they were fiercely critical of other elements of the series and the harmful influence such things might exert on younger children. For example, they maintained that portrayals of Angie's drinking and her subsequent behaviour set a bad example, but they reserved their strongest criticism for the amount of swearing which they saw as being totally unnecessary.

Rhonda (10):	"They have too much swearing as well, because - like - 7-year-olds could watch it and they're always swearing on it."
Denise (10):	"It's not like an adult film [she explains further] ... It's on the usual - umn - half-seven, so it's on the usual child's watching time."
William (10):	"And if it's not after 9 o'clock, it's meant to be for children and the family."
Int:	"Do you think it's suitable for children or not?"
William (10):	"Not for some children."
Emma (10):	"But for children below the age of 9, they could pick up bad language easily."
Darren (9) [protesting]:	"I'm 9!"
Emma (10):	"Well, alright - 8 and 7 then!"

The Characters

As with *Neighbours*, questions were asked about the characters and events, not only in terms of their likes and dislikes but also for their degree of realism. Some of the responses to this line of questioning were very ambiguous; characters were criticised for being unrealistic in certain situations but at the same time, according to some youngsters, the East End setting and the way that people behaved were charged with being so real, so much like what the children already knew, that it was boring. For example, at one point, the youngest children concentrated on the realism of Dot and Ethel, who are both depicted as old ladies with slightly eccentric habits.

Anthony (8):	"I like Dot and Ethel" [he laughs].
Int:	"Do you think Dot and Ethel are like real old ladies then?"

Joanne (8):	"Yes - they're funny!"
Kelly (8) [agreeing]:	"With her Willy [Ethel's dog] - and she's always carrying him and she's always seeing miracles in the cups and saucers. [All laugh]."
Int:	"Are Dot and Ethel more like real old ladies than Mrs Mangel?"
Joanne (8):	"Yes - because old ladies are funny, aren't they?"
Kelly (8):	"Yeah - because she makes - like - umn - old miracles, by throwing cups on the saucers. She says 'What's this I see?' and - umn - she keeps talking ... " [This group found the concept of trying to foretell the future with the aid of tea-leaves as very odd indeed.]
Ian (8):	"I remember that night and it was so boring because Dot and Ethel were just sitting there talking all the way through."

Another character, Michelle, also came in for some criticism; she appeared to be viewed as an atypical teenager; although this was excused to some extent by the fact that she had a baby.

Int:	"What about Sharon, Michelle and Ian - do you think they're like real teenagers or not?"
Kelly (8):	"Sometimes I do."
Joanne (8):	"Ian's alright, but not Michelle."
Kelly (8):	"Because she don't look like it - she don't look like - umn - like with no make-up and that - she just looks like - umn - ... "
Joanne (8) [interrupting]:	"She does *look* like a teenager because she had loads of spots and that."
Kelly (8):	"Oh, yes - sometimes that makes her - but she don't act like one."
Denise (10):	"I'd just like to see her smile."
William (10):	"She just keeps on about the baby."
Denise (10):	"I don't like Michelle - well, I don't like her now - because before she was even thinking that she had a baby, she was a nice little girl. She was fun! But now when she's started knowing she's had the baby, she's miserable in the house - from now on, she's just boring."
Rhonda (10):	"But in that house, it's always dull!"

It was during the discussion of *EastEnders*' characters that it became apparent that younger children, despite their sophisticated references to adult affairs and sexual behaviour earlier in the interview, still have difficulty in following certain aspects of the narrative in soaps, particularly when the plot has no real relevance to their own lives. Both younger and even some of the older age-groups found the behaviour of the unemployed Arthur, who attempts to defraud an insurance company in order to obtain some much-needed cash, difficult to fathom. Presumably, their lack of understanding occurred because of their own limited financial knowledge; our children therefore perceived Arthur's behaviour in this instance as totally unrealistic and struggled to articulate their reasons for this.

Joanne (8):	"But he robbed his own house once, didn't he? That was really strange, robbing his own house."
Ian (8):	"And then he got arrested for it."
Joanne (8):	"And then all of a sudden, he just went mad, didn't he?"
Ian (8):	"It was strange."
Int:	"Do you think that robbing his own house would happen in real life - the way that part was done?"
Kelly (8):	"Well, no - not really. Because you know it's your own house, don't you really? - because you'd be robbing yourself."
Joanne (8):	"You can't really rob yourself, can you?"
Int:	"Why do you think he did it?"
Joanne (8):	"Well, he just started going mad all of a sudden."
Ian (8):	"He wanted money."
Kelly (8):	"Yes - he wanted money." [The rest agree.]
Int:	"Why did he rob his own house?"
Ian (8):	"To get more money."
Int:	"How would he get more money that way?"
Ian (8):	"He'd get it - umn - find - umn - ... " [He tapers off in bewilderment].

Matthew (8)[The only one in this group who appears to have some glimmer of understanding]: "To get the insurance!"

Joanne (8) [in relieved tones]: "Yes - that's what he was trying to find."

If certain of the characters and events were perceived as unrealistic, were there any incidents or behaviour that did bear some resemblance to the children's own environment? The only characters they mentioned as being more like people they themselves knew were Pauline (Arthur's wife), described as "just like a real mum", although she was universally disliked for her continuous nagging and miserable outlook, and Sharon, who acted realistically but looked too old, "more like 30", to be a teenager. Angie's character was appreciated, hence their regret at her having been written out of the series, although the extent of her drinking was seen as greatly exaggerated.

Ian (8):	"I don't know how Angie can get through all that drink. She probably should be dead by now!"

Angie's husband, Den was also perceived as a lively and interesting character when compared with the other inhabitants of Albert Square, although they found his criminal activities difficult to accept.

Daniel (10):	"It's not life-like ... Like Den - he's always dealing in bent gear and going off into drugs - it's silly!"

The general consensus then was that characters and events in *EastEnders* were less realistic than those depicted in *Neighbours*. What had once been an exciting and stimulating series had now deteriorated as far as our children were concerned.

Learning from *EastEnders*
As with *Neighbours*, children were asked whether they thought they could learn from *EastEnders*, particularly as it has deliberately set out to dramatise

current social issues such as alcoholism, drug dependency, homosexuality, unemployment and so on. However, when questioned, the 8-year-olds in particular, maintained that some of the events in *EastEnders* might set a bad example for today's youth and even when prompted to consider the disastrous results of drinking and drug-taking as portrayed on the screen, refused to regard this as a way of encouraging positive social behaviour. In fact, on the subject of drug-taking, they pointed out that Ian was helping to cover up the fact that Mary (an unmarried mother portrayed as a punk-rocker) was becoming drug-dependent.

Int: "You said you thought you could learn how not to argue and get on with people from watching *Neighbours*; can you learn things like that from watching *EastEnders*?"

Kelly (8): "No - because like *EastEnders*, they smoke, drink and take drugs - umn - Mary does - so you wouldn't learn nothing ... You know, he [Ian] found out that Mary smokes - umn - is taking drugs, right? But he don't tell anyone, does he? Ian knows that she's taking drugs!"

What became apparent from this line of questioning, was the younger children's tendency to see issues in terms of right or wrong, refusing to acknowledge any possible in-between areas. On-screen behaviour was regarded as either good or bad, with little allowance made for mitigating circumstances as a means of explaining individual characters' responses to social problems. However, it must be remembered, as the children themselves pointed out, that problems portrayed in soap operas bore little resemblance to any of their problems, so why should they be expected to learn from this style of programming?

The Albert Square Environment

And what about the Albert Square setting? How did the children react to a soap opera set in the East End of London? Did they perceive this as being of particular relevance to them, situated as they were just on the outskirts of the East End - and to what extent did that make the series more or less appealing?

Their first response to this was that many of them would not like to live there; unlike Ramsey Street, which was perceived as bright and "colourful", with "lots of kids" and "nice trees in the gardens", Albert Square was universally disliked for being "sooty", "smelly" and with "loads of rubbish in the streets". The absence and presence of "colour" was commented on by both secondary and primary children alike.

Carrie (12): "In Australia, it's so colourful but there [*EastEnders*], it's all just black and grey."

Denise (10): "But that [*Neighbours*] is always colourful - but in *EastEnders*, it's always dull."

Emma (10) [agreeing]: "It's always grey!"

But did the unappealing environment of Albert Square make the series seem more realistic as far as our children were concerned? The younger children seemed convinced that it was an accurate portrayal, but that this

47

feature also detracted from the programme's appeal.

Denise (10):   "But I think with *EastEnders* - it's like when we said in Australia - the people in Australia don't watch *Neighbours* - so really the way I take it, I know about the East End and everything like that, so I don't really want to see *EastEnders*."

Int: "So do you think *EastEnders* is too real?"

Emma (10):   "For some people who live in the East End - yes - but for other people who don't live in London - like in the north of Scotland - it would be interesting for them because they don't know what it's like."

But the older children were less convinced about the realism of the Albert Square environment, with one of them quoting her grandmother to emphasise the point.

Victoria (14):   "It's nothing like the East End because all my family, they're all from the East End and all you hear from my nan when she's round watching *EastEnders*, she says 'They make us out to be poverty cases'. She goes 'If that's the real East End, I come from the north of Scotland'."

It seems then, that as far as our groups were concerned, the stereotypical nature of the Albert Square environment was more easily recognisable than that of Ramsey Street; it seemed to be yet another reason as to why it had diminished in popularity for them. Did they perceive other soaps in a similar way? Briefly, we turned our attention to other UK soaps as well as some of the American imports.

Other Soaps

Although children were questioned briefly on other British soaps, most of them maintained that they rarely watched these on a regular basis. The main reason they gave was that they were boring and were of no relevance to their age group. For example, one 14-year-old boy criticised *Coronation Street* for its lack of younger characters.

Daniel (14):   "It's the same as it's a community but different things go on - there's not as many kids in *Coronation Street* as there are in *Neighbours*."

In fact, older children were more likely to watch American soaps as opposed to other British offerings; although they rarely perceived these as being realistic in any way. American soaps seemed to appeal strictly as an 'escape' vehicle, although they were still critical of what they regarded as 'fantasy' elements and appreciated that they rarely portrayed realistic views of the US way of life.

Natalie (13):   "I think it's somewhere to escape to - like you watch *Dynasty*, you don't think it's like real life at all ..."

Sandra (14):   "There's some you can relate to and some you can dream about - say like *Falcon Crest* and *Dynasty*; no-one ever walks around with shoulder pads like Krystle."

Samantha (14):   "Well, JR and Sue Ellen, they just keep - umn - she

	goes on the drink and then they split up."
Caroline (14):	"Yeah - that's been going on for the last 10 years."
Samantha (14):	"It's alright if they do it once or twice, but they keep doing it over again."
Paul (13):	"Well, it's like they're on another planet - nobody goes around kind of living in massive buildings ... "
Michaela (13):	"They make me laugh though, because they're all living under one roof, all the brothers and sisters-in-law and if that was a real family, they'd be at each others' throats all the time."

The younger children were critical of the unrealistic nature of some of the storylines, particularly those that involved roles being taken over by other actors and actresses. They were quite incensed at the idea that the producers of some of the glossy US imports believed British audiences to be so gullible that they would fail to notice changes in a character's appearance.

Denise (10):	"When I used to watch, I think one of the last programmes I saw was when somebody and somebody else was going to get married and the bride ran away. It was either after or before she got married and then, I used to start slowly taking it up again - and then it was somebody completely different that came back as her. And for them to think that we think that that's the same person, I think it's ridiculous! I think that when that person goes out, they should leave them out."
Darren (9):	"They even did it once when somebody had died or something!"

The youngest group was also asked what they thought it would be like to live in America; this was an attempt to discover if watching the expensive, materialistic life-styles portrayed by series such as *Dallas* and *Dynasty* had influenced their perceptions of the US way of life. In this age-group only one child was aware that America also had its share of poor as well as rich people, even though this knowledge still appeared to derive from the visual medium.

Int:	"If you lived in America, what sort of house do you think you might live in?"
Kelly (8):	"Very expensive one - like a mansion."
Joanne (8):	"Yes - very expensive."
Kelly (8):	"With waterfalls and swimming pools and all that sort of thing."
Joanne (8):	"And you'd have servants."
Ian (8):	"But in America, there's poor people as well."
Int:	"There's poor people as well?"
Ian (8):	"Yes - in some films, there's like alleyways down the side - and some of the people are all in rags."
Int:	"Do you ever see people like that in *Dallas* and *Dynasty*? "
Ian (8):	"No - they don't show things like that!"

Int: "When you see *Dallas* and *Dynasty* then - are they showing you what America's really like or not?"

All of this group, except for Ian, maintain that they are, but even Ian manages to find a reason for the *Dallas* and *Dynasty* portrayals of US life, which he relates to the tourist industry.

Ian (8): "They're trying to make it look good so that people will come over there!"

However, in spite of their criticisms, *Dallas* still seemed to be one of their favourite viewing choices. All groups were asked to list their three favourite soaps out of a list that comprised *Neighbours*; *EastEnders*; *Brookside; Coronation Street; Dallas; Dynasty*. As was expected, *Neighbours* was first choice with nearly all of the children, irrespective of age or sex, with *Dallas* coming a close second; *EastEnders* occupied third place followed by *Dynasty* in fourth. Only one child put *Brookside* in his top three, but when questioned admitted he only watched it occasionally "when there was nothing else on" and only three included *Coronation Street*.

Conclusion

What can we make of children's soap opera preferences? In particular, why does *Neighbours* remain a first choice with children? The initial response of the ones we spoke to indicated that it had to do with the "cliff-hanger" endings and the realism of the characters. But as further questioning revealed, for them, *Neighbours* seems to have got the balance between "participation" and "escape" just right, as opposed to *EastEnders* and *Dallas* which in each case only offers one or the other. Many of the *Neighbours'* characters are perceived as being just like people they know, caught up in situations that children can understand, but at the same time, the colourful, sunny setting and comfortable homes offer them a 'fantasy' world to 'escape' to; a world where "*Neighbours* really are good friends".

What is also apparent from our discussions is the extent to which children are 'active' rather than 'passive' soap viewers, regularly discussing and arguing among themselves about characters' responses to different narrative situations. Although issues highlighted in soaps often appear to have little relevance to their own lives as yet, children are still being offered some insight into the kinds of problems they themselves might be faced with one day. The 'active' as opposed to 'passive' way in which they are prepared to discuss the rights and wrongs of individual characters' behaviour reflects the manner in which soap operas (derided as they may be by some) may still have a role to play in assisting children's moral and social development.

References

1. Durkin K, (1985) *Television, Sex Roles and Children.*
    London: Open University Press.

    Gunter B, (1986) *Television and Sex Role Stereotyping.* London: John
    Libbey and Co. Ltd.

2. Buckman P, (1984) *All for Love: A study on Soap Opera.*
    London: Secker and Warburg p.168

3. Allen R C, (1985) *Speaking of Soap Operas* Chapel Hill and London:
    University of North Carolina Press

4. Wylie M, (1942) "Washboard Weepies" in *Harpers.* Nov. p 635

4 Situation comedy

The genre of television comedy covers a wide spectrum of programming ranging from the stand-up comic, who has a five-minute spot on a variety show, through various types of situation comedy to the biting satire of *Spitting Image*. Although audiences reveal preferences for more than one kind of comedy, each individual viewer needs both to understand and recognise characterisations or events in terms of their relevance to real life situations, if they are fully to appreciate the comic effect. This requirement is necessary for both children and adults alike, irrespective of the form of presentation.

Some Likes and Dislikes

We began our discussion of comedy shows with children by trying to establish which types of programming today's youngsters preferred and whether there was any pattern to their responses. Did all the children, irrespective of age or sex, appreciate the same kind of humour or did certain differences emerge? It became clear right from the outset of the discussion that most of the children we spoke to seemed to prefer situation comedies (sit-coms) to stand-up comedians although only a few had any real understanding of the meaning of the term 'sit-com'.

Gil (11):   "It's kind of bad but they make it funny - it's a bad

52

	situation but they laugh about it and make fun out of it."
Youssef (12):	"Sit-coms like - um - *No Place Like Home* - it's all based on the house and the family."
David (12):	"It's like *No Place Like Home* because it's based on real life."
Stacey (13):	"It's things that could really happen."

The popularity of situation-comedy as a genre has grown in conjunction with the popularity of television itself, although the style of sit-coms has changed over the years (just as the nature of society itself has changed) and they are now less likely to command a top-ten position in the ratings than they did in the 1950s and '60s.

In the past, both US and UK sit-coms tended to feature traditional family situations; for example, two parents, two children and their everyday life as depicted in the US series *I Love Lucy*, frequently regarded as the prototype of all sit-coms. Nowadays, programmes are more likely to concentrate on the problems encountered by divorcees, single parents and live-in lovers as this is deemed to be a more accurate reflection of modern society; for example, *Kate and Allie* (US) and *Dear John*(UK).

It seems then that just as the structure of audience groups has altered over the years, so has the sit-com itself. However, there are still a few that cling valiantly to the old standards, continuing to reflect the stereotype of the dependent housewife and more dominant male struggling to survive under the pressures imposed by the ever-increasing demands of their offspring, for example, the BBC's *No Place Like Home*, which was the show cited most often by our children as a 'typical' sit-com. However, even this programme could be regarded as nontraditional in that the children have reached adulthood and are no longer wanted as permanent members of the household. In *No Place Like Home*, each week's story is devoted to the theme of how to persuade grown-up children to flee the nest so that their down-trodden parents can recapture their own zest for life which apparently disappeared with the arrival of the first baby. This recurring theme is the one that audiences are expected to identify with and it is this concept of identification that lies beneath the whole structure of sit-coms. According to Newcomb[1], viewers are expected to like and believe in the characters and to admire the way they react to the pressures of modern society by saying and doing things that viewers themselves have always wanted to but have never had the nerve for.

The children we spoke to also appeared to respond in accordance with Newcomb's ideas, revealing direct preferences for verbal humour and the way characters interact with each other in recognisable situations to that of the more traditional slapstick comedy or joke-telling. Comedy partnerships such as Cannon and Ball were criticised as being too "predictable" as were some of the stand-up comics such as Lenny Henry.

Peter (10):	"Well, if you think of the ones like Lenny Henry, you might as well look in a joke book because they're all exactly the same."
Richard (10):	"Because on Lenny Henry, he says - um - sometimes he says the same jokes as before and you think 'Oh

I've heard that one!'."

However, some "alternative" comedians such as French and Saunders and Rowan Atkinson were greatly appreciated, particularly by the secondary children.

Robert (12): [discussing French and Saunders]: "Their comedy is so unfunny that it makes you laugh *because* it's so unfunny. Like they're sitting in the house and someone kicks the door in - and everyone bursts out laughing - it's not funny but everyone laughs anyway."

And on Rowan Atkinson:

Daniel (13): "He's just so witty."

David (13): "He's so sarcastic."

Daniel (13): "Even on that *Live Aid* right? - they was just sitting there talking and he was coming out with all these sarcastic things, weren't he?"

Stacey (13): (agrees) "Yeah - he just makes a joke - um - he makes fun out of everything."

In contrast to this, Benny Hill and Kenny Everett were universally disliked, particularly for their visual, sexist style of humour.

Mollie (10): "It's Benny Hill as well. He doesn't set a very good example for children ... it's always rude!"

Inderpal (11): (criticising Benny Hill): "There's no noise - only music - there's no words and where there is talking, it's all put on, it's like somebody else talking, not Benny Hill."

Cheryl (14): "Nothing's hardly ever funny no more. It's (Benny Hill) always got these dirty men running after women with no tops on. It's really stupid!" (This in spite of the fact that Hill's Angels are no longer as scantily clad as they used to be).

And on Kenny Everett:

Angela (14): "He's boring."

Mark/Andy (14): "He's suggestive."

Cheryl (14): "He's a dirty old man!"

Once they had articulated their likes and dislikes of individual comedians, the children turned their attention to sit-coms. Only one boy was critical of the genre, maintaining:

Youseff (12): "But some of the problems (in sit-coms) never happen.... They (comedy sketches) are more sharp and to the point but in a sit-com, it (the joke) takes a minute to appear."

The other children did their best to explain their preference for sit-coms.

Mollie (10): "You can find more jokes in it - even if there's something that's not meant to be funny, you can still find a joke in it."

Gil (11): "Because it's all one story and not different clips."

Denise (12): "They're more like real life."

Cheryl (14): "Because you can continue the story. It's sort of funny - I mean the characters are always the same -

like Alex in *Family Ties* - he's always bossing about and it's really funny with the different views he gives."

One 13-year-old boy was particularly appreciative of the character of Alf Garnett and the way he is portrayed in *In Sickness and Health*, regarding his outspoken bigotry and self-centredness as a true reflection of many of today's older generation.

Daniel (13):   "I think it's true - like - it's what all old people say. It's like they expect to get their own way with things because they've been in the war. It's like he's been in the war and he displays things - like his blazer or jumper and it's got all these medals on it and when you're waiting for a bus, all the old people push in and they think they've got a right to do that."

However, when questioned further about the realistic nature of sit-coms, some were perceived as being more realistic than others, although this did not necessarily mean that they were better liked.

For example, although none of the groups cited *No Place Like Home* as one of their favourites, it was this programme that appeared most likely to fall within the realms of their own experiences, particularly where the parent/child relationships were concerned. This was despite the fact that the 'child' characters in the series were grown-up.

David (11):   "It (*No Place Like Home*) gives out all - um - like what you get in a family home. Like all the sons come round to use the car and ask for money!"

Leigh (14):   "Yeah - because they're always trying to get rid of the kids .... Because they have big arguments over the same sort of things (as would happen in real life)."

Angela (14):   "Yeah like they'll have arguments about which side to watch as well, like people do."

Leigh (14):   "Yeah - like what to have for dinner and all that stuff."

The US series *Family Ties* was also perceived as realistic, although this did not appear to be the case with *The Cosby Show*. Both of these programmes examine the lives of middle-class US suburban households. The main difference between the two is that one family (The Cosbys) are black and the other (The Keatings in *Family Ties*) are white. However, characters' ethnic origins were not a consideration as far as our children were concerned; their perceptions of realism were linked to the type and amount of humour that was present.

Cheryl (14):   "Like - you wouldn't get sort of *The Cosby Show* in real life. Like *Family Ties* is more realistic than *The Cosby Show* because in *Family Ties*, there's some serious bits as well."

The programme that many of the children had problems with, when discussing degrees of realism in the opening part of the interview, was *Bread*. Although they perceived the situation i.e. a close-knit unemployed Catholic family from Liverpool as being realistic, some of the family's individual behaviour appeared to be alien to the children's own experiences, particularly the manner in which the Boswells derived their income.

Robert (12):	"It's not! (real) Because - like - the things that go on - like he goes into the DHSS office and he bribes the money out of them. No-one could do that in real life."
Peter (10):	"In *Bread*, I don't think that is quite - um - well, it is like fantasy though, because they've got about six people in the family and they're all going down the dole and getting their money and none of them really are trying to get a job."

But Andy, one of the older children saw it differently drawing on his own knowledge of Liverpool's unemployment problem.

Andy (14):	"*Bread*! That's based on life. They're acting as a poor family and they're acting in the neighbourhood where there's - um - a lot of unemployment, but at the same time they're cracking jokes as well."
Cheryl (14):	(disagrees) "Well, you don't send your dog down to the - um - thingy to pick up your wage packet."

Recording Comedy Shows

One further area explored at this stage of the discussion concerned the likelihood of video-taping comedy shows. Few of the children appeared to do this and also admitted that although they enjoyed watching sit-coms they rarely made a point of staying in to do so. Our youngsters' comments on their individual recording behaviour seems to reflect the behaviour of UK families in general. Research into family use of home video carried out by the IBA in the mid-1980s[2] revealed that drama series, films and children's programmes were the most likely programme types to be recorded, with only a small percentage of the population recording sit-coms.

Robert (12):	(on taping) "I only do that with the comedy films. Like I'll record - um - like a comedy film so that I can have - um - put towards my collection, so that when I'm bored I can just put a film on."
Dean (13):	(on regular viewing of sit-coms) "Well, I watch some, but I don't say I've got to watch them. I watch them if they're on."
Leigh (12):	"Well, if you're not doing anything - then, you'll make sure you watch them."

However, there were one or two programmes that the children regarded as exceptions and therefore worth recording but these tended to be the 'classic' repeats such as *Fawlty Towers* and *Steptoe and Son*, both of which appear to have stood the test of time as far as our children were concerned.

Angela (14):	"We've taped every episode of *Steptoe and Son*, - it's really funny."
Andy (14):	"Yeah - you still end up watching it again and again, although I never tape it for myself."

Attitudes Towards Three Sit-Coms

Having explored the children's general attitudes towards humour and sit-coms, we probed further by showing them clips from three current sit-coms, *Me and My Girl*, *Family Ties*, and *Bread*. All three series reflect family relationships but there are inherent differences in style and format.

Me and My Girl features a teenage daughter living with her widowed father who runs his own advertising agency; the programme seeks to examine the problems of a one parent family from both the child and adult perspective. *Family Ties* is a US import that presents Michael J. Fox (who has now achieved box office success in films) as a teenage son of a white middle-class family, constantly harassed by two younger sisters. *Bread* examines the lives of an unemployed Catholic family in a working class area of Liverpool and their attempts to defeat the constraints imposed on them by a capitalist society. The humour in this particular programme is far more sophisticated than that of the other two and contains an underlying element of pathos.

All the groups were shown a five-minute clip from each programme, each clip deliberately chosen to reveal as many of the regular characters as possible and to give some insight into their individual personalities. After being allowed to express their general likes or dislikes of each programme and whether they were regular viewers or not, each group was asked in some depth both about individual characters and the 'situation' itself; the questioning format followed similar lines for each clip.

First Reactions: *Me and My Girl*
The usual response made by many of the children after having viewed the first clip, *Me and My Girl*, was a heartfelt criticism of the amount of canned laughter that burst forth from the screen at every conceivable opportunity. They were not only indignant about the inappropriateness of its use, when as far as they could see there was nothing on screen that justified such loud mirth, but also because of the way it interfered with their ability to follow the narrative by drowning the characters' voices.

Andy (14): "You know when they keep on laughing in the background on the TV? - Well, I never seem to laugh when they laugh ... it's everytime they say something."

Cheryl (14): (agrees) "You can't hear some of the words because everyone's laughing."

Richard (10): "Yes - and when they (the audience) are giggling and they (the actors) carry on talking, you can't understand what they're saying ... it just spoils it, because you think 'Oh, ha! ha! ha! - They're laughing so I am laughing'."

Darshi (10): "I say 'What was so funny about that?' and I can't laugh ... well I laugh sometimes."

Having expressed their distaste for canned laughter, a reaction which occurred spontaneously throughout and across all the age groups, the children turned their attention to specific likes and dislikes of individual programmes.

Me and My Girl was only watched regularly by the older children, notably the 14-year-olds, who were appreciative of the way in which narrative events centred upon the actions of Sam (short for Samantha), the teenage daughter, each week.

Cheryl (14): "It's the situation they get in when Sam's growing up."

Mark (14): "She's always concocting something - dreaming up some plan to mess up something."

The younger children seemed more attracted to the events and situations as opposed to individual characters, maintaining that it was the events that created the humour.

Jessica (11): "Different *things* make you laugh each week."

David (10): (agrees) "Yes - it's the things they do."

The middle age-range, the 12- and 13-year-olds were the most critical of the programme at this stage of the discussion and none of them admitted to watching it regularly, although all had seen it at some point. The 12-year-olds felt that the series lacked humour, a fault they ascribed to the characters of Simon (Sam's father, played by Richard O'Sullivan) and Derek (Simon's partner played by Tim Brooke-Taylor).

Robert (12): "They're boring - they don't make it funny."

Gary (12): "They're so old-fashioned! They don't do anything - it's just work! work! work! ... office! office! office!"

The 13-year-olds criticised the realism both in terms of character behaviour and interaction.

Daniel (13): "It's so untrue - like they're in an office and in an office you'd probably have to get on with work, but they're just talking to other people. They're just not good actors. I don't like no-one."

David (13): (agrees) "They just get on (with each other) *too* well."

Sandy (13): (agrees and thinks of an example to support David's comments) "Like when she (Isabel, Simon's housekeeper) smashes something, he (Simon) just looks at her like that (Sandy pulls a face). He don't say 'Oh! No! You smashed one of my plates!' He just stands there as if to say 'So what?' He's not bothered."

Int: "So you don't think that's very realistic?"

Sandy: "No - because if someone came into your house and started smashing all your stuff, you wouldn't be pleased!"

First Reactions: *Family Ties*

Family Ties received a slightly more positive response, although it tended to be the secondary-aged children who were the more regular viewers. Part of the show's attraction seemed to be that Michael J Fox (a current favourite amongst today's teenagers) had a leading role, even though the series had been made before he achieved super-star status. In fact, some of the children admitted that they had discovered the show almost by accident, mainly when channel-hopping, and then became hooked once they realised that one of their favourite personalities was in it. Both younger and older children volunteered this information, although one fourth-year primary girl admitted that it was her older brother who had first encouraged her to watch.

Jessica (11): "My brother told me it was on, so I saw it and I got into it. He says 'It's a good programme'. He goes 'Turn it on Channel 4' and there's this thing that says Michael J Fox - so I was watching him - I really got into it."

However, even though Michael J Fox had been the initial attraction, his portrayal of Alex (the teenage son) and the way he interacts with the rest of his family (in particular, his youngest sister, Jennifer) was also appreciated by those who were regular viewers. Gil (11), liked, for example, the way they have arguments over "silly things". Sandy (13) had a similar view:-

Sandy: "Like that girl (Jennifer) is always in it; he's her brother, Michael J Fox, and she takes the mickey out of him and that's funny."

Trying to articulate *what* made a series funny caused problems among many of the groups, but the older 13- to 14-year-olds struggled manfully to explain the programme's appeal for them.

Int: "What is it about the programme that makes you laugh?"

Sandy (13): "Everything they say."

Daniel (13): "It's the situations - every situation that happens."

Angela (14): "It's Alex. He's really stroppy and he's always trying to take the lead in everything."

Andy (14): "I like the way that everything that's said is kind of meant to be funny - and usually is - they don't end up saying things and then people (the audience) laugh when they're not funny."

However, there were still some children who were critical of the series. A few of the younger ones for example were bothered by the amount of family in-fighting that appeared to go on.

Peter (10): "I think they make good jokes but they get on in the wrong way."

Int: "What do you mean, they get on in the wrong way?"

Peter: "Well, he doesn't really care - um - Alex - he doesn't really care - and the two sisters, they're always on his mum's side."

And some of the 11- to 12-year-olds disliked the *entire* programme for a variety of reasons, although they did admit that they had hardly seen it.

Youssef (11): "Well, I watched that once before and it was *so* silly!"

Gary (12): "I don't like anything corny."

Robert (12): "That's the first time I've seen it. I thought it looked boring."

Suzida (12): "I don't really like it that much, because the family like - um - they're so unreal. They're just dull. They're boring and they're dull. I don't like dull families."

First Reactions: *Bread*

The third series examined in depth, *Bread*, turned out to be the most popular and the one that was watched regularly by nearly all the children. However, there was a range of different responses to it in terms of likes and dislikes, notably amongst the younger children. Although the majority of 9- to 12-year-olds claimed to be regular viewers, they tended to be very critical of its realism, particularly in terms of character behaviour.

Peter (10):	"I think they're all sort of make-believe - none of them are really real."
Youssef (11):	" ... they're Catholic and they had the baby christened - it was silly ... she didn't have to keep going like that [crosses himself] ... It was overdone, because Catholics don't have to keep going like that every second."
Denise (12):	"I don't like the way they all sit round the table - they're always talking and eating - you don't really see much going on. I know you talk but you don't all sit round a table and preach. You just see them driving around in their cars or talking - like - they're always walking along, you never see them in a job or - um - they just come back and talk about it."

However, the 13- to 14-year-olds were far less critical, maintaining that the series was both realistic and funny. They were particularly appreciative of the way in which the family interacted and supported each other.

Stacey (13):	"They look after each other."
Sarah (13):	(agrees) "Yeah, it's like a big family, like that."
Sandy (13):	"If one of them is in trouble, they help them out."
Mark (14):	"And they're all together; they all stick together."
Cheryl (14):	"It's a really strong Catholic family."

They believed that the humour was produced in a variety of ways; for example, the 13-year-olds were amused by the different schemes that household members thought of to get money, particularly if they turned out to be unsuccessful.

Daniel (13):	"It's just like a typical Liverpool family. They're all trying to get money ... like they're all trying to turn a pound note into two pounds - like everyone's trying to do different things."
Sandy (13):	"They've got different ways of trying to get it. One buys and sells antiques and goes through the books to see if there's any money there. One just makes and sells sandwiches and Joey just gets money from somewhere. All of a sudden he's got money."
Sarah (13):	"Or they're fiddling the Social."

Stacey (13) attempts to identify the humour inherent in the various money-making schemes and recalls an incident when Adrian and Jack (two of the Boswell sons) "fiddle" a woman out of a painting in their search for valuable antiques; a "fiddle" that inevitably backfires on them.

Sandy (13):	(interrupting Stacey's lengthy opening description of the incident) " ... it was worth a lot of money and he

60

	(Adrian) got it off her cheap."
Stacey (13):	"And then like - Adrian was in the back [of the van] and he went through it, didn't he? He went through the painting."
Sandy:	"It was all ripped, so he lost a lot of money."

The 14-year-olds were the most perceptive in identifying other sources of humour in the series. They were aware that the constant jibing at other family members often mirrored happenings from their own lives; they were also the only group who recognised some of the underlying pathos in the programme citing a recent episode that had featured the loss of a pet dog belonging to Joey (the oldest son). These children obviously identified with Joey's sadness and his subsequent dilemma when he discovered that his dog was now being looked after by someone whose need for a pet far outweighed Joey's. It was also the 14-year-olds who were able to appreciate the repetitive nature and inherent incongruity of the weekly prayers around the Boswells' dinner-table, a feature that was criticised by the 9- and 10-year-olds as both boring and pointless.

Darshi (10):	"In *Bread*, whenever they start eating, they're always praying."
(The rest agree):	"Yeah, always praying."
Peter (10):	"That gets so boring."

But the 14-year-olds see it differently.

Cheryl (14):	"I think the prayer they do before their dinner - that's funny because they do it every week."
Mark (14):	"Yeah, but you listen to what's in the prayer."
Leigh (14):	"Yeah, the prayer's always different. It's like - um - 'And God help our Joey'."
Cheryl (14):	"Yeah - and they like - um - say their own prayers - like - um - 'Thank you for ...' - um - they come out with stupid things like 'Thank you for Grandad's cabinet I bought'."

These older youngsters appeared to draw on their prior knowledge of the conventions of praying and were aware that the Boswells' prayers did not follow the lines of a traditional and often meaningless 'Grace'. They were therefore able to appreciate the humour in the family's attempts to speak to God as though He were a close friend with a personal interest in their day-to-day happenings.

The need to relate television events to real life experience in order to understand and appreciate the humour in sit-coms became most apparent when considering the younger children's responses to these scenes at the dinner-table. Not only do the Boswells indulge in personalised family prayers before eating, they also have their own way of encouraging each family member to contribute to the household budget. Each of the Boswells' offspring has to donate a percentage of their income (irrespective of how it has been obtained) to the 'common pot', in this instance a china hen which is placed in the centre of the table. Just as the 9- to 10-year-olds saw no purpose to the praying, they also failed to understand the point and, inevitably, the humour of the 'hen ritual'. In contrast to this, the older children we spoke to seemed aware that many of today's parents expect grown-up children to contribute to the household expenses, and thought the Boswells' solution to the problem highly amusing. The younger children had obviously not yet had these kinds of financial dealings explained to them, hence their perplexity at being faced with the hen ritual. As far as the primary children were concerned, the hen served no real purpose other than being an open invitation to burglars.

Mollie (10): " ... they have that hen where they put all the money ... they wouldn't just leave that hen in the middle of the table with money sticking out of it because it's bound to - um - if they did have a robbery, they're bound to rob all that money."

Peter (10): "Yes, it's bound to be stolen!"

It also interfered with the meal and placed the contents of the china hen in something of a hazardous position according to one worried 10-year-old.

Richard (10): " ... But a real family wouldn't actually put money near food because if, say, like - um - one of them knocked off the top of a thing and while they went like that [mimics someone knocking something over], they knocked it over on top of the money, then it ruins the money!"

Having explored children's initial reactions to the three series, we turned our attention to more specific details, notably the characters and the narrative structure.

The Characters in Sit-Coms

According to Feuer[3], sit-coms in recent times have evolved from an instantly recognisable formula of visual jokes and one-liners (as in *I Love Lucy*) into what Newcomb describes as a 'domestic comedy' where the emphasis is placed on characters and their emotional problems instead of complicated and confusing situations that are successfully resolved each week. The humour in these early sit-coms relied on characters involvement with the situation; that is, the scrapes they got themselves into and eventually extricated themselves from.

Traditionally, then, the comic effect in a sit-com arises from a feeling of superiority to the main character, although this reaction only occurs provided the stereotypical nature of the character is recognised. A good example of this is the bigoted outspokenness of Alf Garnett in *Till Death Us Do Part*, whom the viewers laugh *at* instead of *with* because of their ability to recognise his self-delusion. Theories of comedy[4], maintain that once the audience feels empathy for a character, the humour disappears but recent television offerings appear to dispute these theories, a fact now recognised by the US TV companies who have coined the term 'warmedy'[5] [see Feuer] to refer to the new-style sit-com which is presented as comedy combined with empathic audience identification.

The US series *Kate and Allie*, which highlights the problems of one-parent, middle-class families in a 'house share' situation, attempting to carve out new lives for themselves, and more recently, *Roseanne*, which explores the ambivalent feelings inherent in parent/child relationships, are good examples of these new-style sit-coms. UK sit-coms have also evolved in a similar fashion, most notably those that stem from the pen of Carla Lane: for example, *Butterflies*, *Leaving* and currently *Bread*.

In these new-style comedies, stereotyping still occurs but this tends to apply more to the secondary characters than to the central protagonists. Out of the three programmes we examined, this contrast between exaggerated stereotypical characters and those who still manage to invoke an empathic response in the audience is present in all of them, though probably most evident in *Bread*. When questioning children about the nature of individual characters, they were asked not only about their likes and dislikes, but how many of them seemed to be more like people they knew or had seen i.e. how real they seemed to them. Were characters who were more realistic, less humorous but perhaps more appealing than those who were easily recognisable as being exaggerated stereotypes? The concept of identification was also explored; did any of the characters inspire empathic laughter as far as our children were concerned - to what extent did they laugh *with* them rather than *at* them?

Characters in *Me and My Girl*
In *Me and My girl*, children were asked to give their opinions of the character of Sam and her relationship with her father. These were presented as the two main characters and seemed to be the most likely to inspire some kind of empathic response. They were also questioned about Isabel (the housekeeper) and Liz (the secretary) both of whom were more exaggerated secondary figures, as well as Nell (Sam's grandmother) who seemed unlikely to inspire empathy yet cannot be described as a stereotype.

Few of the children perceived Sam as a very realistic teenager; the younger ones were critical of her appearance maintaining that the programme was trying to present her as being younger than she really was (they estimated her real age as 16), although they had their own theory as to why this might be so.

Darshi (10):	"She looks like a little girl."
Mollie (10):	"Yes, she looks more like eleven years old."
Int:	"Do you think they try to make her look younger than she is?"
Mollie (10):	"Yes - because they've been having her for a time, so she was a younger girl before, so they've still got to try and make her look young."

The 13-year-olds were critical of her life-style seeing it as an inaccurate reflection of the average 14-year-old.

Sarah (13):	"You never see her go to school!"
Dean (13):	"She hasn't got any friends - she's always on her own."
Sandy (13:	"She never asks about her mum ... she hardly ever says 'Was my mum nice?'."

The father/daughter relationship was also perceived as being unrealistic.

Int:	"Do you think it's how it would be in real life?"
Richard (10):	"No, he'd be really strict."
Mollie (10):	"He'll just give in to her, but it wouldn't really be like that."

63

Richard (10):	"I think he would be more strict because if he hasn't got a mother [he means wife], he'd need to pay more money and everything ... because he'd be saying 'You can't have this because we haven't got enough money and that."
Int:	"And he never says that?"
Richard (10):	"No. She goes up to him and asks him 'Can I have - um - a new pair of ear-rings or a new jacket' and he says, 'All right, go and buy one!'."
Inderpal (11):	"They should have more arguments."
Jessica (11):	(agrees) "Yeah - sometimes like in real life, dads and teenagers do have rows."

However, the 14-year-old girls did have some feelings of identification with the character of Sam.

Leigh (14):	"She's our sort of age and does the things that we'd want to do."
Int:	"Is she like a typical 14/15 year old?"
Angela (14)	"In some parts - like - when she tried to run away from home because she was upset about her mother ... [but not when] she's always sort of trying to match make it too much. Like you don't walk up to your dad's firm and say 'Nell, there's someone here' and fix up one of her old buddies for her."

There were mixed responses to the characters of Liz and Isabel in terms of liking, although all the age groups were aware of the stereotypical nature of their roles. Isabel seemed to be the least popular; the general opinion appeared to be that she was just "too silly" and therefore not worth discussing in any detail. Liz's lack of realism was criticised but she was still appreciated as a source of humour by some of the children.

Peter (10):	"She (Liz) chats too much - she isn't even part of the programme for me - it would be a lot better if she wasn't even in it."
Mollie (10):	(disagrees) "I think she gives quite a tinge to it - at the office - she sort of makes fun of Derek as well and things like that."
Uzair (9):	"I think she should be in it; there has to be someone like that."
Gil (11):	"She's funny - but - she isn't serious enough ... she does no work."

Liz's portrayal of a secretary was also criticised by some of the secondary children.

Andy (14):	"She's ridiculous ... they [real secretaries] wouldn't just - um - start talking to their boss as though they were their best mate or something, would they?"
Youssef (11):	"She's always doing her finger-nails ... and she does her own type of shorthand and she forgot how to read it."
Denise (12):	"And you never see her using a typewriter or nothing."

All of the children seemed to have a fixed idea as to the kind of tasks a secretary has to carry out and the way she ought to behave both to her boss and others. Presumably none of them had any direct experience of secretaries except for those sitting in the school office, but they all seemed convinced that real secretaries were serious, conscientious and supportive towards their employers. One perceptive 11-year-old boy pointed out that sit-coms often present secretaries as flighty and irresponsible and was aware that this was a form of stereotyping which could then reflect on real-life secretaries.

Youssef (11):   "It teaches you how they stereotype people ... like the secretary, they're stereotyping - like, as if all secretaries are like that. Like in *My Husband and I*, where all the girls in the typing pool are going like that [mimics someone filing their nails] and they're not talking about work, they're talking about other things."

The children finally turned their attention to Nell (Sam's grandmother), who seemed to be the character they appreciated the most. They admired the way she obviously cared about Sam and also her quick-witted responses to some of the other characters, which they believed produced much of the humour in the series.

Mollie (10):   "Well, she's actually sensible and she doesn't make everything so silly - she is comedy but she's not silly comedy."

Peter (10):   "She adds a bit of flavour to it."

Darshi (10):   "Without someone like that, the film's not right, not as it's supposed to be."

Peter: "She does make it funny more than the others; she's like the funniest person in it."

Int: "Why do you think she's the funniest person in it?"

Peter: "Because when the others are telling jokes, she's always giving the reply - which makes it funny."

And what about her role as a grandmother? Jessica and Gil both perceived her to be like a real grandmother, as did Robert who maintained it's because she's always willing to hand over money to Sam, which in his experience was how grandmothers usually behave.

Jessica (11):   "She speaks right."

Gil (11):   "It's how she acts - how she dresses - she's very gentle with Sam."

Robert (12):   "Oh, I think she's real! She's like my grandmother anyway ... When Samantha asks for money, she'll give it to her and that straightaway. Like she [Sam] says 'Oh, can I have some money?' - she asks for money and things and like she gets it."

However, the 14-year-olds regarded Nell's role as being more complex, possibly because of her relationship to Sam who responds to her both as a mother and grandmother figure; Cheryl maintained that this causes Nell to act younger than she actually looks.

Cheryl (14):   "She has to play like a grandmother and a mother, doesn't she? She acts really younger, but that's the

	funny part about it!"
Andy (14):	"She's like a grandmother when you see her in scenes when she actually gets down to talking seriously, but like other times, when she's cracking jokes against Derek and that - it's like - um - well, they [real grandmothers] might crack one or two jokes, but they wouldn't go too far like she does on there."

Characters in *Family Ties*

The next programme the children were asked to turn their attention to in terms of characters was *Family Ties*. As had been obvious from their first reactions to the clip, their favourite character tended to be the oldest son (Alex played by Michael J. Fox) and the source of identification appeared to be his relationship with his youngest sister, Jennifer, who seemed to be the funniest person in the show as far as our children were concerned. They admired the way she interacted with Alex although they appreciated that many of her responses were far too witty and sophisticated to be realistic.

Gil (11):	"She's too funny (to be real) - and for most people too saucy. Most people about 10 years old don't go out and learn jokes."
Sandy (13):	" ... she says things that aren't really real - like they're written in a script - I mean a little sister might not say it!"
Daniel (13):	"She wouldn't go that far - if a little girl had that much wit then it would be funny like in real life."
Sarah (13):	"She talks like she's older than she actually is."

But it was the older children who were the *most* approving of Alex.

Angela (14):	"He's appealing isn't he?"
Joel (14):	(admiringly) "He's flash!"
Mark (14):	"He's different from all the others - he doesn't want to go into business; he always wants to be in politics and everything."

They were also aware that his relationship with his sisters not only created the comic effect but was also a situation that they could identify with to a certain extent.

Suzida (12):	"The brother's quite funny - the way he treats his sisters."
Denise (12):	"Yes, he bosses them about and makes them do the washing-up."
Angela (14):	"He's always stopping his sister - he's so protective of his sister with boyfriends and that. He goes 'You can't go in that car - you don't know what's going to happen' - you know what I mean? ... that's the funny part, I wouldn't like it but that's the funny part when it's on TV."
Int:	"Do you think they behave like real brothers and sisters would?"
Angela (14):	"Well, sometimes, when they're arguing - because

	they fight."
Andy (14):	"Yes, because I've got two sisters ... only with Alex though, it's better to be the older brother - because I'm the youngest. I'm always arguing with my older sisters but if I were older it would be different."

In Andy's eyes, it would be wonderful to be in Alex's position and dominate younger members of the household instead of being on the receiving end; Alex says and does all the things that Andy himself would like to do but never quite has the nerve for. Angela, however, sympathises with the sisters, appreciating how she would feel if placed in a similar position.

Angela (14):	"I think they (the sisters) must feel a bit trapped; he's right over-protective for a brother - I mean you can expect a father to be like that when she's got to that age but not a brother."

The characters that all the age groups were the most critical of in *Family Ties* were the parents; not only were they regarded as "dull", they were also perceived as being far too lenient with the children.

Peter (10):	"She (the mother) gives in too much."
Mollie (10):	"Also, whenever she - um - shouts, she feels embarrassed and with a real mum, I don't think they would."
Uzair (9):	(disagrees) "I think the mum is real but the dad's not as real."
Int:	"Why not?"
Uzair:	"Because he doesn't really care much and he's too soft on the children."
Richard:	"He's never in a scene much - he comes in a scene and then he goes out again and then he comes back and then he goes out again; he's never in it much."
Robert (12):	"He's plain and boring."

But Mark is aware that the main characters in the series are the Keating *children* and not the parents; the parents are only necessary because the narrative structure of sit-coms requires TV families to have some kind of parent figure if they are to reflect real-life situations.

Mark (14):	"They're just there. They need to have parents so they've put them in it ... the actual parents in it, they don't seem like the rest of them, because they seem so dull compared to - um - like the kids."
Int:	"Do you think the parents treat the kids as parents would in real life?"
Angela (14):	"No, the mum is like a best mate towards them, isn't she? And the father - um - gets on well with Alex, but the oldest girl is like a best mate."
Int:	"And you don't think that's very realistic?"
Angela:	"It is in some cases, but only when it's a one-parent family normally."

Characters in *Bread*

Finally, the children turned their attention to the key characters in *Bread*. Were there any members of the Boswell household that they admired or could identify with? Did some characters lack realism because of exaggerated personality traits? If so, did this detract from or add to the comic effect?

The oldest son, Joey, was perceived as one of the most realistic members of the household, although the younger children maintained that he took his position of seniority a little too seriously.

Richard (10): "He always acts the best and he's always in charge, but if my brother did that to me, I'd punch him in the face."

Uzair (9): "I don't like him - all the time he bosses them around."

The secondary children, however, admired his forcefulness, maintaining that he was the person responsible for keeping the family together.

Suzida (12): "He's so smooth and he's like their big brother and every time he comes in ... "

Robert (12): (interrupts) "He's like the dad of the family. [He thinks of an example] - he walked in the police station last week, and all the others were having a row. Then everyone stopped because he went 'Greetings!'" (Robert mimics Joey's catch-phrase).

Stacey (13): "He's keeping the family together - under control like! He's a cool dude!"

Dean (13): "He never panics or anything - Billy always panics and Joey calms him down."

Cheryl (14): (describing Joey in similar terms to Stacey, although they are in different groups) "He's a cool dude! He organises everything."

Mrs Boswell, the mother was also perceived as realistic particularly in the way she cared for her family. None of the children seemed to regard her as a stereotypical Catholic mother whose main concern was that her family should both eat and pray regularly; their only criticism was of the way in which she controlled the household budget by means of the china hen.

Richard (10): "I think the mum is more like other people because - um - she is! ... Except for the bird that she puts on the table."

Darshi (10): "I think she's the only one who's real."

Daniel also perceived the mother to be the most realistic character thus providing some insight into how he felt mothers should act. It was while they were discussing the character of Mrs Boswell that it became apparent as to how traditional some of the children's ideas were concerning the role of motherhood; but was this motherhood as it is portrayed in sit-coms or as it is in real life?

Daniel (13): "She feeds them and everything ... she holds the family together and makes them still pray and everything."

Leigh (14): "It's really the mum who makes sure that they go to

	church and that - and dress up."
Angela (14):	"And that they eat their dinner."
Int:	"Does that make her more like a mum in real life?"
Leigh (14):	"It might be ... but then they all go to put money in the pot ... "
Cheryl (14):	(interrupts) "If they don't, she like - um - stares - she'll really give them a stare if it's only a fiver."
Int:	"Don't you think that's very real then?"
Leigh:	"No, they all look at each other. I mean, my mum wouldn't do that. I'd kill her if she did."

As far as our children were concerned, neither Joey nor his mother were regarded as the main source of humour. So who were the characters that made them laugh? And how did they fit in with the children's perceptions of realism?

The characters whom the children described as being the funniest were those with the most exaggerated personality traits, that is, Aveline, the only girl in the Boswell household appreciated by the older age groups, and Grandad, who lives next door and was enjoyed by all. Of the two, Aveline was regarded as the least realistic, although it was the primary children who seemed incapable of perceiving that her outlandish appearance and behaviour combined with her own inflated opinion of her attractiveness was what made the character amusing.

Darshi (10):	"I think the worst - um - the one who's not real, is that girl. She's really over the top!"
Richard (10):	(agrees) "Yes, there was one time in the *Bread* series, she said to her mum 'Can I have some money?' and her mum said 'No!'. And then when they were all in bed, she crept down and stole some money and I thought, 'Well, girls wouldn't really do that!'."

The secondary children were more aware of the comic effect of Aveline's appearance.

Sarah (13):	(sarcastically) "She's a model!"
Stacey (13):	(laughs) "Well, I don't think she's going to make it! ... and the mum's always saying 'Take a whistle with you in case you get raped!'."

(All laugh, obviously recognising that Aveline's bizarre appearance is more likely to repel rather than attract a rapist).

Stacey:	(continues) "And the way she walks down the street (giggles)."
Dean (13):	"Oh, yeah - she was walking down the street with the dog and the dog was pulling her along. You should have seen the way her legs were going."

The 14-year-olds held similar views:

Leigh (14):	"Oh, Aveline - she's out of this world! (laughs)."
Cheryl (14):	"Her colour scheme's hideous."
Andy (14):	"She's just funny."
Leigh:	"Yeah, the way she walks down the road with this great big hairy mongrel [laughs]."
Cheryl:	(agrees) "Yeah - and the way she talks is really

funny."

Grandad Boswell's lack of realism was put down to his outrageous behaviour more than his appearance; but it was his anti-social activities that were most appreciated by the children. Here was an old man being allowed to indulge in rude, aggressive behaviour, something that they knew they themselves would never get away with. In their eyes, he is deliberately flouting authority (symbolised by Mrs Boswell) and yet he receives no recriminations or punishment.

Int:	"What makes him funny?"
Cheryl (14):	"He's so unfriendly ... he's so ungrateful!"
Joel (14):	"He's got no manners."
Cheryl:	"He slams the door in your face."
Joel:	"He doesn't say 'Thank you' for anything."
Youssef (11):	"It's the way he swears and he goes 'Where's me tea? Where's me other things?'" (mimics the 'old man' voice of Grandad Boswell).
Gary (12):	"But no Grandad goes and swears at you for not giving him enough food."

It seems then, that children's appreciation of the comic effect of characters in sit-coms is dependent not only on their ability to perceive stereotypical behaviour and personality traits, but also the extent to which they are able to identify with portrayals of family relationships and interaction. Are the same pre-requisites necessary in order to appreciate the humour of narrative *events* in sit-coms?

The Situation and Narrative Events

Having discussed characters, we turned our attention to the 'situation'. What kinds of events happened each week? Did they appear to follow any kind of set pattern or formula and if so did this kind of repetition enhance or detract from the children's enjoyment of the programmes.

What Happens in *Me and My Girl*?

Children's appreciation of the story-lines in *Me and My Girl* seemed to depend upon whether they were regular viewers or not. Those who only watched occasionally, "when there's nothing else on", maintained that events tended to be unrealistic. In their view the narrative appeared to follow the structure of more traditional sit-coms in that a complicated and confusing situation occurs at the outset and is then, without fail, successfully resolved. In the case of *Me and My Girl*, they were also aware that this successful outcome was invariably due to Sam's interference, which many of them believed not only made the series too predictable but also increased its lack of realism.

One 10-year-old girl, for example, managed to think of two recent episodes which, in her view, centred around unlikely events. As she pointed out, some elements could conceivably happen in real life, but because the programme tended to over-dramatise the situation, an element of fantasy then crept into the plot.

Mollie (10):   "Well, in a recent series that there's been, her (Sam) friend's got a single parent as well and she (Sam) tries

	to get - um - they both try to get them (the two parents) together but I don't somehow think that would really happen."
	(She thinks of a second example).
Mollie (10):	" ... they're having an interview, say, and he (Derek) will get all tense. Well, that's real - but at the actual interview where everything goes wrong and it turns out to be a woman (Derek has to interview) and they thought it was going to be a man and they don't think women are better - *then* it's not real! It just turns silly rather than funny."

Two 11-year-olds (one boy and one girl), became quite heated over the realistic nature of the plots and their predictable resolution, with the girl, Jessica, maintaining that she liked these kinds of programmes to finish up on a happy note each week and that a resulting lack of realism was immaterial as far as she was concerned.

Jessica (11):	"I think it's a right ending."
Gil (11):	"But it isn't that realistic because - um - [he thinks of a recent episode] - um - if somebody falls in love, it lasts more than one day."
Jessica:	"He doesn't always fall in love though."
Gil:	"Sometimes he does - every two weeks."
Jessica:	"Well, only sometimes."

But it was the secondary-age children as a whole, who were the most vociferous in complaining about the predictability of the plot resolution.

Int:	"What usually happens in the programme?"
David (13):	"They've got a problem and they sort it out."
Sandy (13):	"It *always* gets sorted out. There's never anything happens - like - where there's a problem and they can't sort it out completely."
Suzida (12):	"It always gets sorted out - *that's* what the problem is; it always gets sorted out."
Youssef (11):	"That's why it's so predictable; it always gets sorted."
Robert (12):	" ... in real life, you wouldn't work a problem out in a day ... they work it out too quick."
Youssef:	(agrees) " ... they do it in about an hour."

The 14-year-olds not only recognised the weekly 'problem' format but also criticised the fact that it was Sam who took on the task of resolving the problem, causing one of them, Cheryl, to contradict what she has said earlier, although she remains blissfully unaware of this fact.

Mark (14):	"There's always problems and it's usually Sam that sort of ends up sorting them out."
Cheryl (14):	"She *really* sorts them out. She's not like one of us (this remark is in direct opposition to something she has said five minutes before). If my dad had a problem at his office or something, he'd sort it out himself, but she goes poking her nose in."

As all the children seemed very aware of some of the contrived nature of the plot structure, questions were then raised as to why certain comedy series tend to stick so closely to a set formula. Some of the replies, even from the younger age groups gave a good indication as to how perceptive many of today's youngsters are in recognising and understanding the conventions of television narratives in general.

Int: "Why do you think it's always sorted out at the end of the programme?"

Richard (10):   "Because they want to leave people without a lump in their throat."

Robert (12):   "To get new storylines every week."

Gary (12):   "Because if it just went on, they'd lose viewers, wouldn't they?"

Dean (13):   "Because they're on a contract for another year!" (laughs).

Mark (14):   "Just to get extra laughs."

Andy (14):   "So that people don't keep on going 'Oooh!' [he makes a groaning noise] - because when everything's sorted out, they go, 'Oh! That's good'."

Because the situations and narrative events in *Me and My Girl* were perceived as unrealistic, the children were unable to identify with them to any extent. Although in their earlier conversation about characters, some of them had been appreciative of Sam's emotional relationship with her father, they were aware that life in their own households bore little resemblance to that in Sam's house. Real-life problems, as far as they were concerned, were unlikely to be resolved as easily as Sam's and Simon's appeared to be.

Leigh (14):   " ... because we haven't got families that are always joking and that - and our problems are never solved like theirs are."

What Happens in *Family Ties*?

Next, the children turned their attention to the plot situations in *Family Ties*, which they perceived as being less predictable than those featured in *Me and My Girl*. All of the age groups recognised that contrived plot resolutions arising from complex and confusing situations were far less likely to occur in *Family Ties*.

Daniel (13):   "Well, some weeks - like - there is a problem, but some weeks like on that one [referring to the clip just seen], there wasn't a problem there - well, it didn't look like it."

Angela (14):   "It's totally different [to *Me and My Girl*]. Everything happens in it; you never know what's going to happen next."

In the children's eyes, this lack of predictable problems meant that the weekly events featured in the Keating household tended to be more realistic than those in *Me and My Girl*, despite the US setting.

Suzida (12):   "In there, it's like something happens to one of them. No-one like an uncle or a grandad comes in with a problem - it's always their own problem ... That problem about the secretary - that was realistic - he

72

went and sorted it out and when he came back, they all knew about it, like he'd promised."

Only one child managed to think of a recent episode that had featured an incident that he perceived as being unrealistic. This was when Alex's father purchased a gun as a burglar deterrent; Gil (11) saw this as being most unlikely to happen in real life, thereby revealing his own lack of knowledge concerning US citizens' rights to carry weapons.

Most of the children maintained that any problems that did arise in the narrative were linked to specific characters, usually Alex. These problems tended to be due to family differences of opinion concerning Alex's behaviour and beliefs, and, if resolution did occur, it was because the family sat down and talked it through so as to achieve some sort of compromise.

Andy (14):   "He's usually the problem - Alex is! Like they get a problem and they're on one side of it and he gets to be the one that's always saying 'Don't do that - do this!'."

Denise (12):   "But they all sit and talk it out."

As far as our children were concerned the way the family talked things through made the programme far more reflective of real life and therefore capable of acting as a model for good social relationships.

Angela (14):   "Well - it's not always kissing each other and that by the end of it ... sometimes they sort of work it out but it's not like *Me and My Girl* when it's always like - um - happy ever after."

Darshi (10):   "I think you can learn to be nice to everyone - I think it tells you how to act as a family - how to be a family."

What Happens in *Bread*?

As usual, *Bread*, because of its complex and more sophisticated narrative that frequently borders on parody, was the series the children had the most difficulty with in terms of comprehension of plot structure. They were aware that there was a certain amount of repetition each week, notably the scenes around the dinner table, but some of them maintained that this added to the humour instead of making it too predictable and as a consequence, boring. At least, these were the older children's interpretations; the younger ones were more critical.

Int: "Does the same sort of thing happen in it each week or not?"

Richard (10):   "Yes - it's always like putting the money in the pot ..."

Mollie (10):   (interrupts) " ... and praying."

Richard: (continues) " ... and having their dinner and then you think, 'Oh, thank God, that's over! - because I don't do that'."

Darshi (10):   "And then they go to sleep - like all they do is go to sleep, wake up, go to work and then again, come dinner, they put money in the pot."

At this point of the discussion, one group also became aware (some of

73

them for the first time) of the use of 'sets' in sit-coms.

Denise (12):	"When I turn over, they're always sitting inside the house."
Youssef (11):	"Or the DHSS office."
Int:	"Do you think a lot of comedy programmes do that?"
Youssef:	"Yeah, sit-coms - because like *No Place Like Home* does - you don't see outside the house."
Denise:	"I've never really thought about that, but you don't, do you? You stay inside and you never really go upstairs."
Int:	"Any idea why?"
Gary (12):	"Because they haven't got nothing to do outside. Because they've got no jobs - their life is inside."
Youssef:	"It's because they're not real houses - because their life's in a set. The lady who writes it, it's up to her."

Youssef also had opinions about stereotyping and how this was a tool frequently employed by sit-com writers to produce humour, an aspect he had touched on earlier when discussing characters.

Youssef (11):	"They always make out that everybody in Liverpool cheats the DHSS. They're saying that everybody in Liverpool drives a Jag and has leather trousers and jeans."
Int:	"Do you think that that sort of programme can give you a bad image of people from Liverpool?"
Youssef:	"Yeah, it can - same as EastEnders does that to the East End."
Gary (12):	"It doesn't say that they *all* con the DHSS though, does it?"
Youssef:	"But they do - don't they?"

And what about the problem format that the children had identified as a major component of *Me and My Girl*, did they perceive a similar narrative structure in *Bread* or was it different in some way? Most of the children appeared to believe that there was some kind of problem each week, but there was a difference in that it did not necessarily get neatly resolved by the end of the episode. This lack of resolution, from which some of the children detected an element of pathos, was seen to reflect real life issues and produced feelings of empathy particularly amongst the older age groups.

Suzida (12):	"There is a problem, but it gets sorted out in detail not just like that."
Youssef (11):	(explains further) "Sometimes there's a bit of it left."
Stacey (13):	"It's always different - because sometimes one of them will get into trouble and they'll all help him out - or sometimes - um - like in that one (Stacey refers to clip which she has seen before) he thought he'd found his dog, but he didn't - so that was different."
Sandy (13):	"Sometimes it is sorted out and sometimes it isn't. Like in *Me and My Girl*, it always is - and it gets boring like that because you know what's going to happen."

Int:	"The fact that it's not always sorted, does that make it more or less real?"
All:	"More real!"
Sandy:	"Because you can't have - um - like problems sorted out every time, because it don't seem right."

And what did the oldest age group have to say on the subject of happy endings?

Andy (14):	"It sometimes has a saddish ending ... but they still have a little joke at the end - always."
Cheryl (14):	"Yeah, there was that time when he [Joey] couldn't get his girl-friend back and ... "
Andy:	(interrupts) "... and he was just sitting in the car all miserable."
Int:	"So it's not always a happy ending?"
Cheryl:	"No but that's the good part about it. Because it's more real - you can understand that happening."

Family Ties had been identified by some of our groups as being a good model for teaching about family relationships. So was there anything the children thought they could learn about social behaviour and family interaction from *Bread*? The primary children thought not, and one secondary-age boy treated the question as a joke.

Gary (12):	(laughing) "Only how to cheat the DHSS!"

However, a 13-year-old thought that there was some attempt being made to impart a message, perhaps one that ought to be regarded as a warning.

Daniel (13):	"It's teaching you about the ups and downs of life - like - in our life, you don't see us struggling to get money and everything, but they're just trying to survive and get money."

It seems then that today's youngsters still expect the events in sit-coms to parallel those of real life. They appreciate that a certain amount of exaggeration is necessary for humour to be produced, but even the youngest are scornful of 'predictable' happy endings.

Conclusion

Having examined children's responses, not only to the genre of TV comedy, but also some specific examples of sit-coms, what seems to be the main factors that influence children's enjoyment? Clearly, there are differences among children, most notably with age, as to what they can understand and identify with. Identification with a leading character and how it affects children's liking for the character seems to work in two opposing ways. Youngsters may become more critical of that character's behaviour if they think he/she is being plain silly, as was the case with the younger children in our sample when discussing Aveline in *Bread*. But this response becomes polarised if the character is more like themselves, as can be seen from their comments on Sam in *Me and My Girl*.

Far-fetched comedies (e.g. *The Young Ones* or *Black Adder*), where out of the ordinary characters may do outlandish things, only really work if they are categorised in some way as 'alternative' or 'zany'. In other words, there are sub-genres of comedy which children come to recognise and in regard to each of which they develop idiosyncratic expectations. *Bread*, with its exaggerated character behaviour and interaction, combines elements of 'alternative' comedy with that of a more familiar sit-com environment. The subtle inclusion of this' 'alternative' element, however, appeared to be beyond the comprehension of our younger children and was only really appreciated by the oldest of our secondary groups, who were thus able to accommodate a perceived lack of realism in certain aspects of the Boswell family's behaviour.

Our youngster's perceptions of the realism of family interaction tended to be judged according to the way the children interacted with their own families, hence their appreciation of the sibling relationships in *Family Ties*. However, it must be remembered that judgements of realism are often a function of comparisons across TV families, and not just those experienced in the real world.

Despite the children's lack of comprehension of certain aspects of *Bread*, this programme proved to be the most popular of the three we discussed in depth, particularly amongst the older children. *Family Ties* was a close second with some of the primary age-group having difficulty in choosing between the two.

The reasons behind these preferences seem to lie with what children expect to get from comedy programming. If today's youngsters are merely seeking a "good laugh", they are more likely to turn to cartoons, stand-up comedians and other traditional forms of humour than they are to sit-coms. From sit-coms they expect more; they want to be stirred emotionally so as to experience moments of sadness as well as joy. For children, just as for adults, modern sit-coms should offer the opportunity for empathy, so that young viewers can laugh *with* characters and their problems rather than *at* them; in this way their popularity as a TV genre may well be retained.

References

1. Newcomb, H. (1974) TV: *The Most Popular Art.* *New York: Anchor Books.*

2. Levy, M and Gunter, G. (1988) *Home Video and the Changing* Nature *of the TV Audience.* *London: John Libbey.*

3. Feuer, J.   (1987)   "The MTM Style" in H. Newcombe (Ed). *Television: The Critical View* (Fourth Edition).   New York: Oxford University Press.

4. See for example: Goudlad, S. (1976) "On the Social Significance of Television Comedy" in G.W.E. Bigsby (Ed). *Approaches to Popular Culture. London: Edwin Arnold.*

5. Feuer, J. *op. cit.*

5   Quiz and game shows

Quiz and game shows are without doubt one of the most popular forms of entertainment programming on television today. They attract large audiences among young and old alike and feature among the best-liked programmes. At the same time, they have, as a genre, probably reached near saturation point. Although clearly enjoyed by mass audiences, there is evidence that many people would not opt for more quiz shows on television than there already are at the moment[1].

Quiz and game shows come in a variety of forms. It would be wrong to assume that this genre consists of a homogeneous category of programmes. Quite the contrary, the games played, the types of contestants featured, the prizes offered and the seriousness as against the light-heartedness of these programmes can vary a great deal. Some shows feature celebrity contestants only, others are played only by ordinary members of the public, while a small number team up celebrities and the public. Some shows offer big star prizes for winners, while others offer only points. Some shows involve a certain amount of skill or put the knowledge of contestants to the test. Others rely mainly on chance and good luck. Some are played by teams, while others pit individuals against each other.

Which among these shows and particular features appeal most and least to children? Are there special ingredients of quiz shows which really attract younger viewers to make such light entertainment regular or even compulsive viewing? In this chapter we take a look at what children aged 8 to 14 have to say about quiz and game shows. What is it, in their own words, that they like or dislike about them?

Six groups were interviewed about their opinions concerning quiz and game shows on TV. Four of these groups were secondary schoolchildren aged 11 - 14 years and the other two were primary schoolchildren aged 9 - 11 years. There were six children per group, comprising equal numbers of boys and girls.

They were asked a range of questions about quiz and games shows in general, and were then in each case shown two or three clips from well-known series currently on television, on which their comments were elicited. The questions we asked took them through their perceptions of what this type of programme is like, which quiz and game shows they watch and prefer, their reasons for watching these shows, and finally, their thoughts and opinions about contestants, presenters, the way the games are played, the prizes offered, and how easy or difficult they find quiz shows to follow and understand.

What is a Quiz Show?

We began by asking children to describe in their own words what they thought was meant by a quiz or game show. Which ones could they name? Was there a distinction to be made between a "quiz" show and a "game" show? Given the names of a small selection of shows, could they say whether each was either a "quiz" or a "game" show?

These sorts of questions are actually quite difficult. Certainly, we probably all feel we know what a quiz show is. We have nearly all seen examples of such entertainment and most of us who have can probably name at least one quiz or game show. However, when asked to describe precisely what this type of programming is, and if asked to draw a distinction between a "quiz" show and a "game" show, how many of us could do so?

What then do children say about quiz and game shows? These programmes are seen variously as shows in which contestants have to answer questions, either to win prizes in the case of a quiz show or to win points and eventually the game in game shows. Not all the children were able to make this subtle distinction; some did not know what we were talking about when we asked if they had heard of "game" shows as a separate category of entertainment from "quiz" shows. Sometimes, the distinction was simply: "they don't ask so many questions" in game shows. This understanding was less well developed among primary-age children than among secondary schoolers.

When asked if they could name any quiz or game shows themselves, the children we interviewed were able spontaneously to think of most of the main ones on TV. Among those named were *Blankety Blank, Blockbusters, Catchphrase, Countdown, Call My Bluff, Every Second Counts, Family Fortunes, A Question of Sport, A Question of Entertainment, Punchlines* and *Winner Takes All*. As can be seen, these include representatives from all the four main broadcast TV channels.

Going back to the subject of what is the difference between a "quiz" show and a "game" show, we asked children to say into which category each of a number of shows fell. *The Price is Right, Play Your Cards Right* and *Treasure Hunt* were all seen as being game shows. So too was *The Krypton Factor*. In the case of two shows, there was some disagreement over which type each was thought to be. *Blankety Blank* was initially described as a game show. But on further reflection, the children felt that because the contestants, who are all celebrities, had to sit and answer questions, this added a quiz show element to it. In sum, it is a bit of both. Another show over which children could not decide was *Catchphrase*, which initially was defined as a quiz show. However, because contestants have to answer questions for which graphic clues are provided, this added a game show element to it.

Perhaps the clearest attempt at drawing the distinction was articulated by one of the youngest children to whom we spoke:

Suki (9):   "On a quiz show they ask you questions about general knowledge and on a game show you play a game where you have to .. um .. like .. um .. have numbers and things."

Which Quiz Shows do Children Watch?

In a series of questions we probed which quiz shows children claimed to watch, how often they watched them, and which ones they liked best. We also asked if they deliberately watched certain shows or if they watched them passively just because such shows happened to be on.

The children gave a range of answers concerning how often they watched and how deliberately they tuned in. Clearly some children really are fans of these programmes and try to watch as many as they can. Others are less strongly attracted and, although they will watch if there is nothing better to do, they do not go out of their way to view TV quizzes.

Most of the leading TV quizzes and games shows were mentioned by the children we spoke to as ones they watched at least on some occasions. These included *Blockbusters, Connections, First Class and Knock Knock* among those made for children, and *Bullseye, Catchphrase, Chain Letters, Every Second Counts, Family Fortunes, Lucky Ladders, Mastermind, The Price is Right, Quandaries, A Question of Sports* and *Winner Takes All* among those made for family audiences.

Favourites among quiz shows were *Catchphrase* and *The Krypton Factor*. Important ingredients of well-liked shows seem to be that they pose a real test of knowledge or skill on the part of the contestants or offer something in which children at home can themselves join in. This seemed to be especially true for shows such as *Catchphrase*.

Sally (12):   "I like Catchphrase because it's good; you can guess at it, and I can answer the questions."

Neil (12):   "It's got common phrases and mostly you know them, so it's kind of an easy show."

Although there was some mention of prizes that could be won on these shows, the central ingredient underlying a telly quiz's appeal is the competition itself. If the quiz involves the right types of questions - the sort the children themselves can attempt at home - then it is more likely to be popular.

A programme which was definitely out of favour was *Mastermind*. This was seen as difficult to follow, lacking in pace and did not invite audience participation. A number of children remarked that it was boring.

According to one girl aged 13 "It's for old people". One boy aged 13 also remarked "... the thing I dislike is there's a black chair".

When we probed the children further as to why they found *Mastermind* boring, a variety of responses were given.

Sarah (13):   "You have to be clever to understand it."

David (13):   "Yeah, the questions - I reckon they're well hard."

Another show which came in for a bit of stick from the children we spoke to was *The Price is Right*. The British version of this show was perceived by at least one child as being inferior to the North American original. For one thing, the prizes were neither as big nor as glamorous in Britain.

Although not always clearly articulated this last point was underlined by one well travelled young man, Stephen (13): "... when I went to Canada, the prizes they get on there, that's what everyone gets when they come in the studio - like they can win about five cars for a caravan over there ..."

Is Quiz Show Viewing Active or Passive?

One of the fundamental questions posed about children's use of television is whether they control the set or it controls them. Children's relative "activity" or "passivity" in their time spent with television can be assessed in a variety of ways. At the level of their behaviourial involvement with television is the question of whether they watch programmes selectively. At the level of their intellectual involvement with television, we can ask how much effort do children invest in trying to follow and understand programmes. The degree of attention children pay to programmes may be controlled both by their personal level of interest or enjoyment and by particular features of the programmes themselves. What then is the nature of children's watching of television quiz shows?

We can begin by looking at children's stated *behaviourial* activity or passivity towards these programmes. Do children choose to watch specific quiz programmes or do they simply watch them because they happen to come on while they are watching television? The answer seems to be that both reasons apply.

Nelson (14):   "Well, *Family Fortunes*, I just come in and watch it because I like that."

Paul (14):   "On a Saturday night, I look for *Catchphrase*."
(Others agree)

Nelson (14):   "Sometimes you turn over and a quiz show just happens to be there.

Interviewer: "What do you do then?"

Nelson (14):   "I'll sit and watch it for a bit, but if it's boring I'll flick over."

Passive watching of TV quiz and game shows by children does not seem to be typical on the testimony we obtained from them. Quiz shows either have some special function for children or they contain particular features which appeal strongly to children's tastes. Another sign of 'activity' in their viewing, was the finding that children experience and enjoy an intellectual challenge while watching some quiz shows. Among the functions recognised by the children we spoke to were that quizzes provide a source of learning. Perhaps more to the point, however, children like to try to answer the questions themselves and see them as a test of their own general knowledge.

Bianca (13):	"Sometimes you think, 'No, I don't want to watch this', but once you've started watching it, then you get ..."
David (13):	(interrupts) "... answering the questions."
Bianca:	(continues) ".. um .. attached to it."
Andrea (13):	".. and if you can answer a question you feel quite good about it."
David:	"And you can play against your brother and sister".
Andrea:	"And, if the person on the TV don't get it, then I'm going 'Yeah!' and I'm getting all excited and going 'That's the answer!' and things like that."
Bianca:	"Yeah, that's it - it adds to the atmosphere."
Sarah (13):	"I get bored every time I get the answer wrong - and I go off .."
Bianca:	"Yeah, because the questions are only for adults; they're not for children."

The appeal of testing their own general knowledge against not only the contestants in the show but against others who happen also to be watching at home was evidenced throughout all the groups we interviewed, even down to the very youngest. In explaining part of the reason why he liked to watch *Family Fortunes*, one 9-year-old boy said "I'm always beating my mum at it!"

Although largely able to follow the rules and understand what is going on in TV quizzes, evidence did emerge that a few children may have difficulties with the language used. Thus, audience participation for some young viewers may be inhibited by an inability to comprehend what the questions mean.

Bianca (13):	"Yes - they keep using long words and you don't even know what they mean - like they could make them into smaller words and then you'd know what they'd mean."

Did the children think they could learn from quiz shows? Some of them did think that they could, but this really depended on whether the subjects were new and at the same time relevant to them, and upon the difficulty of the language used in the show.

Andrea (13):	"Sometimes with questions - if they're like history or geography and you don't know it."
Bianca (13):	".. if the questions were at a more simple level, then we could learn, because then we'd know what they were talking about .. like if they asked them in simple ways instead of using big words."

Appealing Formats
Difficulty for Contestants
Some TV quizzes have a continuity to them in that contestants who win one week may be invited back to carry on playing or to defend their positions as champions the next week. Young viewers claim to be pulled back to the

show when this happens, especially when a contestant has been champion over several games or weeks.

Angela (13):   "I like to see what happens to the contestants."

Shane (13):   "Yes, to see if they're going to get knocked out or if they're going to do the fifth gold run" (referring to the final stage of *Blockbusters*).

The appealing nature of quiz shows in which the contestants are made to sweat for their final rewards is further underlined by children's remarks on the kinds of quizzes they would like to see more often on the box.

Sally (12):   "I prefer things where you have to work at it - rather like *Treasure Hunt* ... because you have to work it out step by step. Like, if there was a kind of murder show ... you'd have to work out who did it."

This opinion was endorsed by others. Shows which have a problem running all the way through - such as *Treasure Hunt* - rather than having lots of different questions, are well-liked by young viewers.

The Appeal of Special Effects and Gimmicks

Children's attention to television programmes is known to be controlled by special sound and visual effects[2]. A child looking away from the screen may still be monitoring it by listening to what is going on in a programme. A sound effect or somebody saying something significant can draw the child's eyes back to the screen again. Continued visual attention may then depend on what's happening visually in a programme as well as what is being said.

Some quiz shows try to be visually interesting by employing technical gimmicks and gadgets. Computer simulations (e.g. *First Class*; *Catchphrase*) and visual displays (e.g. *Family Fortunes*) feature among these special techniques. Both of these features were found to appeal to some of the boys. This was true in particular of *Catchphrase*.

Int: "Why do you like *Catchphrase*?"

Martin (11):   "Because there's computer graphics in it - you've got to guess the pictures."

Int: "Do you like computers in quizzes?"

Martin: Yes, it's good (Probe: Why?) It's more modern than just sitting answering questions ... it's more interesting."

The special, technical gadgetry of *Catchphrase* was liked by even the very youngest children we spoke to.

Stephen (9):   "I like the computer and the pictures."

Suki (9):   "Yeah, I like the buttons that they have to press and that big computer screen."

When asked if there were any quiz shows on which they themselves would like to appear, the attraction to technical gadgetry emerged yet again.

Martin: "I'd like the one with Eugene, but I don't remember the name (*First Class*) - it's really good and you work as a team and they do everything ... it's about pop groups, there's a computer."

The Contestants

Quiz shows revolve around the performance of their contestants. Different games are played in different ways, however; some involve competition between teams, while others pit individuals against each other. We asked children whether they preferred seeing contestants compete as individuals or as part of a team. We also wanted to find out if young viewers felt that quiz show participants have to be a certain type of person.

Singles or Teams?

On the question of competitors appearing as singles, in pairs or in teams, there was quite a strong liking for team games. For one thing, some children felt that contestants themselves were more confident when part of a team than when playing on their own and as a result performed better. In this way a TV quiz could be altogether more entertaining to watch.

Nelson (14):   ".. in pairs, because when you're on your own you're a bit nervous, but once you've got someone next to you, you're OK."

Paul (14):   "Yeah, they come out with some funny things .. they bring up their past."

The preference for teams was found among younger children as well. Nine- and eleven-year-olds enjoyed watching contestants compete as pairs or larger teams. They especially seemed to enjoy seeing the teamwork element, whereby members of the same team could help one another with tricky questions. It was felt that there was more chance of getting an answer correct in a team situation. A romantic element crept in from one of the girls who liked to see couples working together for the benefit of each other.

All these points are illustrated by the following set of remarks from primary-age children in response to the question "Do you prefer quiz or game shows where contestants are on their own, in pairs, or in a team?"

Kylie (11):   "I like when there's two."

Bradley (11):   [breaking in] "Because say one of you gets it wrong - but if there's two of you, one might get it wrong, but the other one might get it right, so that means you've still got two chances of getting it right".

Louise (9):   "I like pairs because it's nice if you get a man and a woman on ... it's as if they're a couple and they're, like, working together."

Not all the children were fans of team games, however, as evidenced by one or two dissenting young voices.

Denny (11):   "... in a team, they're always rowing about which answer they should give ..."

Martin (11):   "I don't like it on teams, because you see them all squabbling ..."

What Type of Person Goes on a TV Quiz Show?

We asked children if they felt that TV quiz show contestants had to be a certain type of person. Their comments, as we show below, indicated that they had mixed feelings about this. Some children did not see that contestants were really any different from ordinary people. Others, however, believed that people with certain qualities or traits would be more suited to appearing on these programmes.

Obviously, because quiz show formats vary quite a bit, the situation will determine to some extent what is the most appropriate way to behave. Thus, the behaviour expected of contestants in a show like *The Price is Right* would not go down well in *Mastermind*. Different types of people will in any case choose to appear in one or other of these two extremes, but the contexts in which the game is played in each case dictate different standards and kinds of behaviour on the part of contestants.

Even in the peak-time game shows where big value prizes can be won, TV producers usually prefer controlled enthusiasm on the part of participants. Anyone who is totally over-the-top or who adopts the wrong kind of attitude is likely to be sifted out before the show is recorded.

The children we interviewed seemed to be remarkably well-informed in some cases, and held clear-cut opinions about the type of person who would be best suited to different TV quizzes. Now let's look at the evidence concerning children's beliefs about fitting the contestant to the question.

Children associated certain types of contestant with particular quiz shows. To appear on *The Price is Right*, for instance, you had to be bouncy and funny. *Mastermind* attracted the 'serious' and 'brainy' types, like a teacher, according to one or two of our young viewers. The latter were not crazy or greedy types as on *The Price Is Right*. *Blockbusters*, which is, of course, aimed at the younger age group, was perceived to have contestants who were clever, intelligent or "boffin" types who were in most cases likely to go on to university.

Even on *The Price Is Right*, contestants had to strike the right balance between being too enthusiastic, and hence appearing silly, as well as distracting attention from the game, and overly quiet and shy - thus making for boring viewing.

Jane (14):	"You can't overact because it puts you off if they overact."
Zoe (14):	"But you can't be shy .."
Jane (14):	"Sometimes everything that's said they laugh at .."
Nelson (14):	"Yeah, sometimes they (the contestants) just go on and on, and the bloke's (compere) trying to get on with the game."

In contrast, the *Mastermind* contestant was classed as quite a different sort of person.

Sally (12):	"Quiet, a quiet, keep-to-yourself kind of person."
Zoe (14):	"They're boring." (*most* agree)
Nelson (14):	"They're not boring; they're just interested in things we don't take much notice of."

The Selection of Contestants

Sometimes the children revealed impressive depths of insight into the processes lying behind the production of TV quiz shows. For instance, one girl was aware of the selection processes employed by some quiz shows in order to choose the best personalities to appear.

Sally (12):	"I think in *The Price Is Right* you have to go and see the director for something - because you get the tickets - but you have to go and see the director to see what kind of character you are .. because they choose you by your character really .. what kind of person you are."
Int:	"What kind of person do you have to be for *The Price Is Right?*"
Sally (12):	"Funny - I mean happy - kind of all jumping about and that. You have to go 'Oh, great, I've got it, I've got it" (mimics excited contestant).

Another group of children were asked if they thought that TV producers tended to favour particular types of person to appear on TV quiz or game shows. On the whole, most felt that this wasn't the case. One dissenting voice, however, believed that there was a tendency for the producers to choose people who would look good on television and hinted that contestants did not represent all sections of the population.

Andrea (13):	".. but that's what they're doing nowadays .. like they're choosing the ones that are .. um .. right for the TV and things like that .. not the ones that are unemployed .."

A little later the same girl elaborated on this point even more, to suggest a middle-class bias in the selection of contestants.

Andrea:	".. but even the ones that have got work and they're like .. um .. they've got a good background and you know, it's sort of like .. um .. posh and everything .. they don't pick the ones that you see everyday. It's the ones that are good at education and things like that."

A perceived middle-class bias in the contestants came through even more strongly in children's opinions about *Blockbusters*.

Int:	"Do you think you have to be a certain type to go on *Blockbusters*?"
Denny (11):	"Intelligent."
Rachel (11):	"I think they have to be quite intelligent and clever, and I think they have to be yuppies to go on it."
Martin (11):	"I reckon you have to be pretty serious, because on some games you can have a bit of a laugh .. but on *Blockbusters*, they're too serious .. why can't they put a bit of humour in it?"
Kylie (11):	"I think that on *Blockbusters*, which is so boring, they're either all boffins or most of the time .. they go .. um .. they're all flash."
Mary (11):	"They all go to college, don't they?"
Kylie (11):	"Yes, they all go to college and they're all flash and they think they know it all and when they get it wrong, I love that bit."

86

At one point, the children whom we interviewed were shown a clip of a children's quiz show, *Knock Knock*. All recognised the show spontaneously although not all claimed to be current viewers of it. We asked the children for their thoughts about the contestants on *Knock Knock*; are they a certain type? A major ingredient in the appeal of quiz shows is that they often feature ordinary people with whom the viewers at home can identify. This certainly seemed to be the case, to a degree, among the children we interviewed. There was still something about people who appeared on television, however, that set them apart from the viewers themselves.

The ordinariness of child contestants in *Knock Knock* came across with such remarks as:

Nelson (14):   "They're just schoolchildren really - just like us."

Jane (14):   "They're not like anybody really."

However, when asked if these children were like kids they knew in school, the distinctions began to emerge.

Nelson (14):   "They're the clever ones and they're willing to be contestants."

Paul (14):   "No, some people aren't (clever), they just pick out of a hat or something like that, because it would be unfair otherwise."

Younger children expressed different opinions about the contestants on *Knock Knock*. They did not identify with contestants on this show. In fact, it was a major bone of contention among primary-age children that the series failed to include competitors with whom they could identify.

Bradley (11):   "They're too old - you don't seem to get ones from primary schools."

Denny (11):   "No, you don't often get them from primary schools, they're high school."

Rachel (11):   "They don't seem to get them from our sort of school - they're more public."

The youngest children of all were the most critical about *Knock Knock*, especially with regard to the contestants. A regional bias was detected by some nine-year-olds and a general perception that contestants on *Knock Knock* often seemed to be miserable. When we asked a group of nine-year-olds whether they thought the contestants on *Knock Knock* are like children they know, we obtained the following replies:

Louise (9):   "Well, it's strange because they always have Scottish and Irish people on there."

Tammy (9):   "Perhaps they just do it in Scottish and Irish places."

Int: "Are they like kids that you know - like in your school?"

Louise: "Well, they're not, they just sort of ... um ... they always seem to be ignorant towards him [the presenter]. They're all, like, long faces and that. They're not happy when they win things."

Int: "So you don't mean ignorant, you mean they don't look happy? They're miserable?"

Louise: "Yes, they look sort of like they've got the hump!"

Tammy: "Yes, say if they've been in the skip and then after that they'll win a prize - well, they'll still be grumpy because they went in the skip."

Getting to Know Contestants

Do children want to know what the contestants are like as people? In general, they do, but children do not like shows which dwell on this for too long. The ones we interviewed felt that adult quiz shows often spent too much time introducing contestants and finding out who they are, while in those shows made more especially for children, too little time was felt to be spent on this. One reason for wanting to know more about the contestants is so that "you know which side to cheer for." This desire for participation, however defined, is a recurring theme throughout our investigations - irrespective of which aspect of TV we were addressing.

One unexpected concern about the quiz show hosts' interviews to find out about contestants as part of the introduction to the show, was the possibility that contestants might be embarrassed to have certain details revealed about themselves on TV.

Sally (12):   "Sometimes it's a bit embarrassing - it's like they say things that have happened to you and you don't really want to tell other people - and then its broadcast all over the nation ... You know that in one show, they said something about this bloke .. um .. something happened to him and he got really embarrassed about it and he got kind of angry because of it. I don't like that kind of thing."

Supporting Particular Contestants

Siding with contestants seems to be part of the fun of TV quiz and game show watching. Children do have their favourite types and look for contestants to cheer for. Those contestants who are seen as funny or who you can feel sorry for are the ones most likely to attract the support of the child audience at home. 'Smart Alec' types are less popular. Sympathy for the underdog surfaced as well, with some children saying they supported contestants who were losing. Here are some of the comments made by the children about this.

Nelson (14):   "Well, some contestants kind of draw you to them .. like they're really funny."

Paul (14):   "Some you take pity on .."

Kevin (14):   "Well, others, they're really boasting and that."

Among younger children, the reasons for choosing to support a contestant tended to be less subtle - favourite contestants may be chosen because they are of the same sex or have the same name.

Scott (9):   "I like the boys to win."

Stephen (9):   "I like it if they have my name."

Once a favourite was chosen, the teenage children usually claimed to stick with that individual or team and to root for them to win and for their opponents to lose.

Int: "Do you ever want certain contestants to win or lose then?"

All: "Yes."

| Andrea (13): | "Some I do, because some I can't stand - like some of the men on *Catchphrase*, they try and act all hard and everything and the other contestant, he's alone and I think 'Come on, come on - beat him'.. and they zoom right past him. I mean the other person snatches all the points off him." |

Younger children showed signs of being more fickle in their support. They tended to want to be on the side of the winners and would shift their allegiances during the course of a show if necessary.

| Louise (9): | "I pick one team, but if they start to lose then I go on the other side." |
| Tammy (9): | "I like it when they're winning, but if I'm playing with my dad and he's on one team and I'm on another, my dad won't swap because they're winning." |

The last remark suggests that children may sometimes be joined by parents and that together the whole family become involved in the fun of the competition.

Why do People Want to be on Quiz Shows?

We asked the children why they thought people would want to appear as contestants on TV quiz and game shows. Is it just to appear on television? Is it to win money and big-value prizes? Or is it because they want to meet the compere? A variety of reasons were identified, including all of the above.

Nelson (14):	"To win prizes."
Jane (14):	"To be on telly."
Zoe (13):	"To meet the presenter."
Jane (14):	"Yeah, the host."
Paul (14):	"Yeah, and to be on telly - then you could tell your friends, 'Oh, I saw so and so'" (laughs).

Younger children echoed these views but also thought that greed and the desire to win money was a major reason for people wanting to appear on quiz shows.

Kylie (11):	"To earn 'loadsa money'."
Denny (11):	"Because they're greedy, some of them."
Bradley (11):	"Some of the people who go on these, they've got mansions and then they want another mansion."
Mary (11):	"I think they do it because they want to win money and they want the chance to be on television."

The children, who were shown a clip from *Knock Knock*, were asked in respect of this show, why they thought child contestants would want to appear. This procedure of asking about a specific programme which they were shown an actual excerpt from, was designed to give our young respondents a concrete and familiar example on which to express their opinions.

The general view was that contestants want to appear on telly or are curious about what it's like to be on a quiz show. Thus, it's a personal experience thing. Another opinion, however, was that they are show-offs who just want to boast to their friends that they've been on the telly.

Int:	"Why do you think they want to go on *Knock Knock*?"
Jane (14):	"To be on telly."
Nelson (14):	"To tell their mates at school - or some people can look back when they're older and say 'Well, I was on it'."
Zoe (13):	"Some people are addicted to them; they're just addicted. They feel they've got to be on a game show."
Int:	"So, it's not to win the prizes?"
Jane:	"It depends."
Nelson:	"I think it's not just to be on a quiz show, it's because you want to see somebody famous."

Younger children's views about why contestants want to appear on *Knock Knock* mirrored those given by their elders.

| Tammy (9): | "They want to be famous ... to enjoy themselves ... to win a prize". |
| Louise (9): | "To show that they've beaten someone - and to feel that everyone's looking at them on TV." |

Do Children Themselves Want to Appear in TV Quiz Shows?

Would the children like to appear on TV quiz shows themselves? We asked children if they themselves would like to be a contestant on a TV quiz show, and if so on which one? In general, most said they would like to give it a go. The shows they wanted to appear on, however, varied from one child to the next.

Nelson (14):	"*Knock Knock*, it's really easy."
Paul (14):	"Yeah, it's easy to win prizes on it, you could just walk away with loads of stuff."
Kevin (14):	"*Catchphrase* .."
Paul:	"Yeah, I'm good at that."
Jane (14):	"*Krypton Factor*."
Paul:	"*Family Fortunes* (Why?) .. to show up my mum and dad."
Zoe (13):	"No, it's because you can say what you think when they ask the questions (the others agree) .. like they say it's something out of a 100 people or whatever, and you can just say anything and you might get it."

The Presenters

Audience research among adult viewers has revealed that the presenter of a TV quiz show can be a crucial factor underpinning the audience's enjoyment of it[3]. As well as the game itself, the way the programme flows is controlled by the host. It helps if the compere is entertaining, but not at the expense of the contestants or game itself. The host of the show must therefore hit the right pitch - being both amusing and getting on with the business of playing the game, and without trying to dominate the programme.

Who among the many quiz show presenters on television these days do children like best?

Nelson (14):	"Noel Edmunds in that .. um .. what's it called?"
Paul (14):	*"Telly Addicts."*

When they were asked why they liked Noel Edmunds we got the following replies.

Paul (14):	"Don't know ... he livened it up."
Nelson:	"Yeah, and I don't reckon he rehearsed anything like he ... (interrupted)
Jane:	"Yeah, he's just a natural."
Zoe (13):	"I liked the way he pulled them out of the audience and took the mickey out of them. It was funny."

(Interviewer probes further about presenters)

Kevin (14):	"Russ Abbott's alright, but he don't do many."
(All laugh)	
Zoe (13):	"He don't do any!" (scornfully).
Kevin (14):	"Well, Les Dennis then .."
Paul:	"No, I hate him .. you watch him, when the ladies come out, he's always hugging them, and going 'cor' and doing that thing with his lip."
Jane (14):	"I like him, I think he's funny."
Paul:	"I like that bloke who does *Blockbusters*."
Kevin (14):	"Bob Holness."
Paul:	"Yeah, he's alright, he's brainy, but he mixes it in so that he's kinda funny as well .. the audience likes him too."
Kevin (14):	"He thinks he's still young, but he's an old geezer."

Further questioning probed whether the children preferred male or female presenters. As the children themselves quickly pointed out though, there aren't very many female quiz show presenters, so there's really not much to choose from. According to one boy, women aren't really clever enough, but on the whole, the children agreed that there ought to be more women presenters than there are at the moment. The ones they did notice were Sue Robbie of *Connections* and Debbie Greenwood who presents *First Class*. One or two of the girls were quite critical of Debbie.

Jane (14):	"Well, she's always talking about her husband."
Zoe (13):	"And whatever it is, she knows about, she always says 'Oh, I've been there' or 'I know it'."

One boy felt that women sometimes show favouritism towards contestants.

Kevin (14):	"Yeah, and the one on *Connections*, if there's someone nice, then she says 'Come on, you can get it, you can get it' and then to the next couple she says 'No, that's not it' and goes back to the first and says 'Come on, come on' - I don't like that. I like her, but I don't like the way she does it, it's as though she keeps telling them the answer and they just get it in the end."

Among the children's favourite presenters overall were Noel Edmunds and Michael Aspel. All children agreed that both of these two are very professional and very good with contestants.

The Questions

One of the things research among adult audiences has found out about the appeal of quiz and game shows on TV is that the viewers at home enjoy being able to join in the fun of the competition themselves. This feature is probably more important than seeing people win big prizes. TV quiz shows which invite audience participation and which require viewers at home to stretch themselves to some extent are likely to prove very popular. From the comments of our respondents so far, this phenomenon also seems to hold true among younger members of the audience. To confirm this, we asked our children directly if they ever tried to answer the questions on quiz shows. The general reply was that this was something they all did.

Kevin (14):   "Yeah, I have competitions between me and my brother to see who gets the most."

Did the children think that quiz show contestants have generally to work hard to win? Opinions on this matter were mixed, with some children feeling that the questions were often quite difficult; others disagreeing.

Some of our young quiz show fans had sympathy for the contestants who froze in front of the cameras. They seemed to realise that it was not the same trying to think clearly and answer even fairly easy questions in the glare of the studio lights and in front of millions of people and doing so while sitting in the comfort of home watching TV.

Nelson (14):   "Well some people, they know the questions but once they see all the cameras and the lights and the audience, well they ..."

Jane (14):   (interrupts) "They get nervous." (All agree)

Kevin (14):   "Yeah, they're scared, their mind goes blank."

Do children think that quiz shows should therefore make things easier for contestants by asking only easy questions? In general, this idea did not appeal. One of the central ingredients of a successful TV quiz show is the drama and uncertainty of who will win. This can really only be generated in a truly competitive environment where contestants have to be stretched. Quiz and game shows, where the children thought contestants had it too easy, and won prizes without really having to work for them, were scathingly treated.

The Prizes

How important are prizes to the enjoyment of TV quiz and game shows? On some shows, the main aim is to win the star prize at the end of the game. In others, the only thing that counts is winning the game itself. In this country there are clearly specified limits to the value of prizes or prize money that can be won in quiz shows. At the time of writing, the maximum value of a star prize that can be won in a single show was fixed at £4,000. Another attitude we probed was whether the games should be all or nothing, with the winner taking all and the losers leaving without a thing?

The relative significance of prizes seems to depend on the nature of the game itself. In the case of some TV quiz shows the game is so simple that it needs a big value prize to lend any excitement or drama to the proceedings. Other games are sufficiently exciting and fun in themselves that they do not need to rely on having large prizes for the winners. For example, our children felt that *The Krypton Factor*, which does have a low-value prize for the winner, is enjoyable to watch for other reasons. The game itself is challenging for contestants and the show's entertainment value derives from seeing which contestant will triumph in the end. The tests to which contestants are put in the studio are also mostly tasks which the audience at home can play as well.

We next asked what would be their own personal preferences, if they were contestants; would they like money or a prize?

Nelson (14):   "I'd go for the money."

Jane (14):   "It depends on the prize .. but if you were to win the money equivalent to it, you could go out and buy it."

Nelson: "Yeah, but you don't know how much money they're going to give you."

In the end, they all finally agreed they would opt for the prize because it would be more interesting and useful. However, one boy perceived a possible problem with prizes, especially if contestants already owned an item like it.

Nelson (14):   "If some people have already got the prize, then they'd want it to be worth a lot so they could flog it."

Prizes and Entertainment Value

The importance of prizes depends not only on the kind of show but also on the age of the children. Opinions about the importance of prizes on quizzes did change with age. Among the youngest children, there was some perplexity about contestants' motives for appearing on quizzes which offered only small prizes. This was true, for instance, of *Mastermind*. For the youngest children, prizes added an element of fun which would otherwise be missing. They had not yet come to understand that for some contestants the main goal was not to win a prize but to win the competition.

There were mixed opinions among primary-age children about whether it is better to win prizes or to win money. One perceived advantage of money is that you can spend it on whatever you like. The disadvantage is that you may end up spending it with nothing to show, while at least with a prize you have something to keep. Of course, with prizes, there is always the chance that you have the item already. Another feature according to one youngster was that it was relatively commonplace to see contestants winning prizes of some sort, but relatively rare for someone to win a really large amount of money.

James (9):   "Well, one person could get a really, really big sum of money and one could get nothing - but - um, like you get a prize all the time if you go on it."

Suki (9):   "I think a prize (is better) because with money you can - um - like spend it, but with a car or something, you can keep it."

Martin (11):   "I like it to be money, because if you give them a prize and just say they've already got it, they'll think 'Oh no, I don't want this'. But if you give them the money, well it's like Christmas presents. If you're

93

given a toy and you're a bit too old for it, you'll say 'Oh, I don't really like this' and you'll put it to one side. But if you're given a voucher, then you go out and buy what you want."

As children get older, the significance of prizes to their enjoyment of quiz shows becomes less central. They begin to see other elements that are important to a quiz's entertainment value. Indeed, some children, as they mature, indicate concerns about the 'greed' factor which they believe motivates contestants to appear on those TV quizzes which offer the really big prizes. Thus, shows such as *The Krypton Factor* come to be more appreciated because contestants enter the challenge of the competition and not simply to win a prize. According to Denny (11), commenting on contestants who appear on *The Krypton Factor*, "They're not too greedy on there".

How Much Should Contestants be Allowed to Win?
Do children think that it is better that contestants be allowed to win prizes only or money as well? Mixed feelings emerged once again, with some children opting for money for successful contestants, while others felt that the winners should be content with prizes. One opinion was that money should be won in the early rounds and that even those contestants not getting all the way to the final rounds, should not leave empty-handed.

Paul (14):   "They ought to win the money getting there, to the final bit and then they get a prize at the end."

For the final round, all the children chose to see a prize as opposed to money for the winners.

We next asked if limits should be set to the value of prizes that can be won? These children were not overwhelmingly in favour of limits to the value of prizes. One advantage of expensive prizes was that if the contestants already had the item in question, they could always sell off the one they had won.

The children were probed further for their opinions about prizes on quiz shows after watching a clip from the children's series, *Knock Knock*. What level of awareness did they have about the kinds of prizes which could be won by successful contestants on this show? Did children think that the prizes were important or not? To begin with, the children interviewed were able to name a wide range of prizes from this show. Primary-age children generally thought that the prizes on *Knock Knock* were good or at least, appropriate for the kind of show it is, though on the whole, they had little to say on this subject. Older children were better able to articulate opinions about prizes on the show.

Jane (14):   "Record tokens,"
Nelson (14):   ".. and records."
Paul (14):   "Hairdryer."
Zoe (13):   ".. and there's cassette players, little and large ones .. it's always the same - they've got little alarm clocks."
Int: "So, it's always the same prizes?"
Zoe: "Yeah, there's the keyboard and the crayons."
Paul: "They probably buy them wholesale and get them

cheap."

Int:	"So, are the prizes better or worse (on *Knock Knock*) than on other quiz shows?"
Zoe:	"Worse really; it's like as we're younger, we're only children, we don't get offered such good prizes."
Kevin (14):	"No, it's not that, it's just that they've been given a certain amount of money, like at the BBC, and they have to spend it on what they think is right."
Zoe (13):	"They don't have to spend it on crayons."

So are the prizes really important or not? To some children they are clearly an important aspect of a TV quiz show. Without them, the drama and entertainment value of the show are diminished. For others, it is the game itself which is central. Games requiring skill and competence on the part of the contestants, which invite viewers at home to join in too, are the ones they most enjoy. Thus, some of the children said they would continue to watch *Knock Knock* even if there were no prizes for contestants; others, however, felt that there would be no competition without them. In the end, the significance of prizes probably depends on the type of game. With some games, in which a good deal of skill or knowledge is required, seeing who wins can be enjoyment enough, especially if the contestants or competing teams have support from viewers at home. Identification with the competitors is important here. With simpler games, where luck rather than skill is paramount, without prizes, there would be little left to generate any drama. Without the drama of not knowing who will win a prize worth winning, the show loses all its appeal.

How the Show is Put Together

The format of TV quiz shows can vary a great deal. Some games or quizzes have complex rules, while others seem to have hardly any at all. Children seem to prefer simple rules. They claimed to be confused when the rules changed from one week to the next, even though they might be relatively simple. *The Price is Right*, for example, fell into this category. The contestants are led through the game by the compere, and don't have to do much more than guess the prices of items which one could argue requires some semblance of consumer awareness. However, their general knowledge is never really put to the test. And yet, the format of the show does not remain exactly the same all the time; the games and the rounds change from one week to the next.

Following the Rules of the Game

Among the secondary schoolchildren, it was difficult to derive from their comments any consistent view about the ideal quiz show format. Some preferred simple rules, while others favoured complex games. A few wanted to have the rules clearly explained at the start of the show, while other, more ambitious types, were happy to be left to work it out for themselves as the show went along. Many did agree that they liked shows which had lots of different events or games.

Among primary school children, however, clearer opinions emerged, particularly with regard to preferences for team games as against contestants competing singly or in pairs. The advantage perceived for contestants playing in teams was that, if one of them failed to answer a question, other team members could help out. The disadvantage of teams was that different members might not always agree on the right answer to give.

Bradley (11): ".. say one of you gets it wrong - but if there's two of you, one might get it wrong but the other one might get it right, so that means you've still got two chances of getting it right."

Denny (11): "Yes, but in a team, they're always rowing about which answer they should give and then one's going to get it wrong and then everybody blames the one who gets it wrong."

Martin (11): "I don't like it on teams because you see them all squabbling and they're really quiet (imitates people whispering) .."

The pace of a TV quiz or game show is important to young viewers. If it slows down too much for any length of time, they begin to get irritated with the show. This was evident in the opinions they gave about *Every Second Counts*, another show from which a clip was presented. We asked our children what they thought about the pace of this programme and whether in their opinion there were too many or too few questions. Although made for a more adult audience, this family quiz was popular with the children we interviewed. The game itself was found easy to follow and the host, Paul Daniels, was very highly thought of by many of them.

The children had no difficulties with the rules.

Paul (14): "They're straightforward - it's like multiple choice, that's what makes it so good."

Nelson (14): "Yeah, it's a chance, isn't it - you can say something and it's going to be one or the other."

Int: "What do you have to do?"

Nelson: "Just say like true or false."

Paul: "Just like that we've just seen (in a clip of the show which was shown to them) where they had to say faster, and he said hare."

Kevin (14): "And they get seconds when they get a question right and it's who's won the most seconds."

Int: "And then what? They go through to the final? What happens in the final?"

Paul: "That's when you use your seconds."

Jane (14): "Yes, the more seconds you get, the more chance they have to win prizes."

Paul (14): "They've got to get four questions and when they keep answering them, the seconds keep going down and once you've stopped, once you've answered all four, it stops."

Nelson (14): "If you've got more seconds, then it's alright, you've got more time to answer."

Int: "Are questions in the final the same as the main part of the quiz?"

96

Nelson:	"No, not quite."
Jane (14):	"It's more like they have three choices instead of two, but when it's still the six people, they've got like, just two choices, but in the final they've got three choices."

Even younger, primary-age children were in a limited fashion able to describe the way the game is played on *Every Second Counts*.

Int:	"How does the quiz work? What happens to start off with?"
James (11):	"They have to change around. The couples change round each question thing and the one with the most seconds wins - and they've got - um - well, say they've only got two seconds on it - say two seconds to answer seven questions on it."
Suki (11):	"... you have to sit down and the contestants change their mind and you have to answer these questions - you press the button if you know it. You have to say True or False."
Int:	"What happens in the end - in the final?"
Louise (11):	"Oh, the lights! They have to put the lights out. Like, they've got a '3' and they have to put them out and they have to get them in so many seconds."

Clearly, children have no problems with following the way this particular game is played. Are there any particular features of the show they would like to have changed, however?

Kevin (14):	"Well, at the beginning, they take too much long to present .. um .. introduce the people - they spend about 15 minutes."
Paul (14):	"Yeah, it takes up too much of the quiz show."
Nelson:	"I reckon they should have a limit on how much time they should be taking up."

Apart from this introductory section during which Paul Daniels meets the contestants and ask them to say something about themselves, where they come from and what they do for a living, the children felt that the rest of the show, where the game itself was actually played, moved along alright.

Quiz and Game Shows: The Key Ingredients
Television quizzes and game shows are watched extensively by children. The young viewers we interviewed were familiar with most of the major quizzes on TV. Furthermore, many youngsters seem to have clear-cut likes and dislikes where this genre of programming is concerned. They know which shows they like to watch and which attributes are central to their enjoyment of telly quizzes.

Children watch quiz and game shows that are made especially for their age group and shows which are aimed at broader family or adult audiences. Although often regarded by critics as lowest common denominator viewing fare children can be very fussy about the entertainment value provided by these shows. Certainly, children are not simply passive viewers of these programmes.

The essential ingredients of a good quiz or game show as far as our children are concerned include:

* a game or quiz which they themselves can take part in at home, either to test their own general knowledge, to compete with the contestants in the show, or to compete against others watching with them.

* a game or quiz requiring a certain degree of skill, and where contestants have to work to win, rather than rely mainly on luck or chance.

* a game or quiz which they can understand and follow, and not one whose language or rules are beyond their understanding.

* a game or quiz whose contestants they can somehow relate to or feel an affinity with, whose side they can then take and offer support to.

References

1. Gunter, B. Come on down : a report on the popular appeal of TV quiz and game shows. *Airwaves : Quarterly Journal of the IBA*, 1986, Spring, p. 5.

2. Anderson, D R and Lorch, E P. Looking at television: Action or reaction? In J Bryant and D R Anderson (Eds) *Children's understanding of television: Research on attention and comprehension*. New York; Academic Press.

3. Gunter, B, 1986, *op. cit.*

6 Music, variety and chat

Light entertainment covers a miscellany of different programmes. Broadcasters tend to distinguish between quiz and games shows, situation comedy, music and variety and chat shows as the main categories of entertainment. Further division can be made in terms of the target audience; thus, children's and adult-oriented light entertainment can be separated. Despite the latter division, however, children watch and enjoy both types of programming, and as they grow older, they tend to turn more frequently towards family entertainment broadcast later in the evening, while showing less and less preference for those programmes made especially for their own age group. During this developmental process, there comes a time when, although they may still watch children's entertainment programming early in the evening, young viewers become less inclined to admit to doing so.

Separate chapters have already examined children's views about situation comedy and quiz and game shows. In this chapter we focus on the rest of light entertainment and discuss what young viewers think about music and variety, and talk shows on television. We also take a look at what children have to say about cartoons.

Altogether we interviewed eight groups of children about television's light entertainment programmes, four groups of primary schoolers (aged 7-11 years) and four groups of secondary schoolers (aged 11-13 years). In addition to asking for their spontaneous preferences and tastes among programmes of this type, we also presented clips from some of these programmes in order to lend more focus to the discussion. Each group was shown three clips, though not every group saw the same clips. Two primary and two secondary-school groups saw clips from *Get Fresh*, *Network 7* and *Roland Rat*, while the remaining groups saw clips from *Emu's World*, *The Chart Show* and the *Les Dennis Show*.

The interview began by asking all children which entertainment programmes they could think of that were specially made for their age group. A number of programmes were mentioned in response to this question - *Going Live*, *Get Fresh*, *Wackaday*, *On the Waterfront*, *Blue Peter* and *Thunder Cats* being named by secondary schoolchildren, and *Rolf Harris Cartoon Time*, *Inspector Gadget*, *The Mysterious Cities of Gold*, *The Movie Game*, *Young Krypton* and *Super Ted* being mentioned by primary schoolers. A number of children also mentioned some drama series in the present context of entertainment.

Research into children's viewing habits and programme preferences has revealed gradual changes in what and how much children watch as they pass from pre-teen to teenage years. As they begin to develop other interests and activities during their teens, the amount of television watching they do drops significantly[1]. Furthermore, secondary schoolers tend to develop a taste for more adult-orientated programming. At the same time they reject programmes customarily thought of as children's programmes.

There was evidence from the children we interviewed of changing taste with age. Older children (12 years and above) were beginning to reject children's programmes.

Interviewer: "Are there any specific children's or teen programmes that you dislike?"
Ayse (13):   "Super Ted"
Int: "Why don't you like that?"
Ayse: "It's for kids."

Another feature of children's comments about television which characterised, but was not unique to remarks about light entertainment programmes, was their varying ability to articulate their opinions. Older children generally had more well-formed opinions about programmes and were better able than younger children to express their thoughts and feelings about television. Thus, age-related differences in opinions about programmes and in apparent viewing tastes may to some extent be accounted for in terms of the differing language abilities of primary and secondary-age children.

The youngest children found it difficult to express what it was that they found appealing or unattractive about programmes and thus rarely elaborated very much on their reasons for liking or disliking particular light entertainment shows. Occasionally a programme would touch on a special interest of the child.

Basere (9):   "I like *Pole Position*."
Int: "Why do you like *Pole Position*?"
Basere: "Because I'm interested in cars and there's cars in it that I like."

Special gadgets seemed to underlie the appeal of this cartoon series.

Keith (9):   [referring again to *Pole Position*] "And they convert to hover-crafts and hydrofoils."
Abbas (9):   "I like *Pole Position* because it's got nice cars in it."

Basere:	"They're all like - um - got electric and that ..."
Abbas:	"Yeah - they've got computers in them that help them."
Basere:	"They tell them where they're going and that."
Int:	"So you like things that have got computers in?"
Keith (9):	"And electronic things - in *The Cities of Gold* there's all mechanical things that are made by the Incas."

Thus, the general discussion about entertainment programmes with this age-group tended to be short-lived as the children quickly ran out of things to say or were able to offer only brief comments about them. More focus was provided by clips excerpted from well-known light entertainment programmes. Before each clip, however, the children were asked for their general opinions about programmes of the type they were about to see.

Music Programmes

When asked which music programmes they could think of, primary and secondary-age children mostly named *Top of the Pops*, *The Roxy and The Chart Show*. The late-night *American Top Ten* was also known to a few children. Preference among these shows varied. Many children were fond of *Top of the Pops*:

| Gillian (13): | "It shows the charts as well as all the records that are in it." |

Others also liked *The Chart Show*

| Robert[1] (13): | "Because it's got a wide selection - it also does heavy metal - but it also does different stuff." |

Children who preferred *The Chart Show* liked it best because it was longer than *Top of the Pops*, and because there were no presenters, feeling this left even more time for the music.

| Craig (12) | "It's on for an hour and it shows more records than you get on *Top of the Pops*." |

Other children preferred *Top of the Pops* because they felt that it played more of the best known music and had more of the most popular performers of the day, who appeared live in the studio. According to Kerry (12), talking about *Top of the Pops*:

"It shows you the whole top 40 and they play the ones that everyone buys."

Commenting on *The Chart Show* Sarah (12) felt that:

"It's boring. It goes on and on. It's got pop groups that you don't really know."

Those children who were questioned about music programmes were then shown a clip of *The Chart Show*. All the children shown the clip were able to identify it and many claimed to be regular viewers of it. *The Chart Show*'s distinctive characteristic which sets it apart from *Top of the Pops* and other similar popular music programmes, is that it has no presenter. In addition to music videos, *The Chart Show* displays written information about singers and musicians and their recording histories on the screen, superimposed over the video footage of the performers. As we will see in due course, the absence of talk appealed to some children because they said it left more time for the music.

The Chart Show also uses special production techniques such as rewinding, pausing or fast-forwarding the video-recording of performers. All these distinctive features were apparent to the children we interviewed.

Int: "Are there any ways in which it's different to other 'pop' shows?"

Ayse (13):   "Yes - *Top of the Pops* because on there it doesn't show you anything about them [the performers]."

Gillian (13):   "And it has the rewind on it."

There were, however, mixed opinions about the rewind, pause and fast-forward features in *The Chart Show*. When asked if they liked the idea or not, contrasting replies were given:

Gillian (13):   "No, they'll get half-way through a song and then they start re-winding it and go back to another one, so you'd rather they just played it all the way through."

Others, however, liked this technique and felt it had certain advantages.

Robert[2](13):   "Well, it cuts out the rough songs - well, like, it just goes through and cuts them out until it gets to a certain one."

Younger children also noticed and were attracted by *The Chart Show*'s peculiar features.

Basere (9):   "I notice that when it rewinds - um - when it gets to number one, it only rewinds all the way to number ten and then it starts at four, three, two, one and then it's finished."

Tulsey (9):   "I like the pop stars and it keeps rewinding and playing."

Binder (9):   "If you come to a song that you like, then it rewinds and it comes again."

Among children who claimed to like *Top of the Pops*, we probed further to try to find what it was about this show that they particularly liked.

Robert[2](13):   "Well, it always gives you a preview of what's come into the charts."

Tracey (13):   "It shows you the new releases and that."

For some children, one advantage of *Top of the Pops* over *The Chart Show* was that the former focuses on the "Top 40" selling records of the week, while the latter might feature any of the "key 100" records. These children preferred to see and hear only those from the top of the charts.

Top of the Pops was not liked in its entirety, however. There were certain aspects of the show which turned some children off.

Gillian (13):   "Some of the presenters, they go on a bit, don't they?"

The children we spoke to had clear favourites among popular presenters and DJs. Overly excitable presenters did not impress; instead young viewers liked a professional style, and presenters who seemed to know about popular music.

In reference to one unnamed *Top of the Pops* female presenter, quite a few negative comments emerged:

Robert[2](13):   "Yeah, she goes over the top."

Int: "In what way?"

Ayse (13):   "I just don't like the way she speaks or anything."

| Robert[2]: | "Yeah, she screams and - hee! hee! hee!" (he mimics a girlish giggle.) |

In contrast, remarks about one well-known male presenter were highly favourable.

Robert[1](13):	"He's funny."
Tracey (13):	"He doesn't go over the top."
Ayse (13):	"He's good - he tells you bits and bobs about the 'pop' stars - he tells you what songs are coming out, like when their albums are coming out."

One particular feature of *Top of the Pops* is the fact that it has a live studio audience, giving the show a disco feel. Most of the children we interviewed liked this aspect of the show and felt that it added to the atmosphere.

| Robert[1](13): | "It's a good atmosphere and the crowd take part in it and everything." |

Occasionally, however, there was a negative side to this aspect of the programme.

| Tracey (13): | "Yeah, but sometimes if it's a quiet song, they all stand there screaming and that ... Sometimes you can't hear the song." |

The camera work on *Top of the Pops* is a further ingredient which was noticed by the children and lends a distinctive character to the show.

Int:	"Have you ever noticed if they do anything unusual with the cameras?"
Tracey (13):	"Yeah, they run about on the stage and try and get pictures - um - like of them playing the organ".
Robert[2](13):	"They do close-ups, but the close-ups are too slow and when the next camera comes along you can still see the other camera getting off the stage."
Int:	"Do you like to see unusual camera angles or not?"
Robert[2](13):	"Yeah, but they must be able to think of a way where they don't show the camera because it spoils the actual show."
Tracey (13):	"It's like you're watching the stars and you see this cameraman running across the back - and the other week you saw the soundman as well running across the back."

Thus, the children did not mind the unusual camera angles, zooms and other techniques, but did not want to be made aware of the cameras by seeing them on screen. Although young viewers know it's a live show, set in a studio and created especially for television, they do not want to be made aware of this; they still want the effect of a transparent screen, so that they are offered a realistic "window on the world". Over-elaborate camera work gave rise to heated discussion by the children we interviewed.

| Keith (9): | "I like the way that the cameras film from above looking down on top of it." |
| Basere (9): | "I don't like it when they do it above because when they do it above it looks a better view looking straight at them to the face and see what they're singing and |

the way their lips are moving - and from there [i.e. above] it just looks like blank heads."

Although some of the youngest children claimed to watch *Top of the Pops*, not all of them enjoyed the show. On making comparisons with *The Chart Show*, those who voiced opinions felt that the latter contained more music. There was also a feeling that *The Chart Show* played more of the kind of music they liked to hear.

Basere (9):   [referring to *Top of the Pops*] "Yes, I used to like it but the music hasn't got any taste to it. *The Chart Show*'s got more taste."

Tulsey (9):   "*The Chart Show*'s got more music in it."

Clearly, tastes vary among children just as they do among grown-ups. For some young children, the setting in which a song is performed is central to how much they enjoy the performance. *Top of the Pop*'s live studio setting did not appeal to one child as much as watching the video performances of *The Chart Show*.

Basere: "On the top ten, they do play the same song sometimes, but in *Top of the Pops*, it makes it sound all blank - um - in the place that they sing in."

Basere went on to say that songs sounded "more lively" on *The Chart Show* than they did on *Top of the Pops*. The different perceptions of this sort which some children remarked upon are probably to be expected given the quite different formats of these two shows. *Top of the Pops* these days comprises a mixture of the studio appearances by groups and solo artists and videos, while *The Chart Show* consists of videos only. The two shows have different atmospheres, which may affect how children hear the music.

Sources of Information about 'Pop' Music

We asked children to name the best source for information about 'pop' records. This included not just television but other sources as well. We found that children do not rely exclusively on television for finding out the latest goings-on in the world of 'pop'; indeed, television in some respects was the least important source. More crucial for being up to date was to listen to the right radio shows and read the right magazines.

Tracey (13):   "Most TV programmes only show records that are going up, not the ones that are going out, and if you like them [ones that are going down] then you don't get to hear them, but the radio still plays them."

Ayse (13):   [referring to radio] "Because on Sunday, they play the whole top 40 from 6.00 till 8.00."

On television, some shows were seen as better than others for keeping them informed about pop music developments. *The Chart Show* may not be rated as highly for its atmosphere, but it was thought to be better than *Top of the Pops* for the amount of music it contained and the extra information about performers it displayed on screen.

Int: "Which is the best for giving you extra information about 'pop' groups?"

All: "*The Chart Show*."

Robert[2](13):   "*The Chart Show* - they play it a lot longer - at least it goes on a lot longer. So it plays the actual song longer, so you hear it more. On *Top of the Pops* you only get half the record."

The youngest children felt that *The Chart Show* provided information about pop stars they did not already know, even though most of the performers were familiar to them.

Basere (9):	"... they'll tell you something about - um - like Bros - and then there's people like - um - Fat Boys."
Int:	"So they tell you about different groups. Is it usually things you already know or is it new things?"
Tulsey (9):	"They only tell you things that you don't know, like once they showed us that Belinda Carlisle has got a pet pig."
Basere:	"When they play the music, they tell you all about them - like they tell you how The Fat Boys got famous."

Generally, children enjoy television's pop music programmes. Different youngsters, however, have their own particular favourites, which are defined in terms of the kinds of music and performers they characteristically associate with different shows and in terms of production format. Some children like to see live bands introduced by presenters, other prefer video performances and superimposed text information about artists on screen. Self-indulgent production techniques are not widely appreciated; many children like to see straight performances when the show is in a studio setting. Production gimmicks are most likely to be welcomed if they add to rather than detract from children's enjoyment of their favourite singers.

Chat Shows

While the concept of a 'chat show' was difficult for some of our young respondents to define, the children we spoke to did become clearer about what it involved with increasing age. Whilst the youngest children we interviewed were confused when asked to describe what a chat show is, the older ones were less so. A chat show was defined simply and in a nutshell by Tracey (13) as "someone goes on to chat to a host". Then when asked to give examples, other 13-year-olds showed that they had grasped what this type of show is by naming Terry Wogan, Michael Parkinson, Michael Aspel and Jimmy Tarbuck. Wogan, Aspel and Tarby were the chat show host favourites among teenagers. Another well-liked talk-show host was Dame Edna Everidge.

For younger children (aged 9) we found that the notion of the chat show covered any programme that involved people talking seriously about serious subjects. *Wogan* was mentioned, but so too were some current affairs and documentary programmes.

Once we explained to them which programmes we were referring to, most of the 9-year-olds who were asked about chat shows indicated that they did watch them. The most clearly articulated opinions about such shows, however, came from older children only.

The older children were able to express far wider views about chat shows. We were able to obtain their opinions about the hosts, guests, format of the shows and the kinds of things the chat is about.

Chat Show Presenters
Wogan and *Aspel* were among the favourites for peak-time chat shows. We found increasingly with age, however, that Jonathon Ross accumulated a following. Teenagers especially liked the rather offbeat style of *The Last Resort*.

So what is it about *Wogan*, for instance, that teenagers like?

Robert[2](13): "Because he talks to them all right but he also has music as well."

Tracey (13): "And he don't care what he says, he's game for a laugh!"

The *Wogan* show does not rely solely on talk, but has musical items too, and this is clearly important to children's enjoyment of it. Further comments underscore this observation. When asked if they liked his personality we got the following replies:

Robert[2](13): "Yeah. Also, they don't just stick to the - like - um - one subject - um - people - they have more of a selection - um - they might have pop stars and then politicians."

Tracey (13): "And they keep the people on; they keep the people they've talked to on there and then they combine the old interviews with the new."

In other words, guests on the show do not just do their spot and then disappear. Regardless of their background or profession, *Wogan* may keep a variety of guests on stage together. This mixture of perspectives in a discussion seemed to fascinate some children.

The personality and professionalism of the host is very important to the success of a chat show. The most successful chat show host makes it all look so easy - as if he or she is not really trying. Children notice this point as well. For young viewers, the host who gives the appearance that he is chatting to his guests as if they were sitting in his living room at home, is one to be admired. This observation came out when we asked one group of 13-year-olds why they liked *Aspel*.

Tracey (13): "I don't know really - it's just some of the questions he comes out with - um - it's friendly - it's not like he's just sitting there asking questions, it's as if they are making them feel at home and that."

Guests and format
There are two main questions under this heading. The first is whether children prefer to see guests interviewed one at a time, or in twos and threes together. We have already seen some views expressed on this question. It appears that youngsters do enjoy seeing more than one guest involved in the chat. However, children also feel that a show should try to avoid having too many guests on, because this could over-crowd the programme. The second question is whether they like guests who do things other than talk. For example, a singing artist who comes on and sings a song before being

interviewed.

A well-liked format, and one which they identified with *Wogan* and *Parkinson*, was where guests may be interviewed at first on their own, and then are invited to stay while the next guest comes on. Sufficient time is always set aside to focus on each guest in turn, before throwing the discussion open to the group.

Kevin (12):   "I think have one, and let it go on for about 15 minutes and then you can get four in an hour."

Tracey (13):   "I think - like on *Wogan*, where he chats to one and they stay and then he chats to another one and then two stay."

There are some kinds of guests whom children do not generally welcome.

Robert[2](13):   "Politicians."

Int: "Why wouldn't you like these?"

Robert[2]:   "They're always going on about how good their party is and once - um - I mean, it's all the same really, even though they've got different views - I mean even if we didn't have Margaret Thatcher - like, if somebody else was Prime Minister, we'd still have the same troubles as what there is at the moment".

Tracey: "Authors ... they're boring!"

Ayse (13):   "Yeah, they're usually oldish sort of people and they've got really old-fashioned views ... "

Other children, while disliking interviews with politicians, exhibited a broader point of view, taking into consideration the possible tastes of others, especially of grown-ups.

Craig (12):   "You have to have politicians on some chat shows because adults like it; but they should have chat shows for children and chat shows for adults."

The most popular kind of guest with teenagers, as with younger children, were pop stars. Some of the children we spoke to enjoyed seeing guests on chat shows do more than just talk. If they were pop stars, young viewers felt that these guests should be given the opportunity to sing as well. Sometimes, therefore, children were disappointed when this didn't happen.

Danielle (12):   "I do like *Wogan*, but sometimes he has guests, like Kylie Minogue and other singers and that, but he doesn't give them time to sing."

However, young viewers are not simply interested in hearing recording artists' latest records; they are even more interested to learn about their favourites' private lives. Even so, the majority agreed that questioners should not go too far with this sort of chat. There were certain things chat show hosts ought not to ask their guests, especially where their private lives are concerned. As Robert[2], aged 13, remarked: "They get all embarrassed".

Guests and format were two topics which our youngest respondents were able to talk about. One nine-year-old liked chat shows when they featured pop stars; in particular, she liked to find out new things about stars and to hear them sing. The only other opinions to emerge from the youngest children concerned their views about how many guests they liked to see interviewed at the same time. However, these opinions were not consistent.

Some youngsters preferred to see guests interviewed one at a time while others liked to see a number of them interviewed together.

Int: "Do you prefer chat shows (e.g. Terry Wogan) to have lots of different people or just a few or what?"

Tulsey (9):   "Just a few because otherwise it gets all crowded if he has a load of them."

Int: "Do you like people to be interviewed on their own or do you prefer it when they're all on together?"

Majority: "On their own."

Basere (9):   "Together."

Tulsey: "On their own because they'll say everything all at once."

Int:[to Basere]   "Why do you like them together?"

Basere: "Because when they do it altogether, it's like - um - it's like they're all one family on there - all sorting it out together - it looks like it is anyway."

Variety Shows

What do children understand by a variety show? Once again, this is a genre which comprises a number of different sorts of entertainment and may be difficult to pin down. Many of the children, especially the youngest ones, had no proper idea of what this type of programme was until the interviewer described it to them and named some examples. Some among the children we interviewed did have a go at defining the type, however.

Ayse (13):   "Oh, it's got all different acts and things in it?"

Tulsey (9):   "Do they say a different variety of things?"

Keith (9):   "They show different acts and things."

Which examples of such programmes could they name? Teenagers were better at recalling variety shows than younger children. One group of 13-year-olds mentioned *Live from the Palladium*, *Wednesday at Eight*, *Opportunity Knocks* and *New Faces*. Nine-year-olds remembered the *Children's Royal Variety Show*.

Some of the younger children could remember particular shows but forgot what they were called or what the name of the host was. One nine-year-old had difficulty remembering the name of Paul Daniels.

Basere (9):   "There's a magic man on TV. I watched that."

Sometimes they could remember specific acts they had seen, but not the programmes in which the acts had occurred.

Keith (9):   "I saw a variety show once with a man from Germany and he had an apple, an egg and an orange, and when the apple went past he took a bit and juggled once and bit the egg instead."

The youngest children were clearly taken with unusual tricks and performances that then stay with them in their memories for some time. Older children seemed to be preoccupied more with talent shows. *New Faces* and *Opportunity Knocks* stood out for teenage viewers, who were not always complimentary about these programmes. On *New Faces* there was some criticism of the judges.

Tracey (13):   "The judges - they can be so - um - they say what they

	feel. I mean, they don't spare people's feelings - they - um - like Nina Myshkov's usually on there and she just moans about everybody."
Tracey:	[continues] "And Marti's (Caine) a bit scatty, the way she runs up and down everywhere."

Les Dennis

We showed some children a clip from the *Les Dennis Laughter Show*, as an example of one of the most popular variety shows on television at that time. It came as somewhat of a surprise therefore when the youngest children misidentified the show and only some of the older ones got it right. When asked to say who it was at the end of the clip, the majority of the nine-year-old group who saw it, thought he was Benny Hill. Meanwhile, among the 13-year-olds, some correctly identified Les Dennis, while others thought he was Russ Abbott.

After being told who it was, we probed both age groups further for their familiarity with and opinions about the show and its star. Was there anything in particular that children liked about the show?

Robert[2](13):	"It's like - um - he does all different sketches - like he may not be the main attraction in one sketch, he may be, like - um."
Tracey (13):	[interrupts] "In the next shot."
Robert[2]:	"Yes, in the next shot."

The earlier confusion about Les Dennis and Russ Abbott may have arisen because the two of them were in a series together, before Les Dennis got his own variety show. This is implied by the comments made by some of the 13-year-olds about how the two of them were together, when appearing in Abbott's show.

Robert[2](13):	"Well, when Les Dennis is with Russ Abbott, it's really good, as it's them two together plus Bella Emberg - I reckon they make a good team."
Int:	"What do you like about *The Russ Abbott Show*?"
Robert[2]:	"Well, they're all good comedians and - um ..."
Tracey (13):	[interrupts] "They do clips and then they do all those dances, when they get all dressed up in the teddy boy suits and everything - and then Les Dennis dances and sings and that."

Having established with the nine-year-olds that Les Dennis is not Benny Hill, they suddenly revealed both watching and enjoying Les Dennis on TV.

Tulsey (9):	"I watch it all the time because it's really funny."
Int:	"What do you find funny about it?"
Tulsey:	"Well, it's the way Les Dennis acts that makes me laugh - like when he ..." [she mimics Les Dennis' actions].

These children also liked Les Dennis' impressions of Prince Charles, Mrs Thatcher and other well-known people.

Children's Entertainment

In our interviews with several groups of children we focused on those entertainment programmes made especially for young viewers. Although, entertainment programming for adult audiences is widely watched by children and teenagers, the major television channels have also traditionally broadcast programmes especially made for children. These children's programmes are customarily shown on weekdays during the late afternoon and on Saturday mornings. What follows is a discussion of remarks the children made about these programmes. We begin with those programmes broadcast on weekdays and then consider Saturday morning's children's programmes in a subsequent section. We also found that the children had some especially interesting comments to make about cartoons, and these are treated under a further separate heading.

Weekday Entertainment for Children

There have been numerous popular and entertaining programmes made for primary and secondary children over the years. To focus the minds of the youngsters we interviewed, however, we showed clips from and asked about two series - *Roland Rat* and *Emu's World*. Both these programmes featured puppet characters with outrageous tendencies, which they got away with because they were puppets.

When asked if they ever watched *Roland Rat*, the majority of secondary schoolers claimed that they did not. Many of them claimed that they used to watch him but that now they had grown out of watching this kind of programme.

Robert[2](13):   "I used to when I was a bit younger - I thought it was funny."

Others in the same group thought that Roland Rat was too outrageous and that his was not the sort of entertainment to appeal to their age group.

Tracey (13):   "He's so over the top and everything."
Ayse (13):   "He's flash."
Robert[1](13):   "It's babyish."
Robert[2](13):   "Yeah - it's really aimed at younger children, like 7- to 8-year-olds."
Tracey: "My friend likes to watch it, so when I stay over there, I have to sit and watch it."

Thirteen-year-olds dismissed Roland Rat because he was a puppet. They claimed that they knew he was not real, but that younger children may not be so clever or insightful. In many ways, they seemed to be claiming a superiority over younger children. It is interesting, however, that older children's negative reaction to Roland Rat on the grounds that he is only a puppet did not appear to colour their opinions about Emu, who was very popular among this age group.

When asked whether or not they found *Roland Rat* funny, typical replies were as follows:

Robert[1](13):   "No, because you don't see a puppet talking, do you?"
Tracey (13):   "Well, it does [talk], but we don't find it funny because we know it's a puppet whereas little kids will think it's real, but we know it's a puppet so it's a bit boring for us - it's like *The Sooty Show* really, isn't it?"

In contrast, most were happy to admit to watching *Emu's World* and in general, the children found *Emu's World* far funnier than *Roland Rat*.

Gillian (13):	"There's more going on in *Emu's World*."
Tracey (13):	"They give prizes away and that - *Roland Rat*'s just all the puppets - there's only one puppet - um - two puppets in *Emu's World*."

Other more cynical youngsters were not impressed, however, even by Emu, although the prizes were perhaps a saving grace.

Robert[2](13):	"I don't like it - it's good in one sense in that it gives prizes away and gets the audience involved but I think it's - um - it's the puppet - I mean that they must be able to see his hand going up inside the puppet".
Tracey (13):	"You can see he's got a false arm, with the other arm underneath it."
Robert[2](13):	"Yeah, they must be able to see that because he never moves the arm, does he?"

Cartoons

We asked four groups of children about cartoons. Which cartoons could they think of and what did they like or dislike about them? The most popularly named cartoons were *Tom and Jerry*, *Scooby Doo*, *Donald Duck*, *Laurel and Hardy*, *Superted*, *Mickey Mouse*, *Bugs Bunny*, *The Flintstones*, *Ghostbusters*, *Centurions* and *The Banana Man*. Others mentioned included *The Bisketts* and *Pole Position*. In other words, both the older, established, and newer cartoons were watched, and to varying extents were enjoyed by children. *Mr Magoo* and *Popeye* were included among 'boring old' cartoons by some children.

Some children clearly preferred the newcomers and, with one or two exceptions, were less attracted to those which have been around for several generations. This observation is encapsulated by a remark by one boy, Andrew (aged 11) who, when asked if he would watch any cartoons or only certain ones, replied:

"Only the good ones, because some of them, like the really old ones, they're really boring."

The appeal of cartoons is difficult to pin down precisely. For children, cartoons can have a variety of attractions. For some it is the animation, others like the humour, some enjoy the colour, and yet others watch them only if there's nothing better on. Cartoon characters can do fantastic things and are not bound by the normal laws of physics or nature. This strong fantasy element is also undoubtedly a central feature underlying their inherent appeal.

Nitan (10):	[referring to cartoon characters] "They can do like- um - different things. They can't just walk around like anyone, they can jump up about 50 feet, but normal people can't."

Over the years there has been concern that despite their fantastic nature, even cartoons may mislead children or encourage them to misbehave. It became clear from the comments of the children we interviewed, however, that even primary schoolers distinguish between what's possible for a cartoon character and what is possible for real people, as shown in the above quotation.

Cartoons are fun. A number of children remarked on how they could be uplifted by watching cartoons.

Andrew (11):   "If you don't feel too good, it helps to watch cartoons."

Fay (12):   "It cheers you up."

Children distinguish between reality and cartoon fantasy. They also know that animated characters on television are capable of doing things which would not be possible for human actors.

Int: "So in a cartoon, they do all sorts of things that if it were an actor doing it, you'd know it was impossible?"

All agree.

Int: "Is that what you like about cartoons, that they really are fantasy?"

All: "Yes."

Andrew (11):   "Like in *Tom and Jerry*, they have a massive fight but they always get up."

Int: "Do you accept that in a cartoon, for example, he gets flattened out and then picks himself up and starts all over again."

All: "Yes." (laugh)

Int: "What if it happened in a real film? What would you think then?"

Jon (12):   "No, that's stupid." (the rest agree)

Int: (to Daniel, continuing earlier conversation) "Why don't you like *The Centurions*?"

Daniel (12):   "Because after the people - um - say someone falls in the lake, they just go - um - they just buzz up to the space ship and then they go - um - what is it?"

Andrew (11):   "The power extreme."

Daniel: "Yes, that's it - and all this equipment comes on and they change into a submarine and that."

Jon: "I don't like that either."

Int: "So you think it's too much of a fantasy?"

Daniel: "Yes, because they've got all this equipment and it just gets them out again by becoming a submarine."

The implication of these remarks seems to be that children dislike productions which rely heavily on simplistic, cheap gimmicks to resolve plots. Special effects and gadgets are liked when they enhance the story, but are not perceived to be sufficient to substitute for a good, well-structured storyline.

In order to sustain the loyalty of young viewers, cartoons must have an interesting storyline. With repeated viewing, children soon become familiar with the plot structures of cartoons. They like to see the way the plot unfolds, however, and we got the impression that each week they would test their expectations of what was going to happen against what actually occurred.

Put simply, children learn to recognise story structures and know what to expect each week. They are intrigued to see if their hypotheses about what will happen are correct and they are also curious to see how the expected storyline will, on this occasion, be played out.

Here are some illustrative remarks made during discussions about two cartoon series: *The Bisketts* and *Inspector Gadget*.

Int:	"... What's good about *The Bisketts*?"
Clare (10):	"King Max is always trying to do things and he never succeeds."
Wayne (10):	"He's always trying to nick the treasure and that."
Int:	"So the same sort of thing happens each week? ... Do you think that happens a lot in cartoons?"
Clare:	"Yes, like *Tom and Jerry*."
Int:	"Do you like the fact that you know really what's going to happen?"
Majority:	"Yes."
Int:	"Why do you think you watch it then - if you know each time that a certain person is going to try and do something but they won't succeed?"
Clare:	"Because they always try and do it in different ways."
Wayne:	It's good fun seeing *how* they do it."

Once again, these remarks underline the importance to children of the storyline. Young viewers' enjoyment of programmes for their own age group stems from the fundamental ingredients of quality television - a good story, which varies from week to week, in a well-made production.

On another occasion, a conversation developed about a different cartoon character, *Inspector Gadget*, to illustrate again that repetition is not necessarily a turn-off, if the cartoon has other interesting features.

Int:	"Why do you like *Inspector Gadget*?"
Jon (12):	"He's funny and he goes over to the same people."
Int:	"What do you mean, 'he goes over to the same people'?"
Jon:	"He fights the same people, but they've different stories and he gets in with the person he's really fighting."
Andrew (11):	"And he's got all funny things coming out of him everywhere."
Daniel (12):	"He's meant to be going after the baddies but he gets it wrong and keeps going after the goodies. In the end it's like his niece who solves the mystery and he doesn't."

Thus, cartoons are characterised by repetitive formulae which children soon learn. Provided there is sufficient intrigue in the way the expected story unfolds or the leading characters exhibit unusual habits or attributes, the repetitive elements do not lead to boredom. Heavily stereotyped storylines or characters quickly cause children to loose interest however. This appeared to be true of *He-Man and Masters of the Universe*. Ten and 11-year-olds we interviewed were sceptical about this series. In many ways, they had come to regard it as so ridiculously stereotyped and repetitive that it had become a joke and attained an almost cult status as such.

Nitan (10):	It's babyish."
Wayne (10):	"Yeah, the characters are."
Billy (10):	"And it's boring."
Int:	"So you think the characters in it are babyish?"
Billy:	"And the way it just changes."
Int:	"What's wrong with the way it changes?"
Billy:	"Well, he just sticks up his sword and says something and then he's changed." (all giggle)
Int:	"Do you see characters change in other cartoons?'
Louise (9):	"In *Transformers* they change."
Int:	"So they change better in *Transformers* than they do in *He-Man*?"
Wayne:	"At least they change into vehicles, whereas in *He-Man*, he just changes into *He-Man*."

He-man and *Transformers* are US imports, which have the additional characteristic of being not only television shows but also toy products which can be bought in major stores. Fears have been expressed by some lobby groups that children can be misled by these programmes into believing that the toy versions are capable of doing things they are in practice unable to do. One might question just how much children are influenced in this way, especially when the production style of such shows is not highly appreciated, even causing some young viewers to reject the characters rather than to want to own toy models of them.

Swedish researchers have observed that identification with the little guy, as we see below, is one important ingredient in the humour of cartoons[2]. The conflict between the little guy and the big guy, though identified as violent in nature, is not taken seriously in the cartoon context.

Int:	Which cartoon do you think is the funniest?"
Majority:	"*Tom and Jerry*."
Int:	"Why do you think they are funniest?"
Billy (10):	"Because they're always running all over the place and whenever Jerry's gone round, he gets something and hides behind the curtain and bashes him in the face?"
All laugh.	
Int:	"Do you think there's a lot of violence in *Tom and Jerry*?"
Majority:	"Yes." (laugh)
Sophia (9):	But I like it because - you see - Jerry's so little and he's got this big thing in his hand and he always beats Tom - like he's after him, but he never gets Jerry."

One of the most popular cartoons of all, and one about which the children had a great deal to say, was *Ghostbusters*. It became clear that young viewers of this series are familiar with the plot structure and enjoy seeing the way the story is worked out each week. The series was thought to be exciting, unusual and filled with special gadgets and effects.

When we asked children to describe what happens in *Ghostbusters* each week, they were eager to tell.

Michelle (11):	"There's sometimes like a haunted house and someone comes running up and she presses the bell and

115

	everyone runs down and like - um - the house is moving, bodies are flying everywhere and that."
Jon (12):	"Yeah, they'll turn their backs and all these books will come flying and when they turn round everything's back to normal and an old lady's there with a parrot who changes into a great big enormous monster ... and ...".
Michelle:	[interrupts] "and he runs out and then he drags all them there and he says 'it's the parrot!'
Jon (12):	[interrupts] "and the lady changes into a massive monster".
Int:	"So is it the same sort of thing every week or not?"
Michelle:	"No, it's always different places with different ghosts. But they're always trying to catch ghosts?"

Although there appears to be a learning value associated with repetitive storylines, which enable children through repeat-viewing of a series to internalise plot structures, the popularity of cartoons can nevertheless be enhanced by unusual twists. Even here, though, the children learn to expect a twist at the end of the tale and look forward to seeing what shape it will take. This feature was seen to characterise the cartoon series, *Scooby-Do*.

Int:	"What's more interesting about *Scooby-Do* compared with others?"
Claire (10):	"Because there's always a twist - it always turns out to be somebody instead of a monster."
Int:	"So although you think there's a monster, there isn't really?"
Louise (9):	"Yeah - it's interesting looking at the clues they leave and where they find them."

Saturday Morning's Children's Television

Saturday morning is traditionally a time when children's programmes are broadcast by the major television networks. These days, typical offerings include magazine formats featuring interviews with TV celebrities, pop stars, sports personalities and experts on different topics. Interspersed with these interviews are musical items, cartoons, games and telephone call-in spots. In addition to studio-based items, there may also be on-location, outside broadcasts showing live events of various kinds.

We asked the children we interviewed for their opinions about Saturday morning's programmes for their age group, and, in order to focus their thoughts, showed them a clip from one current show - *Get Fresh*. Practically all those interviewed about the clip claimed to watch this programme. Different youngsters had different favourite spots. Some liked the cartoons best of all; some liked the musical items, others liked the games. Opinions were generally positive, although there were one or two sour notes.

One problem pointed to by several children was that the show is rather 'frantic' and crams in a lot of material.

Andrew (11):	"It's too frantic."
Jon (12):	"It gets on your nerves - you can't understand what

	they're saying - they talk too fast."
Int:	"Is it just the talking too fast or is the rest of it too frantic as well?"
Daniel (12):	"Most of it's frantic."
Jon:	"I think they try to fit in too much."
Int:	"Is it frantic because they have lots of different things and you only see sections for a very short time or is it lots of things happening at once."
Daniel:	"Yeah, like the cartoon's in about four different parts."
Jon:	"It goes on until about half past eleven and it starts about eight, and you have to keep on watching it, don't you?"

It is worth pointing out here that Jon's last remark was mistaken as far as the start time of *Get Fresh* is concerned. In fact, the programme did not start until 9.30 am. It is possible that he began his viewing at eight o'clock in the morning, starting with breakfast television's children's programming and then continue watching until *Get Fresh* came on. The interesting part of his remark, however, which applies to a lot of children's programming on Saturday morning, is that programmes tend to consist of lots of short sections and bursts of energy. The pace never lets up and this may be designed to produce a series of what psychologists call 'orienting responses' to the television screen. In other words, the programmes are presented at a frenetic pace and maintain heightened stimulation all the time. The children cannot pull themselves away from the screen because as one item ends, another equally stimulating one begins, causing them to orient towards the screen once again.

The characters featured in *Get Fresh* have strange idiosyncrasies which mostly appeal to young viewers as well. The puppet character called Gilbert stood out for many of the children for his outrageous personality, often rude remarks and occasionally disgusting behaviour. Despite all these, he proved to be very popular, especially with children aged 11-13 years.

Mark (13):	".... he does outrageous things and does impressions of people."

The game element of *Get Fresh* had special appeal because it featured computer simulations (something which crops up again and again as holding a strong attraction for young viewers) and because of the way contestants are treated. When asked why he liked the game part, Daniel (12) replied:

"Because if they lose they get all this slime and that all over them and I like the actual game they play."

The game turns out to be a space-invaders type game which is played on a computer. Some of the children claimed to have the game at home and to have played it themselves. This item generally appealed more to the boys than the girls.

The girls were more likely to enjoy the music and interviews, and were most likely to mention phone-ins. They were not always complimentary about the latter, however.

Michelle (11):	"I think they're all right if they're like 'phoning famous people, like they 'phoned Kylie Minogue before."

117

The presenters were criticised, however, for talking too quickly. Another opinion was that the presenters were sometimes rather too full of themselves.

Int:	"Anything you dislike about the presenters on *Get Fresh*?"
Daniel (12):	"Yeah, they talk too fast - and they talk too much".
Fay (12):	"They're too leery."
Int:	"What do you mean 'they're too leery'?"
Fay:	"Well, they're a bit full of themselves."
Andrew (11):	"Like when that lady just took that animal - when she went over to Gazza and said 'Dear, oh dear, I can't understand him'."
Fay:	"It's like they take the mickey out of them sometimes, if they're not so friendly or something, they take the mickey out of them and go on to something else."

As well as criticising their presentation style, the children we interviewed were also unhappy with the celebrity guest interviews in *Get Fresh*.

Int:	"What about the way they do their interviews; do you think they do that quite well or not?"
Fay:	"No, sometimes they don't ask them enough."
Andrew:	"And they go on too much."
Fay:	"They never ask them the right question; they ask them all the stupid ones."

Continuing this discussion, we asked the children to describe what they meant by good and bad questions. In what way did the presenters of this programme fail to ask guests on the show the kinds of things children in the audience wanted to know about?

Daniel (12):	It depends; if they're like a 'pop' star - like a different question would be 'What's the first record you bought?' or 'What's the first record they ever recorded?'."

The plea seemed to be for a more carefully thought-out and in-depth interview which probed aspects of a star's personal background and tastes in music.

The children we spoke to were also concerned about the range of guests featured on *Get Fresh*. Some of them felt that the show focused on a fairly narrow range of celebrities, mainly from the pop music world. While they were interested to see such people interviewed, they also wanted more variation. The children felt there was room in the show for guests who were not in the music business.

Jon (12):	"Sports people."
Andrew (11):	"Presenters of other children's programmes."
Jon:	"Yeah, or people that might have done something that week."

Get Fresh was not the only Saturday morning show these children watched. A number of them also tuned in to *On the Waterfront* which was shown at the same time on a different channel. The pace of this show was perceived to be slower and this was generally welcomed.

Jon (12):	"They speak - um - not so quick - you can understand more because they finish what they're saying."

Michelle (12):	"You can learn things from it - they have like - um - that mysterious thing - um - what is it? - oh, I don't know."
Fay (12):	"They have - um - nearly everybody they have on there are more well-known."
Andrew (11):	"And they don't keep on having the same ones all the time - like they have different subjects, they don't keep talking about the same subject for weeks on end."

On the Waterfront was well liked also because the presenters showed you how to make things.

Jon (12):	"And they showed that - um - sausage thing - like how they get all the sausage through and after they have Beat the Expert - like after the expert's shown them what to do they have to do it in so many minutes."

In fact, Jon was describing a kind of studio competition between children on the show, who were required to perform a task or make an object having seen an expert do it properly first. This idea was featured on British television some years earlier in a show hosted by Bruce Forsyth called *The Generation Game*.

Network 7

Continuing the discussion about light talk programmes aimed at younger viewers, we showed children a clip from *Network 7*. This member of the genre of so-called 'youth' programmes consisted of a mixture of interviews with celebrities and ordinary people, and reported in an upbeat current affairs style on topical issues presumed to be of special interest to young viewers, on the brink of adulthood.

This programme hit home with teenagers more so than with other children. Primary schoolers either failed to recognise the programme from the clip or, if they did, had relatively little to say about it. Secondary schoolers, at the younger end of the age range, 11- to 12- year-olds, were just beginning to get into the show. However, even the latter saw it as a programme for viewers just a year or two older than themselves.

Maria (12):	"Well, most of it's stuff you can't really understand - it's for teenagers really."

Viewers in their early-teens still preferred pop music to the more news-orientated elements of much of *Network 7*.

Claire (13):	"It don't have much pop groups; it's all about facts and that, and they have job interviews in it."

Network 7 was therefore just beyond the reach of pre-teens although among those children who had watched the programme, the occasional item stood out.

Daniel (12):	"Yes, well, the one I saw was where a man went out and he only had £10 to spend and he had to find somewhere to sleep."
Int:	"So what did you like about that?"
Daniel:	"Um - the way he actually found a home to stay in."
Int:	"What other sorts of things do they usually have on it?"

Fay (12):   "Well, there was this woman who wanted her nose
                 changed, because she had this terrible nose and she had
                 plastic surgery and it was completely different after.
                 And there was a bloke that had committed a crime and
                 he had three days to live and he had to be put - um -
                 killed in the electric chair."

What emerged from this and further discussion among 12-year-olds was
that *Network 7* was something they only watched every now and again. The
series contained some items of interest to them but it was mainly the unusual
which stood out in their minds and which they subsequently were able to
remember. While the content of the programme held some appeal, however,
these young viewers were not so impressed by the style in which *Network
7* was presented. The presenters in particular were criticised by the 11- to
12-year olds.

Daniel (12):   "They don't know what to say, because they're new,
                 they're not sure what to say whereas with interviewers
                 like Terry Wogan, they know exactly what to say."

Even slightly older children were unhappy with what they perceived to be
an awkward, jerky style of presentation.

Claire (13):   "I don't like the way it keeps jumping about. It tells
                 you a bit about something and then it goes on to
                 something else."

One real worry was that *Network 7* dealt in too much detail with certain
social issues which might have potentially undesirable side-effects. One
group of 13-year-olds related their concerns about one item which dealt with
the subject of burglary.

Philip (13):   "It tells you about AIDS, burglars and things."
Int: "What do you mean, it told you about burglars and
                 things?"
Philip: "Well, like, um, it was telling you how they do it and
                 how they went through your home while you used to
                 live there ..."
Int: "Was it actually showing you how they actually did
                 it?"
Philip: "Well, sort of. It showed you how they were getting
                 in and that, and it was showing you what sort of
                 people they were."
Mark (13):   "And they had an ex-burglar on there and he showed
                 you how to get in and how easy it was."
Int: "Do you think they should show things like that?"
Philip: "No, 'cause anyone could go out. You can get a piece
                 of plastic and run it down the side of the door and you
                 were in a house."

Not all the children in this group agreed with Philip, however. For
instance, some thought that such things should be shown,

Jay (13):   " .... because if they show you all the places where
                 they can get in, you can check on all that."

Clarifying his earlier points, Philip explained:
                 "They should say you should beware of all that, but

they shouldn't show you how to do it - how they get in."

Conclusion
This chapter has explored children's views about a miscellany of light entertainment programmes not previously covered in earlier sections on quiz and game shows and situation comedy. In addition to the latter two popular programme genres, television's entertainment fare includes a number of further, distinct kinds of programmes, principally, music and variety shows, chat shows, and entertainment programmes made especially for children and finally, cartoons. Once again, the children we interviewed provided a range of opinions about the programmes they knew and watched. Some programmes were praised, while others were criticised. Criticisms made reference to aspects of programme content, style of presentation and the behaviour of presenters and guests in programmes.

One clear pattern to emerge, which has been observed already in respect of other programme types, was a change in viewing tastes and preferences with age. As youngsters mature through their pre-teen and early teenage years, so the programmes they like, and perhaps more importantly, which they believe they are expected (by peers) to enjoy, alter.

During primary school years, although young viewers may prefer to watch some children's entertainment programmes more than others, they exhibit inhibitions about admitting that they watch such material. As they progress through secondary school, however, teenagers openly turn against some "kids" programmes because the latter are associated with a different age subculture. Even though they may still steal a look at these so-called "kids" programmes from time to time, they seldom admit doing so voluntarily.

As children get older they become both more perceptive when assessing what they like and dislike about entertainment programmes, and better able to articulate their opinions. They show increased awareness with age of production tricks and techniques. Some of these techniques may be designed to enhance the appeal of a programme to young audiences, but actually produce the opposite results. Unusual camera angles in pop shows are acceptable provided they are not overdone and do not interfere with the viewer's ability to watch and enjoy the artists performing. Rapid cuts from sequence to sequence or from one camera angle to another can spoil enjoyment and is perceived by some children to be unnecessary.

Despite these few gripes about certain light entertainment shows, children mostly appreciate this genre as entertaining, light-hearted fun. Any show which contains current, popular music items is almost guaranteed to appeal, although different youngsters have different favourites among the pop stars of the day. Too much heavy talk can be a turn-off, but much depends on the subject matter and who the guests are.

In entertainment programmes with a dramatic narrative, such as animated cartoons, unusual characters with special powers or unusual skills, qualities and gadgets are popular with most children, though younger ones are most ready to admit to liking these shows. However, nearly all the children agreed that special effects can't compensate for poor stories. Clichéd characters and repetitive use of super powers and techniques can quickly lose their appeal in shallow cartoons with little else to offer. The success and enduring popularity of a show depends on interesting new turns of events each week. In some respects, children take even entertainment television seriously. They were critical of poor quality, badly produced, overly-repetitive material. The provision of escapist and relaxing entertainment is one of the central functions of television. But in this context, slapstick must not be confused with slapdash. *Light* entertainment should not be taken *lightly* by broadcasters if it is to earn and retain the loyalty, respect and appreciation of young viewers.

References

1.   Gunter, B., and McAleer, J. *Children and Television: The One-Eyed Monster?* London: Routledge. 1990

2.   Schyller, I., and Rydin, I. *Children and Humour.* Paper presented to International Association of Mass Communication Research conference, Barcelona, Spain, August, 1988

7 Sport

Sports coverage has been a regular feature of the television schedules and can attract large audience, at least for major events. Over the years, however, the nature of sports coverage has changed both in terms of the sports most on television and where they occur in the schedules. Future broadcasting developments promise to bring further changes to the amount and the type of sports being transmitted.

What do the public think about television's sports coverage? The research that is available is relatively consensual. Thus, most people are satisfied with the nature and amount of sport shown on television. A *Which?* report[1] indicated that, against this background, while 7% (of 2000 adults) wanted more sport on television, 16% wanted less. Reardon and Wober[2] reported that both men and women are more interested than not in seeing sport 'on the box'. Within this overall liking, however, women appeared to prefer watching sports involving artistic expression, and did not like sports characterized by aggressive bodily contact. Men, on the other hand, did like this type of sport but also liked viewing snooker and angling.

Both Reardon and Wober[3] and Gunter[4] showed that major points of contention were the overall amount of sports coverage, the showing of sport on both major channels at the same time, and the need for more variety of sport on television. Nearly three out of four viewers agreed that the amount of coverage television gives to certain sports is often excessive and six out of ten wanted to see more coverage of sports not usually covered by television, and less emphasise on traditional sports.

Sex differences are commonly found when people are asked about sport and sports coverage on television. Thus, Gunter found that while 50% of

124

n answered 'yes' when questioned about whether there was too much verage of football on television, 65% of women offered this answer[5]. .iis male-female difference was again shown by Gunter when - following 1any months of absence of football from the screens of ITV - men and omen were asked if they welcomed its resumption[6]. Men were much more ppreciative of its return than women.

In general then viewers are broadly satisfied with sports programming, ut they would like to see greater variety and there are clear sex differences 1 responses to what is being shown. These views seem to mesh omfortably with the current changes being seen in television programming f sport: But what about the audiences of tomorrow? Do they appreciate the new sports currently being given increased coverage? Do they look forward to satellite and cable television channels devoted solely to sport? These and other sports-related questions were addressed to our primary and secondary school aged boys and girls. Some of their answers were quite surprising - especially when viewed against the back drop of the strategic planning discernible in television's coverage of sport currently underway.

General Levels of Appreciation

The vast majority of our school aged respondents watched sport on television, but a few girls stated most emphatically that they didn't watch any sport at all. A general finding in fact was that as girls got older they lost interest in sport on television, except perhaps for major events. The preferred television fare was wide and varied and not specifically sex-linked. Not surprisingly, the first-mentioned sports were those traditional taught in school, played by the respondents and given most coverage by television. Thus, Tennis, Football, Athletics, Swimming, Cricket and Gymnastics were frequently cited as being most watched on television.

When asked if there were any sports on television that they did *not* like watching, a varied and mixed bag was offered.

Emma (10): "Boxing - all that sweat dripping off them - yuck - I don't like that at all."

Mark (10): "Sumo - that's just so boring - pushing and slapping - and those costumes! Table tennis I don't like either because its just knocking that ball about all the time."

Michelle (11): "Cricket and Football - they go on for so long and you just sit there and watch it, but you don't really know what's going on."

William (11): "Horse racing and golf - they're just both boring."

Simon (11): "Rugby -they're just beating people up all the time and you don't even see where the ball is."

Oskar (13): "Volleyball - its a woman's game, not really a man's game."

Annalise (13): "Football - that's boring because its all men."

Gary (15): "I don't like Bowls - its so boring watching the bowl trying to hit the white thing at the end."

This wide range of dislikes of individual sports poses a problem for commentators because the basis of most dislikes seems to be rooted in a lack of awareness of the finer details of the rules and regulations that govern

125

each sport. A failure to explain the rules and the tactics employed within these rules may result in the perception by young viewers of frenetic or lethargic movement with no clear purpose, thus the feeling of boredom - the most frequently given reason for dislike by our respondents. This argument was nicely put by one of our 13-year-olds.

Tammy (13):   "If you don't understand a game you find it boring because I used to think cricket was boring when I was about 7 - but when you get into it - now I understand it and it's great."

This desire to be told the purpose, and the means of achieving the desired ends, especially of new sports, places an onus of explanation on the commentator which may be difficult to discharge because of the danger of alienating, and thus losing, audience members who *do* know about the game. This fine line between "being informative" and "being a prat" (Gary, 15) was frequently transgressed by commentators, according to many of our children. Interestingly, this aspect of commentating was remarked on by many respondents in Gunter's and Reardon and Wober's adult surveys also[7].

Perceived Balance of Coverage

Passing on to the actual *amount* of sport shown on television, the vast majority of our young respondents said there should be more, and more variety, thus both agreeing and disagreeing with the opinions of adults, presented in the Introduction, where it was shown that most adults felt the balance was about right, with a desire for greater variety.

Emma (10):   "There should be more hockey."
Paul (10):   "There should be more underwater sports."
Richard (12):   "There's too little wrestling - and they're going to stop it altogether!"
Mark (11):   "There's not enough basketball."
Sarah (12):   "There's not enough swimming."

Our older groups felt that the "balance was about right" (Michael, 15), but there seemed to be a specific effect caused by several big events coming together at the time of our interviewing. This view echoes the view of adults discovered by Gunter[8] : there are times, such as the World Cup and the Olympics, when there is just 'too much sport' being presented on TV.

Gary (15):   "Yeah - there has been too much just recently - there's been too many big competitions at one time and - um - sport's taking up more time on telly than I like."

Favourite Sports Programme

The children's programme awareness was examined by asking if they could name any sports programmes. Universally *Grandstand*, *Midweek Sports Special*, *Match of the Day* and *Sportsnight* were named. The decision as to which of these programmes was best was largely a function of its scheduled presentation time and the respondents availability for viewing.

Shahida (15):   "I like *Grandstand*. It's Saturday afternoon, so I can watch it all. It covers every sport - like what's going on today."

Gary (15):   "Well *Grandstand* is on in the afternoon and I don't

126

really stay in on Saturdays, but with *Sportsnight* it's on at nights - so I've got time to watch it."

Others liked *Grandstand* because it was 'topical' (Richard, 14) and 'seasonal' (?) (Tammy, 13). *Midweek Sports Special* was regarded as better than *Sportsnight* because the former had ' better coverage' (Mark, 14) and the latter was perceived as 'talk only' (Joe, 13).

Aspects of Viewing
Recording Sport
As an indicator of the children's commitment to this aspect of television ware, we asked whether any of them ever videotaped any sports programmes or sporting events. All groups had members who taped at least some of the time, and many more boys than girls taped such programmes. Football was the chief sporting category that was time shifted or stored for late viewing and analysis by the boys. This heavy taping of sports programmes by our youngsters is in marked contrast to the recording of sport by adults. Levy and Gunter showed that only 4% of all programmes recorded by adults were of a sporting kind[9]. However, if the situation demands it videos are also used at a higher level by adults to record sport. Thus, Gunter demonstrated a marked increase in video usage by adult males during the 1986 World Cup[10].

The major reason given for taping by our respondents was either that 'it was a main event' (e.g., Paul, 10), or because it was going to be missed when transmitted because the child was away or otherwise unavailable to view.

Simon (11):   "I tape them because I want to keep good matches, like in the European Cup."

Joe (13):   *"Sportsnight* - I tape it all the time. It's got good games to watch again."

Late Viewing
Another indication of sport-viewing avidness could be the tendency for the children to "stay up late" to watch particular sporting events. Were our respondents keen enough sports viewers - and negotiators with parents - to do this? From the earliest age groups it was obvious that they were - although in several cases while the spirit was willing the flesh was found to be weak.

Simon (11):   "Well I've got up when there's been football on - I creep out of bed when my Mum and Dad don't know."

William (11):   "Well - if there's something really good on - like a boxing match - then I'll set my alarm for 3 o'clock so I can see it."

Int: "Did you get up for the recent title fight?"

William: "Yeah - I got up from about quarter to two till a quarter to three - I started reading and went back to sleep.

Interviewer: So you missed it?"

William: "Yeah!"

This was a World Heavyweight Boxing match that lasted 90 seconds! Some of the girls in one group thought it incredibly funny that boys would make the effort to get up and watch something that could last 90 seconds, or even less.

Valerie (12): "I stay up late every Saturday night to watch the basketball."

Joe (13): "I stay up till half past 11 to watch Calypso cricket."

Angela (13): "I watch show jumping no matter what time its on - um Mum lets me."

Gary (15): "One time I stayed up until 4 o'clock in the morning to watch ice-hockey because they've got late night sports and - um - recently they've got this new soccer thing from America which is very popular - so I've stayed up to watch that - that's if I'm not too tired."

Non-viewers and Non-viewable Programmes

While a number of our secondary school girl respondents claimed that they watched very little sport on television, they were willing to admit that this non-viewing could be overridden by the hype of major events. Only two of our respondents (out of 36) claimed *never* to have watched a main event in *any* sport. Thus, while horse racing was perhaps the most disliked of all sports, the Grand National was viewed by 34 of our 36 children. This level of popularity held for most 'major' sports events on the television. When asked why they watched major events but not minor events in the same sports category, a coherent answer was difficult to find. At base, however, it does look as if 'big events' are cultural events. That is, being aware that a majority in the country will be watching a 'big' event, it becomes an 'in' thing to do - being a part of cultural heritage, even if not openly realized or admitted by our children.

Shahinda (15): "The big stars usually come out in the finals, so it's more interesting, because the people are better at the sport - like if you have just little stars, they're not very good at it."

Harjeet (15): "There's more competition going on between the top people and that makes it more interesting."

Kirshie (13): "I watch to see people that I don't like get beaten in important competitions."

Oscar (13): "I watch the main events because there's usually a title in it, it's just not ordinary."

Valerie (12): (talking about the Grand National) "I watch it because it's the best race."

Mark (11): (talking about boxing) "I watch the big events because it's more exciting, its for more money and so they go at it harder. You also see more famous people. In the little events they just go pat-pat (imitating light sparring)."

Simon (11): "Well we all watched it (the Wimbledon Final) at school because at school we were allowed to watch it in the class."

Michelle (11): "It's like - um - if you said - um - most people are just beginners even though they can do it, but the two people who win are the champions so their game is chosen because there's usually more action (the rest agree in this group)."

Certain of the youngest age group argued that the reason they watched the main event but not the preliminary skirmishes, or the 'ordinary' matches or events, was purely a scheduling matter:

Kerry (10):   "Lots of sport is on at school time while the main events are on when you're not at school - like - on Saturdays or Sundays. That's why I watch the big events only."

This, it should be noted, was factually incorrect, only horse racing was on regularly at school time.

As an example of only watching main events, all this group agreed that while they did not watch a great deal of athletics normally they were all watching the Olympics, which were taking place at the time of our interviews, especially on breakfast time television.

Views about Different Sports on Television
The next set of questions we asked our children concerned the coverage of specific sports on television and we tried to elicit what they felt about aspects of the style of presentation.

Our respondents were divided upon the issue of protracted 'build ups' and discussion sessions before and after a game. While this is similar to the adults views[11], which felt this was over played, in our sample the issue clearly demonstrated the anti-sport attitudes that developed in girls with age.

Helen (11):   "I think they do it too much on TV."
Michelle (11):   "It's dead boring - I just wish they'd shut up."

Others however (mainly boys) felt that talk about the game at half time was interesting.

Paul (10):   "They can talk about how they feel and they can discuss it between them."

Throughout our sample, and especially for the boys, there was a fairly common desire to have 'experts' analyses and evaluate at half time what the children had just seen for themselves. This adult, expert, consolidation phase seems important for overall enjoyment of the sport being viewed.

When we discussed tennis all the children appreciated that this sport was covered mostly by the BBC. Our younger groups found the extended nature of a tennis match a little difficult.

Valerie (12):   "It goes on too long, it gets boring."
Richard (12):   "I watch it for about 20 minutes and turn it off - I'm not interested in how they play - just who wins."

On the question of whether there should be more tennis, opinion was divided, but girls more than boys argued for its increased coverage. All watched some of Wimbledon but only if a 'favourite' was playing or if it was the semi finals or finals.

We next asked about snooker. With this sport however it was not so much the game as the atmosphere and monetary rewards that our respondents wished to talk about.

Oskar (13):   "That Scottish one (Stephen Hendry) won £100,000,

	something like that."
Joe (13):	"It's crazy, just because you win one game - just hitting silly balls."
Angela (13):	"No - if the public's ready to give the money for it."
Tammy (13):	"It's fair, because they have a bigger following."

Our older groups appreciated that snooker represented a different type of sport to that of, for example, football, where there were physical thrills and spills.

Mark (14):	"In football you sometimes challenge the person - but in snooker it's just so slow and hitting silly balls of different colours."
Neescha (14):	"I think it's the atmosphere (of snooker), the crowd is hushed and the commentators just whisper, Oh, - it's really about suspense and that."

This hushed suspense however was just too much for some of the children, who wished to break out of it.

Gary (15):	"Yeah - but the commentator should talk a little more to liven the game up."
Cheryl (15):	"Yeah - that 'whispering Ted Lowe' - he's a scream, you'd think he was telling a ghost story."

With snooker, it was clear that our respondents either liked it or loathed it - but this polarization cut across both age and sex.

Of those who watched athletics, they would like to have more: for those who did not watch, the thought of more was not appreciated!

Highlights or Extended - Coverage?

We were interested to find out whether our children preferred 'highlights' or the more extended coverage of the whole event. Do they watch one or the other, both, or neither? It was clear that the answers to those questions depended on the interest in the person, team or event concerned. If the children were interested, both types of presentation were viewed; if they were not interested, neither type of programme was watched. 'Highlights' programmes were used very much as a second-hand means of catching up on an event that had been unavoidably missed, or as a way of recapturing moments of excitement. Knowledge of the result - 'inadvertently' given by a rival channel - had no effect upon this avid viewing. It is thus clear that children watch sport for reasons over and above finding our about eventual results.

This involvement, that went beyond just knowing "who won", was made clear when we raised the topic of 'build up' to and 'discussion' about events before, during an after their occurrence. We have already mentioned certain specific responses to this type of 'sports televising' but the overall impression gained was that such programming techniques were found satisfying by those who were interested - especially as the discussion gets close to, and involves, the actual people involved. As an example, many of our children liked the FA Cup 'chats' with players in the changing room after the match. Such intimate tête-à-têtes with the combatants served to create the illusion of actually participating in the event on the part of the viewer. In opposition to those who disliked sport, and all the discussion around it (see earlier comments), this involvement seems critical for sports viewers who have an interest in the sport.

Paul (10):   (commenting upon 'build up' discussions) "It makes it more exciting and makes you want to play - um - watch - even more."

Emma (11):   "Yeah - I like it in the changing rooms because it is good to find out how the players feel."

But, of course, all this ego-involvement is numbing to those who have no interest in the sport being covered.

Venessa (14):   "I prefer to have all the discussion and interviewing at the end - so I can turn it off!"

New Sports on Television

So far then we have been concerned to investigate how far television in general satisfies children's needs in terms of showing them sports which they have, mostly, had first hand experience of playing. Television, however, also has the potential to open up new vistas on sport and to introduce the population to games and competitive situations that they have not experiences before. Did our children appreciate this exposure to new sports offered by television? We were concerned to find out if they had seen any new sports on television lately, and whether they had liked them or not. We were also interested to find out if this exposure had whetted their appetites for more and whether they felt that increased television exposure could render the sports covered more popular.

Kelpia (10):   "I saw a game called curling, where you had to slide this big stone with a handle down ice and team mates had to sweep away the ice in front of it to keep it going. I liked that."

Basketball and American Football was also mentioned and apparently well-liked by our 10- and 11- year olds. Several of the older children also mentioned these sports favourably. All however found the actual time of showing quite inappropriate.

Sherhinda (15):   "American Football's quite good but they show it very late."

Mark (10):   "There was also American Basketball - but it's on about midnight. I liked that, but I'd like it to be on earlier then I don't have to fight with my Mum and Dad about staying up to watch it."

William (11):   "They should show more basketball but it's on in the middle of the night (the rest of the group agree)."

Emma (11):   "There's another thing - it's like hockey but it's on roller-skates - that's good."

Gary (15):   "Roller hockey - on Channel 4 - that was terrific."

William: "I like water polo as well - that's very good."

Some children were keen to see new sports substituted for some of the older, more traditional, sports currently covered.

Joe (13):   "They could drop horse racing - it's boring - and put on things like ice and street hockey - and roller skating - I've seen that on BBC1."

131

| Joanne (13): | "I think they could put on more car and motor bike racing - at the moment all you see is Grand Prix." |

Sumo wrestling was a topic that generated quite a bit of mirth with our respondents.

Tammy (13):	"Sumo wrestling - that's good: the way they do it though - it's only on for about 5 seconds. That's too short."
Kirshie (13):	"Oh no! Sumo is horrible - all those fat men slapping and pushing each other - its really silly - and those costumes - that's repulsive."
Cheryl (15):	"I switch over straight away."
Gary (15):	"They're so big, they look ridiculous."
Herjeet 15):	"Yes (laughing) I've watched it once in a while but that's all."
Int: (to Gary and to Cheryl)	"Why was it funny, and why did you turn over straight away?"
Cheryl:	(giggling) "I didn't like it."
Gary :	"It was their backsides wasn't it (laughs)"
Cheryl:	"Yeah - both of them (all laugh)."

Martial Arts also caused some interaction within various groups.

Talat (14):	"Martial Arts should be shown more - and Thai Boxing (kick-boxing) - it was good, because it had women for a change."
Richard (14):	"Thai boxing - that's vicious ... "
Talat:	(interrupting) "Yeah its vicious but it shows you how the head can get damaged."
Venessa (14):	"Seeing one woman kicking or punching another is silly."

Squash and volleyball, likewise, were mentioned as 'new' sports that were appreciated by most, although with squash many children mentioned the difficulty of following the flight of the ball despite the appreciation that the television companies had been instrumental in trying to make it easier for viewers - by using glass walled courts and 'white' squash balls.

| Richard (14): | "My Dad watches and plays squash, but I always find it difficult to see where the ball is. It moves too fast. It's better now thought because they play in glass courts." |

Our older viewers appreciated that television could both lead and follow in terms of promoting less well-known sports. To the question 'do you think they (the television companies) should show more new sports or not?'

| Gary (15): | "Well yes - they should because people react to it - they like it more. I don't like the girl's hockey -I think *that's* boring, but the men's is good. Like the World Cup, it was brilliant - I mean since Great Britain did well in the Olympics and since our other competitions, hockey's become quite big now." |

In summary, then, our young viewers had seen 'new' sports on television despite, rather than because of, their scheduling slots, and had, in the main, appreciated the exposure to them. They felt that if the television were to show more such novel sports they could grow in popularity.

Children in Sport?
Throughout the book we have constantly come across a desire by our children for more child-orientated or child-participatory based programmes. Did the same hold true for sports coverage which, almost by definition, involved adult players and competitors? Strangely, in sport, there was no great desire for more children's sports programmes. However a few did say that they would prefer better coverage of certain sports, participated in mainly by their own age group.

Mark (12):   "Yeah - I'd like to see more things like *BMX Beat.*"

Oskar (12):   "Oh Yeah - things like *Superchamps* and *Skate Board Beat* should be on much more - activities with kids doing it."

Others, however, disagreed - violently.

Gary (15):   (discussing *Superchamps*) "It's rubbish! - rally naff. It's for little kids."

New ventures in sports coverage like *Run the Gauntlet* and *Survival of the Fittest* were generally well received by all our age groups.

Michael (15):   "Yes I've seen it (*Run the Gauntlet*) - it keeps you interested because difference sports are in it - like when you've got those little hovercrafts and that -I like that sort of thing."

Annalise (13):   "I liked the different machines they had."

Mark (14):   "I liked the way they went through the water with the explosions."

Joe (13):   (Talking of *Survival of the Fittest*) "It was good - lots of competitions with sports you never do. I liked the water parachuting - you should be able to do things like that."

Our youngest age groups were the most enthusiastic about these programmes based on the latest technological gizmos - often getting quite tongue-tied in trying to communicate their enthusiasm.

William (11):   "They have like - um - dinky-toy cars and parachuting. It's Holland against England and - um."

Simon (11):   "It has-like-obstacles-with-um-motor bikes and water jets - and ...... "

Paul (10):   (interrupting) "and parachuting. It's really exciting and they get all muddy and dirty."

Mark (10):   *"Run the Gauntlet* is great. It's very exciting and fun - lots of water sports and getting hosed off logs."

Daniel (10):   "Yeah - it's really different and I would like to see more things like that."

Violence in Sport
It was clear to us during the interviews that the children related strongly - positively or negatively - to contact sport in which opponents tried to inflict physical damage on each other. We have already seen that kick boxing was disliked by some children for this reason. This view also held for

wrestling, and American - no holds barred - wrestling in particular. We raised this issue of violent sports, such as the above, and whether they should be televised.

Gary (15): "I don't think boxing and wrestling are really violent, but I saw something - just a bit on *Network 7* - um - Thai boxing - that was very violent. It was just like having a fight - it was all kicking and punching."

Int: "Should this be shown on TV?"

Gary: "Only late at night - not in the afternoon because people could copy it."

Mark (12): "Kick boxing shouldn't be shown - I've seen it once on TV."

Kirshire (13): "In one, an English girl won and the Dutch girl had brain damage and she almost died. That certainly shouldn't be on the box."

Generally, however, the youngsters felt that there was "not much violent sport on television" (Neescha, 14), and some events that looked violent weren't really because "they are all fake" (Annalise, 13). A sizeable minority however did say that they would not like to watch "all the time" when an apparently violent sport was on. One reflective 13-year-old ventured the opinion that violent sport on television can mislead or give the wrong impression.

Joe (13): "I watched boxing once and I thought punching didn't hurt - a few days later I got into my first fight and found out that it did."

Sarah (12): "Boxing's soft really - they have gloves on."

Valerie (12): "I wouldn't go into boxing because most boxers have brain damage - I wouldn't go in for that sort of thing - but its OK to watch it."

Joanne (12): "Wrestling is violent - they probably need an operation after the bout - but they sometimes act."

Tongue in cheek, one of our respondents had the benefit accruing to a relative uppermost in mind when she answered our question concerning the showing of violent sport on television.

Angela (13): "Yeah - so your silly old granny can sit there going 'yeah - bash him up'."

What was very clear was that our *youngest* children had very definite views on whether violent sports should be shown and why.

Kerry (10): "No - it could increase violence."

Emma (10): "No - it gives nightmares to young children."

Paul (10): "No - it can lead to imitation with your friends."

Violence on the Terraces

We next turned to violence on the terraces and whether the cameras should show this. The consensus was less than uniform and the reasons differed across our age groups.

Our youngest group all said such violence should not be shown because it could encourage people to imitate it. However, they all felt that viewers should be told that it was happening.

The majority of our next-oldest group felt that viewers *should* be presented with pictures of terrace unrest "to show what's happening" (Simon, 11), but a majority felt, like the previous group, that "they should say what's happening but not show it" (Michelle, 11).

Our older groups were aware of the surveillance aspects of training the television cameras on crowd trouble.

Richard (14):   "The public will know who the hooligans are."

Joe (13):   "Yeah it should be shown because the police can then get them - because their faces are seen."

Int: "But can't it encourage violence?"

Oscar (13):   "If they know they'll be filmed they won't do it so much."

Angela (13):   "It also shows other people not to go - not to take their children because there will be fights."

One boy however was quite frank:

Gary (15):   "It should be shown because it's exciting."

These last two comments testify to the ambiguity over whether crowd violence should be shown or not, and this issue was debated at length, spontaneously by our oldest group.

Herjeet (15):   "I reckon they should show it - because football used to be a friendly game and now people are going to matches just for fights."

Int: "So why should they show the fights?"

Herjeet: "Because - um - they ... "

Shahida (15):   (interrupting) "To stop families going - so they know not to go."

Herjeet: (getting her thoughts together) "But it's not just warning families, its telling the people what's going on. They're ruining the football - I mean the game -they're no longer going to watch the game."

Michelle (15):   "I think showing it will lessen the violence because if people go there for the violence and they've watched it on TV they're going to know that they're being filmed and everything. It will put them off being violent because they will know they'll get picket out on the film after."

This last comment may be based upon the fact that the interviews we conducted took place shortly after there has been reports in the press about police watching television coverage film to identify soccer hooligans, If this is so, then here we have evidence of cross-media learning: television interpretation and reflection was being influenced by knowledge gained from other media.

Impact of New Television Services

Another issue that we were keen to explore with our children was their knowledge about and anticipation of cable and satellite television as it concerned sport. We began by asking them if they had heard what might happen to sports programmes or events when they bring in cable and satellite broadcasting. The majority of our older groups averred that "there will be more sports coverage".

To the question of whether there would be better or worse sports coverage, opinion was divided.

Shahida (15): "It will most probably be better because they'll have all different sports on different channels."

Cheryl (15): "No - I don't think so - I think in the end you're only going to want to watch British programmes because they're going to show all the American ones and half the people don't like them."

Venessa (14): "I think the sports coverage would be worse because there would be less competition."

Mark (12): "Better coverage, because there will be more competition."

Tammy (13): "And because there would be more variety."

Sarah (12): "I think we'll need sports on satellite and cable because there's going to be less on normal TV because it's becoming so expensive."

Paul (10): "I think when satellite comes in, sport will be better because it will give a better coverage and it will introduce new sports you would never really see."

The spectre of new channels specifically devoted to sport was raised by our fourth oldest group. When asked if there was too much or too little sport, Mark (12) reeled off comparative figures world wide.

Mark: "I think we need more channels - the USA have about 50; Japan has 7, and we have four."

Pardip (12): "Yeah - I'd like to see a sports channel."

The idea of a dedicated sports channel was endorsed by members of other groups. Most respondents said they would watch such a channel, at least some of the time. Some of our less sports-oriented viewers, however, saw the benefit of a single sports channel along lines other than viewing sport from dawn to dusk.

Michelle (11): "A single sports channel would be good. It would all be on one channel and you wouldn't have to waste time on sports programmes if you didn't want to."

Gary (25): "Like - there are two sports channels in America - they've got two world sports channels and if its all kept to the same channel then people wouldn't keep complaining that there's too much sport on TV."

As to what they would like to see on such a sports channel, views ranged from "all the major events" (Pardip, 12), to "loads of new and unusual sports like parachute jumping and abseiling" (Mark, 12).

Sponsorship in Sport

Having sought the opinion of children to one contentious aspect of television sports coverage - terrace violence - we then raised another more subtle issue: that of sponsorship. Did all our children understand what sponsorship was and were there any sponsorships our respondents took exception to? Now while sponsorship takes several forms: sponsoring of television programmes, of sporting events, and of particular teams and individuals, our respondents were only aware of the latter two - and it was these that they discussed.

Even our youngest group could name individual sponsors "Echo Trust - West Ham" (Paul, 10); "JVC - Arsenal and Aberdeen" (Mark, 10). Coke was associated with the Olympics, and Mars with the London Marathon (Kerry, 10). When asked whether sponsors should be involved in sponsoring the whole of an event or just individuals, this youngest group clearly felt that the event itself should be the recipient of the sponsor's money. This group could not think of any sponsors who should not be allowed to participate in sports funding.

Our second youngest group, in addition to mentioning those already spotted by their younger counterparts, instanced "Puma - tennis" (William, 11); "Barclay's Bank - Football" (Paul, 10).

Emma (11): "Well all round the world you always see on these different shots that Coca-Cola's sponsoring different things, and its sponsoring the Olympics this year."

This age group was beginning to get an inkling about the paradoxical nature of advertising in sports. To the question of whether any sponsors should be banned.

William (11): "Coca-Cola - they get too much advertising - it should be the companies that make sports things that should do it (the rest agree in this group)."

On probing this issue further only Pepsi was mentioned as a reason for not allowing Coca-Cola to participate in sponsorship. Thus, only a rudimentary awareness of something amiss was present in our 10-11 year olds.

Our third youngest group mentioned "Benson and Hedges and Superkings - Motor racing" (Pardip, 12); "Embassy - car racing" (Mark, 11), and "Mobile - car racing" (Sarah, 12). By this age, the alcohol and cigarette sponsors were clearly perceived as interlopers in the field of health and sports, and as such, should be banned.

The 12- to 13-year-olds mentioned, in addition to all the above, "McKeowns lager - Ranger's football club" (Oscar, 12); "Cornhill Assurance - cricket" (Joe, 13); "Texaco - cricket" (Tammy, 13). Again, alcohol and cigarette sponsorship were argued to be inappropriate "because they've got nothing to do with sport - its bad for your health" - Angela (13), and "it's just another way of advertising" - Kirshie (13).

Our second oldest discussion group cited Guiness, Embassy, Marlbro, Access Credit and Rothmans, in addition to many of those already mentioned by younger groups. Clearly, then, all our children were being exposed to sponsors in a way that those sponsors would appreciate. By this age however the good and the bad points of sponsorship were clearly perceived and the nature of the paradox understood.

Venessa (14): "They (sponsors) give a chance for your talents to get better, and gets more money into the sport, making it better."

Talat (14): "Cigarette sponsorship should be banned because they do the opposite: sport makes you healthy, cigarettes make you unhealthy."

All the pro's and con's of sponsorship as our children understood it were discussed fully by our oldest group (15-16 year olds), with the parthian shot going to Gary.

Gary (15):   "I don't think people pay any attention to them."

It was not for our youngsters to solve this question of whether advertising has an effect or not - older heads than theirs have been greatly exercised by this difficult question. The fact however that they could articulate the major arguments was pleasing. As has been said, sponsorship is a complex subject. By the examples cited it is clear that at least our older children were aware of sponsorship of sporting events shown on television, and sponsorship of individual sportsmen or teams. It is clear also that they could distinguish between 'sport' advertising in commercial breaks and the presence of a brand name on a player's shirt. They also, however, saw the connection.

Conclusion

From the foregoing discussion with the children it can be seen that they reflect, but also go beyond, the adult views sampled in the introduction to this chapter[12]. Our children both wanted more, and more varied, sports coverage by television. They looked forward - eagerly - to the new developments of satellite and cable television both as vehicles for presenting more sport, but also more sport of a varied nature. Indeed, our children expressed a strong feeling that not only could television satisfy felt needs for viewing sport but could also act to create interest in and enthusiasm for sports that had not yet been experienced first hand. This is a nice example of the power of television to both satisfy and stimulate needs, expectations, and knowledge on the part of the viewer.

However, as we have found throughout the book, interest is the chief motivation for viewing: where there was no interest there was little or no viewing. Active selection rather than passive exposure characterised our respondents' replies. Thus, there were a small minority who looked to all-sports channels simply because this may keep sport off all the other, more general, channels.

Perhaps of all the television genres we have asked children about, this is the one that exhibited the clearest age-related sex difference in viewers. In our older secondary - age groups the majority of girls contributed very little to the discussion, whereas this was not the case at the primary level. One secondary aged girl was totally hostile to the idea of discussing the subject of sport at all. Older girls only volunteered opinions when minority sports were being discussed, or major events that may have cultural importance. It is hard to avoid the conclusion that as they mature, girls are being socialized into the attitude that sport is for boys and men and that it is unfeminine to display an interest in it.

However, the majority did watch and appreciate the sports programmes currently on offer. They were not however uncritical of these offerings. Our young viewers had clear preferences both in general and for specific types of sport based mainly upon the quality of production and the amount of pre match discussion.

While our respondents were appreciative of the presentation of new sports on television they were fairly critical of how sports were scheduled. However, many of our children were willing to miss sleep or change habits in order to view sports of interest to them. While they did use video fairly extensively it was always as a second best - usually because they were unavailable to view because of school or other commitments. For those without videos, or who had no control over their operation, late night sports programmes presented real problems.

It was pleasing to find that children of all ages had some formed views on issues that, while not central to sports coverage, are central to sport as a national pastime. Thus, our children offered views on violent sports being transmitted; violence at sporting events being shown; and violence to the spirit of sport, health and fitness, as manifest in sponsorship by tobacco and drinks companies. In all cases the range of views present matched those found in adult society. For instance, some children thought violent sport precipitated imitation,while others didn't; fighting on the terraces was seen as exciting by some but as shocking by others; and sponsorship from tobacco and drinks companies should be banned, according to some, while others said, it shouldn't be, because nobody took any notice of it anyway.

In terms of presentation formats a fairly strong message came across that while viewers like some discussion before, during and after the sporting event, this should not be overdone. Where discussions do take place, discussion involving the combatants is preferred. Children want much more than the cool clinical results. They wish to know the feelings, the anguish and the disappointment or elation of those who have just 'given their all.' These emotive aspects should not be neglected by the programmers. In this sense watching football or tennis is no different from watching a soap or a drama. They all involve the observed participants attempting to overcome hurdles to achievement and their reactions to success or failure in this. And it is these reactions to success or failure that the viewers wish to imbibe. The last word resides with one of our 11-year olds.

Emma (11):   "I watched Chris Evert crying - she had tried so hard against all the obstacles - but it was fate. I cried too."

References

1.   Which? *TV The Viewers' View*. London: Author. November, 1983.

2.   Reardon, G. and Wober, M. *Interest in Sport on Television*. London: Independent Broadcasting Authority, June 1982.

3.   Reardon, G. and Wober., M., 1982 *ibid*.

4.   Gunter, B. *Attitudes concerning Televised Sport* London: Independent Broadcasting Authority, November, 1985

5.   Gunter, B. 1985, *ibid*.

6.   Gunter, B. *Television Coverage of the 1986 World Cup*. London: Independent Broadcasting Authority, September, 1986.

7.   Gunter, B. 1985, *op.cit*.
      Reardon, G. and Wober, M., 1982 *op.cit*.

8.   Gunter, B. 1985 *op.cit*.
      Gunter, B. 1986 *op.cit*.

9.   Levy, M., and Gunter, B. *Home Video and the Changing Nature of the Television Audience*. London: John Libbey. 1988.

10.   Gunter, B. 1986, *op.cit*

11.   Gunter,B. 1986, *op.cit*
      Reardon, G. and Wober, M., 1982, *op.cit*

12.   Gunter, B. 1985, 1986, *op.cit*
      Reardon, G. and Wober, M. 1982, *op.cit*

8 News and current affairs

News and Current Affairs programmes are a prominent and ubiquitous feature of the television schedules of the modern world, which, over the last few decades, have exhibited a marked expansion in the number of hours devoted to them. This increased coverage of world and local affairs seems to be appreciated by the general public, because in numerous national surveys, both in the USA and the UK, it has been shown that people attach importance to the news, and claim that television is their major and most trusted source of news about the world[1].

However, within this global appreciation of television news as a chief information source, there do seem to be differences between sections of the population in their uptake of the news content. Survey research in Britain has indicated that males and older people have greater knowledge of recent news events than females and younger people[2], and older people were observed to recall more from an evening's news broadcast than younger people when questioned on programme content shortly after transmission[3].

In the light of the fact that the provision and purpose of news is justified on grounds of the right of individuals living in a democratic society to know what is going on around them, and that if has been found that television news may play an important role both in the political socialization process among young people[4], and in learning about their own and other environments[5], the above findings are a little worrying. Children do not seem to be availing themselves of television offerings.

This is one problem: there is another, and they may be linked. The production of television news is, of necessity, a highly routinized and selective process. News broadcasts do not consist simply of a series of stories put together in order of decreasing importance. There is generally some underlying aesthetic ideal of how the well-structured news programme should look and sound. News programmes are planned so as to create and then maintain a level of audience interest, and this in turn is linked to the goal of maintaining audience size. With this essentially entertainment function in mind, programme concepts therefore incorporate assumptions about content, organization and presentation format that will command the audience's attention. However, the danger is that news production based upon a desire to hold audience attention through entertainment value or emotional impact, carries with it the inherent possibility that news will produce transient satisfaction but ineffective communication of meaning, and possible perceptions of bias, exaggeration or untruthfulness.

In this chapter these two worries are investigated: first, that children may not be availing themselves of the news and current affairs programmes being offered. Secondly, that, if they *do* watch, there may be problems about production, organization and presentation of news bulletins that are serving to 'switch children off' or preventing acceptable levels of understanding or appreciation to occur. It is obvious that the extent to which children are able to remember and comprehend television news depends upon their attitude to the news and on the level of sophistication they bring with them to the viewing situation. It is with these 'attitudes to' and 'levels of sophistication with' the news that this chapter is concerned.

To gain insight into these areas of child viewing we interviewed 5 groups of children aged from 11 to 16 years of age. We began by getting all the children to discuss their attitudes and behaviour towards the news, and then, in order to obtain more focused, critical judgements (concerning content, presentation and organization) they were offered three news items from three different news programmes which they were encouraged to discuss freely and on parts of which the interviewer sought answers to prompted questions.

Frequency of Viewing the News

We began by asking our respondents if they watched the news, and if so, how often. While all age groups said they watched either "regularly" or "sometimes", the frequency of viewing increased steadily with age. So, while the most frequent response from our younger groups (aged 11 to 13 years) was that they watched the news "about 3 times a week", the older group members (14 to 16 years) responded most frequently with "everyday". In addition, the majority of our oldest group watched both the early and the late news, whether on BBC or ITV.

For the few who said they never watched, the following reasons were given:

Samantha (11):	"You can read about it in the papers - it's about the same."
Claire (13):	"It's boring and there are better things on the other side."
Nicola (14):	"There's just too much of it."
Ian (15):	"I read it on Ceefax."
Binitshah (13) &	

Helen (12):	"Just not interested."

Among those who did watch, viewing the news seemed largely to depend on either interest or circumstances.

Chris (11):	"Because I'm, interested in what's happening in the world, I watch both sides."
Terry (13):	"Anything - whatever sounds interesting."
Paul (16):	"It depends which channel is on - I don't actually, like, - um - I just watch a programme and if the news follows sometimes I'll watch it."
Mervyn (15):	"In the morning I watch ITV and at night its BBC."

Likes and Dislikes in the News

Adults have given numerous reasons for why they watch television in general, and news in particular. One research programme has distinguished between people who watch to fill time, and for companionship, relaxation, arousal and escape; and people who are more selective, who seek information, and watch news, talk and magazine-type programmes[6]. Where would our children fit in?

When asked why they liked watching the news, the younger respondents tended to give a diffuse answer.

Martin (11):	"It's just interesting."
April (11):	"Dangerous issues."
Samantha (11):	"Interesting features - like the Olympics."

But with increasing age the reasons became a little more specific. For example, a chief motivation for viewing seemed to be to fill out a story they had heard elsewhere, or to get details on something they found interesting. That is, news was serving as an information - enlargement source, much as it does with adults. For example, it has been shown that, of all motives for watching television, information or learning was given as the chief reason by over 70per cent of an adult sample[7].

Natalia (15):	"I only watch it if something big happens."
Paul (16):	"I usually watch the headlines at the start and if there's anything interesting I'll watch it."

For most of the children, however, prior interest was not the main determinant of whether they watched or not. Many said they watched in order to find out about what was going on in the world. Bradley is typical:-

Bradley (12):	"It tells you what's going on in the world and that."

The various groups were a little more certain about what they *disliked* in the news. The youngest respondents, while appreciating that disasters and violence had to be presented, did not like it - especially if there were 'blood and guts' vividly portrayed. Interestingly, all groups were prepared to debate the need for and the value of showing realistic violence on News programmes.

Apart from violence and disasters, the only other spontaneously mentioned dislike was:-

Matthew (13):	"The Royal Family".
Paul (16):	"The way the Royal Family are reported everyday in the news - it really gets up my nose (all laugh)."

This anti-royal sentiment grew in intensity with age.

Paul goes on:	"I think it's - um - like - if - um - well it's getting to the point where if 5,000 die in an IRA bomb blast but Princess Diana has gone off to Australia on a tour that comes first."
Mervyn (15): (interrupting)	"It's trivia - you don't need to know about it - my mum goes on holiday but its not on the news (all laugh)."
Natalia (15):	"They never criticise them either - I mean the newspapers will say 'Didn't she look fat' but especially Alistair Burnett - Oh God! (mimics) "Didn't she look lovely today'."

Wishing to probe their likes and dislikes more thoroughly we asked all groups whether they liked to see specific topics covered in the news bulletins.

From the second year of secondary school onwards it seems as if children like to hear about home and foreign news about equally; only the youngest children preferred UK news items.

Politics was universally disliked. The youngest respondents equated political items with:-

April (11):	"Boring, shouting and arguing."
Lize (12):	"You can't understand it."

While the older groups could see the need for political coverage, they had serious reservations about its treatment.

Louise (15):	"Well they go overboard on that as well - and I think it's all just exactly the same."

Strikes were seen as more entertaining than informative:

Louise:	"There's usually rows aren't there when they shout and that - its kind of like entertainment."

But, while generally disliked, all ages showed some interest if the strike being covered had some direct or indirect relevance to their own lives. When asked about whether she was interested in the coverage of strikes by News programmes,

Angeline (12) replied:	"Not really, but if it's about your school - if it's relevant to you then it's interesting."
Hailey (13):	"Yes because my dad was on strike."
Benitshah (13):	"The ferry strike was interesting because they were to do with the British families going on holiday."
Terry (13):	"The postal strike was relevant because you needed to know if you were going to get your letters."

The economy got a universal thumbs-down, but with increasing age the respondents appreciated that there was a need for this type of information.

Christopher (11):	"No its boring - but my mum and dad go on about it all the time."
Natalia (15):	"They have all pretty diagrams for that now."
Paul (16):	"It might be better if they put it right at the end of the programme say, after the weather - so that anybody who isn't very interested in the city - well they can watch it all the way through up to the weather and then turn it off."

Somewhat surprisingly the weather was enthusiastically endorsed by all children, although the older age groups were a little more sceptical of its accuracy and informational qualities.

Mervyn (15):   "You don't really need to (watch the weather) - it's always the same every day."

Paul (16):   "Usually I watch it - but it's always all wrong anyway!"

Motivations for Watching the News

Different children seem to watch the news for different reasons. We have already seen that they watch for amplification.

Dipty (11):   "I watch it if I have heard something - a story or something - and I'm not sure about the details. I watch it for the details."

Dean (14):   "I watch it if I want to know something more about what I've heard."

Others watch it for the 'continuing saga': an ongoing event or issue is of interest to them.

Paul (16):   "And a continuing story - like Ben Johnson being accused of taking drugs - so to see what's happening - I'm going to watch again tonight, definitely."

Yet others watch the news as a matter of routine.

Martin (11):   "I watch it because different things are happening."

Mark (11):   "I always watch it at 6 o'clock for the sport."

Mandy (15):   "I'm interested in knowing what's going on."

Lastly, some respondents watch the news if some personal involvement or relevance is involved.

Ian (15):   "I watch it if something has happened that somebody you know is involved in."

Of course, several of the less frequent viewers only watch if the news appears just before or just after some preferred programme. Alternatively, there may be no perceived alternative channel offering at the times news programmes are scheduled. In this case news programmes may be 'watched' but without any great enthusiasm.

Relative Merits of Television Versus Other Sources Of News

Public attitudes towards various possible sources of news (for example, television, radio, newspapers) have been tracked continuously for many years in the United States and the United Kingdom. To the question of where they usually get most of their news about what is going on in the world today, a survey in the USA in 1959 found 57 per cent said newspapers, 51 per cent said television and 34 per cent mentioned radio[8]. Since 1967, television has taken the lead and remained there. Similarly, national samples in the UK have indicated, since 1963, that television is regarded as the most important source of news[9].

However this perception of the effectiveness and informativeness of television as a principal or best news source is not constant across all kinds of news. Newspapers are frequently rated better than television for local news[10].

145

Does this media preference for different types of news manifest itself in young viewers, in the 11 to 16 age range? Pleasingly, all our groups both read newspapers and listened to the radio. However, they had fairly clear views both as individuals, and within groups, as to which media were better for different types of news. For local news our 11-, 13-, 15- and 16- year-old groups felt that radio was best, while the fourth year group felt that newspapers were better. From discussion with this latter group it was clear that the newspapers they were referring to were 'freebies' that are common in London. For national news there was a complete consensus that TV was best. Sport was felt to be well served by both TV and the newspapers, in different ways. Those respondents who favoured the papers felt that they could go into more detail but lacked the immediacy of the television picture. An interesting observation from the youngest group onwards was that newspapers were seen as a little untrustworthy.

Mark (11):   "You don't always get the truth in newspapers."

Dipty (11):   "Yeah - newspapers exaggerate more."

And by the end of our interviews it was also clear that some of our respondents were aware that the television news could be equally 'untrustworthy'.

Transmission Time and the Nature Of News

Our younger respondents tended to reason rather than recall to this line of questioning because few of them had actually watched the late news. But their reasoning was accurate. For example, they believed that the late news showed much more violence because smaller children would be in bed by 9 or 10 o'clock.

April (11):   "More terrorist things are put on late because -like - all the young children have gone to bed."

This reason is in line with broadcasters' own Family Viewing Policy which employs a 9 o'clock watershed, following which programmes are broadcast which may not be suitable for child audiences.

In addition, our younger respondents believed that the later post-watershed news would have more detail, because news editors have had more time to put the news together.

Dipty (11):   "There is more detail in the later ones because they've had more time."

Samantha (11):   "The early news doesn't know much of what's happened but later (news) knows more."

By the age of 14 or 15, however youngsters are more aware of the reality of coverage, apart from the sex and violence content, and have experienced it first hand.

Mervyn (15):   "They're the same - I think - they carry exactly the same things - there's hardly any difference."

However some youngsters appreciated wider considerations that could apply.

Natalia (15):   "Well - because of time differences they can get some new foreign news in the later programmes."

Presenters

As a means of assessing their involvement with news programmes, we asked the children if they could name any newscasters. They could: Gordon Honeycombe, Sue Lawley, Martyn Lewis, Trevor McDonald, Michael Buerk, Moira Stuart, Sandy Gaul, Robin Houston, Alastair Burnett and Peter Sissons.

While the respondents did have their individual pet hates and favourites, what was interesting about comments on presenters here, compared with other programming areas which we have looked at, was their desire to treat presenters not as individuals but as groups. Thus, they were concerned to stress that women presenters were better groomed than were the men; that this grooming was important; and thirdly that, in a sense, because of the nature of the subject matter, it was right and proper that news readers should not be treated as individual personalities.

Nicola (13): "I think if you look at the ladies side and then at the men's side, the ladies seem to have smartened themselves up - but the men are all scruffy."

Christopher (11): "I think it's important (that they be well groomed) because they are telling the truth and so they have to look good."

Paul (15): "I just listen to what they say - you can't really judge someone from what they read on the news - I mean, they're not sort of expressing their personality that much, so you can't really judge them."

When asked if this meant that he thought newsreaders should not project a personality, Paul continued.

"Well I wouldn't like it if they were just sitting there going 'Today there was something happening' (mimics a monotone) - they've got to put some expression into their voice - obviously - but -you know, it doesn't really matter about their personality as long as you can understand clearly what they're saying and they make it sound interesting."

News: Biased, Truthful, Exaggerated?

While there is a legal obligation laid upon broadcasters to ensure that the news observes "due impartiality" in the coverage of matters of political and industrial concern, the TV news is frequently criticised for being politically biased. At times of elections, news broadcasters go to great lengths to ensure that leading political parties get equal amounts of coverage. This need to observe fairness and impartiality requirements at this critical and highly politically sensitive time often interrupts the usual journalistic news worthiness criteria.

Research among viewers, however, has repeatedly shown that a majority perceive the news to be trustworthy and fair. How do our children perceive it?

The 11-year-olds felt that the news was truthful but they did perceive a little exaggeration and felt that a lot of 'bits' were left out of stories, but not in any malevolent way.

147

Mark (11):	"They just tell you the endings. They just show the results."
Hailey (13):	"Sometimes they tell you someone is lost but they never tell you if he has been found or where he could be."
Binitshah (12):	"Oh yeah - if they are doing a strike they show you both sides."

Where the younger respondents perceive less than full information, they see it as a problem of getting everything in.

| Bradley (12): | "Sometimes they go onto the next thing too quickly." |

By the third year, however, the children were beginning to be a little more sceptical.

Hailey (13):	"Sometimes they exaggerate - eh - twist it - go over the top."
Terry (13):	"Sometimes they make it sound worse to get someone to do something about it, or to keep you watching."
Mathew (13):	(talking of strikes):" They put over their point of view - not the workers, only the managers."
Roy (14):	"Yes they're biased - they just push one view."

At this stage, it was unclear whether these views or perceptions were based on experience, or whether these teenagers were paying lip-service to this sort of opinion. However, by the end of the interview it was fairly clear that what we were witnessing was the development of political awareness.

Some older children were not prepared to over-generalise, but did feel that in certain areas the news was concerned to stress a particular perspective.

| Ian (15): | "In some cases they tell the truth and let you make up your own mind but - eh - in other cases they give a biased opinion." |

By the fifth-year adult perceptions and an acute understanding of what motivates television programme producers were beginning to show through. An extended part of the discussion transcript is given to show this increased sophistication.

Paul (16):	"Well they don't tell lies - they just don't tell you all of it. What they tell you - obviously there's got to be an element of truth in it because otherwise they'd be liars - but if there's something they don't want you to know, then they don't actually tell you (the rest agree)."
Mervyn (15):	"Yeah - say - um - a UFO landed or something - I don't think they'd actually tell you about it in the news because people would get - really - um - upset - but they'd probably say a UFO was seen - you know - but they wouldn't actually confirm it."
Mandy (15):	"I think they also distort by over-hyping things."
Int:	"What do you mean?"
	"Well - Michael Jackson for example - there's too much coverage of it."

Mervyn:	"Yeah - they had the Amnesty International concert on, which was for a good cause - and they didn't get half as much coverage as Michael Jackson."
Int:	"Why do you think this was?"
Louise (15):	"It's because he's got a big following - it'll put their ratings up."
Int:	"So you think they adjust the news for that reason?"
Louise:	"They have to."
Paul (16):	"It's just the popular opinion - it's like the majority opinion gets the news."

Here then we have direct reference being made to the second problem we raised at the beginning of this chapter: the fact that television news uses 'entertainment' techniques to compete with entertainment programmes in a medium which is, for most people, for most of the time, an entertainment medium.

Prohibited Topics

There are government-lead guidelines concerning what news broadcasters are permitted to show, and the ITC and BBC have their own self-generated codes of practice. Indeed the BBC are currently drawing up a simplified code of practice for general public consumption. In addition, news editors use their own discretion in deciding how much detail of a news event to show. Against this is the belief that part of the function of news is to tell it and to show it 'the way it is'. The concept of *Eyewitness News* emanating from America endorses this latter concept of news on the box. As we will see our respondents were also split as between the 'sanitized' editorial versus the 'warts and all' eyewitness, approaches to news content.

We asked all our young people if there was anything they considered should not be shown on television. While there were a few idiosyncratic answers, like "manure when you're eating your dinner" (Liza, 12), the major issue was violence in its many manifestations. The youngest group argued strongly that "bad killings or murder" should not be shown, while the oldest group seemed to operate with the principle that anything should be capable of being shown provided that it was necessary and contributed directly to the issue being broadcast.

| Paul (16): | "Yeah - they should show things that are necessary basically - not things that aren't." |
| Mervyn (15): | "Yeah - but only if it has something to do with the point of the bulletin." |

Very clearly then with increase in age the realistic content of the news programmes was being judged less by horrific vividness and more by story integrity.

Interestingly, even with the youngest group, the idea of imitation of television violence was present and seemed to be the chief motive of this group for arguing against the inclusion of explicit violence in news bulletins.

Dipty (11):	"Bad killings or murder."
(probe-why?)	"Because children will learn from it - it does give an example."
Martin (11):	"It can encourage people like Hungerford. The man

was watching television since he was small."

April (11):   "They should tell you but not show you."

The problem of imitation of television violence was solved by a second year, Bradley (12), who suggested that because we needed to see what had happened it should only be shown after 6 o'clock "because all the little kids would be in bed".

By the third year all the respondents agreed that news programmes should show scenes of disasters, war and violence "to let you know what's happened" (Nicola, 13) and to "let you know how bad it is" (Duncan, 14).

Thus, progressively, our young adolescents were arguing that the exclusion of violent scenes was not an option but rather that they may be necessary both to show what had taken place and also perhaps to persuade the viewer that something had to be done about the topic being featured.

Paul (16):	"Well I don't think they should turn it into a horror programme - but I think it should be realistic."
Mervyn (15):	"I reckon there's nothing they shouldn't show on the news if it's actually happening - if something's happening they shouldn't just not show it because that's just covering it up."
Paul:	"But if they start showing a lot of violence people would start saying they were doing it deliberately - like if they showed bomb blasts and they started zooming in on all the bodies and that - with all the details and everything."
Louise (15):	"But they've got to make the public aware of what's happening."
Paul:	"Yeah - they've got to do something like that to make the people shocked - but they can't do it - um - they can't over-exaggerate it because then it would start getting out of hand - you know - getting like a video news nasty."
Mervyn:	"Well - that's what it is - that's what's happening and I think they've got to have the right to show things."
Natalia (15):	"If they don't show the violence they're defeating the object."

Following the youngsters discussions of violence and violent scenes in the news we asked if they had ever been shocked by anything they had seen.

Louise:	"When they showed you that man who was shot up on Gibraltar - they showed you that."
Mervyn:	"Sometimes - when you see - like - um - dead bodies being dragged along - you think 'that person is actually dead'."
Natalia:	"I saw something about a year or two ago on the news and it was about - um - Muslims or Sikhs or something - their ritual killing of animals to eat - and they showed you a picture of it being held up in the street and its throat being cut - and blood running into the gutter and I thought they shouldn't have shown that."

Animals were also mentioned as a topic that had shocked our younger respondents.

Claire (13):   "Anything to do with animals - showing work like by scientists. Trying to get it stopped in China where they put their dogs in their curry."

Clearly then for all our interviewees violence against the person and animals was a topic which caused concern. Our younger respondents wished such issues to be prohibited from appearing in the news. With increasing age, however, the necessity of realism became more appreciated and to a certain extent regarded as necessary for achieving full impact on, and generating indignation in, the viewers. All were aware of the current debate about the possible effects of televised violence on children but most felt this could be avoided by scheduling explicit violence or aggression after 6 o'clock.

Newsround and *Newsround Extra*

Newsround was the first-ever news programme especially for children, and began in April 1976. It was decided by the BBC that children should have a news programme of their own that put over the main news stories of the day in a way that was aimed directly at its younger viewers. *Newsround* had a huge advantage in that it had the support of the BBC's adult news department. This meant that reporters in hotspots all over the world were not only filing for the Six and Nine O'Clock news, but also for *Newsround*. Did our youngsters appreciate this pioneering news programme specifically designed for them?

Generally, *Newsround* was appreciated by all our groups for what it was - a special news programme for younger viewers. This appreciation was captured by Louise.

Louise (15):   "It's a shorter programme with more interesting things for a younger age group, so it will keep their attention through a longer time span."

They all agreed that *Newsround* explained things better, by using shorter words, talking more slowly, and using film footage to good effect. They could also see a difference in the items covered: "less violence" (Bradley, 7), "they've got more kids stuff" (Angelina, 12); "more animal features" (Zishaan, 12); "less politics" (Helen, 12) and "less argument" (Lisa, 12).

However, as the respondents became older all these aspects were seen to be double edged. What for the younger viewers was 'clear speaking' was now "too slow and up and down" and caused the programme to "drag on a bit" (Dean, 14).

Whilst our oldest group still watched *Newsround* regularly, except Paul who couldn't "bear it", they now watched it more reflectively. They expressed difficulty in locating the programme's precise audience and how it should be treated.

Ian (15):   "I just like watching it to see how they express the news for children, but I can't see any age group for it because when I was really little I didn't really understand it - I thought it was a 'Big Boys News' (laugh), but when I grew up I thought it was for kids."

| Natalie (15): | "I think they treat children a lot more immature than what they are." |
| Paul (16): | "Yeah - they patronize them a bit - because I always thought that John Craven's *Newsround* was a bit babyish - it was either too serious or too babyish - I can't decide." |

The appreciation that young viewers have of programmes that feature children in them appears here again, but this time the inclusion of children is viewed more critically. We followed up a suggestion by Angelina (12) that *Newsround* was "good because it involves kids" by asking our other groups for their views on this. Several thought there was a danger of trivia. As an example, an item involving children opening up a bank in a school was roundly criticised.

| Bradley (12): | "That's silly news - that's stupid stuff. It's not real news." |
| Liza (12): | "None of it's interesting." |

Newsround Extra on the other hand was accorded a good rating.

| Mandy (15): | "There's *Newsround Extra* - that's good." |
| Mervyn (15): | "Yeah - because it concentrates on one subject." |

However, Ian was a little more sanguine.

| Ian (15): | "When I've seen them, they used quite a large vocabulary for small children and I've thought - um - like-10-year old kids wouldn't be able to understand that." |

Overall, however, the children could recall many *Newsround Extras* with a great deal of clarity and thus provided good evidence that learning was easily achieved from such programmes and that knowledge gained endured over time.

These impressions of knowledge gain, based upon recollections by our group members, were borne out by the second of the three clips of news programmes that we presented to all our groups, which involved a Newsround item on gold mining on a tributary of the Amazon and the resulting pollution caused by the use of mercury in the extraction process. There was clear evidence that all age ranges of respondents had understood the major points made in the clip and that comprehension of the serious side-effects of even such a simple process as 'pan-handling' had been achieved. On many indices, then, *Newsround* can be seen to be a programme that is evaluated highly by its viewers and that presents material and topics in a way that can be easily grasped, retained and understood by them.

Response to News Bulletin Clips

Having discussed a whole range of topics relevant to news bulletin viewing we presented each group with three news clips, each clip followed by spontaneous and prompted discussion of it. This part was designed to do a number of things. A group's facility in recognising the actual bulletin would confirm or deny that group's stated viewing frequency and regularity. Their previous responses to general questions about production and content variables could be checked by their ability to evaluate specifically presented clips within these same categories. This phase of the interviews also afforded an opportunity to test, somewhat haphazardly, immediate recall and understanding of factual material presented in news broadcasts.

The first clip involved Motorway tailgating - the dangerous practice of driving too closely behind other motorists on motorway, and suggested procedures for combating it in Britain, drawing on foreign experiences.

All age groups correctly identified the clip as coming from BBC News at 6 o'clock. The bases of the identification were the studio setting and the presenter.

Recall was very good, as can be seen from one 12-year-old.

Bradley: "Tailgating - it said that the cars were getting too close and they're setting up cameras to - like survey it all. Cars are getting close to each other - um - and they said that - learners who had less than 6 months experience had to have green number plates."

All felt that the content was comprehensive, truthful and without exaggeration The basis of judging the truth of the film footage, and the overall news item, was frequently given as the presence of film, or a visual representation:

Zishaan (12):   "Because we saw the accident (rest agree). (But the 'accident' was in fact a still shot at the beginning of the bulletin and was used to illustrate a point - it was 'old' material and not a scene from an accident that had just happened - but this groups of 12-year-olds did not appear to be aware of this)."

This 'seeing it with my own eyes' was involved as a justification for believability in all three clips shown: if it is presented visually then it must be true.

The mixture of visuals and talking in this clip was felt to be about right, but some respondents claimed that there was "too much talking across the films" (Duncan, 14).

While the younger respondents felt that the content was easy to learn, somewhat paradoxically, the older viewers in the 15 to 16-year-old group found that the information density was a little too much to fully understand *all* that was being said, and went on to make the general point that at certain times children may not be in the mood to devote full concentration to serious television material.

Paul (16):   "Well at 6 o'clock, when you've just got in from school and you're lying down and everything - looking at the telly - like *Neighbours* isn't the most scintillating thing ever, is it? - so you're not really in the mood for taking in all this complex information."

Overall, however, this particular item was fairly well received in terms of communicating information and as having been produced with an appropriate balance of visuals and talking that held the attention of all age ranges.

As already indicated, the second clip shown came from *Newsround*, and comprised an item on gold mining in a tributary of the Amazon. It focused upon the pollution caused by the use of mercury in the extraction process.

The level of recall was good - with all groups and members within them comprehending the major points of the bulletin. Most groups however felt that the level of detail was insufficient concerning the extent of the pollution. It was felt that there was too much talking, and talking across pictures, although all agreed that the talking was clear. However, precisely this clarity began to grate with older viewers.

Matthew (13):   "They all speak rather thick (slowly) la-la-la."

Hailey (13):   "They spoke too slowly - too up and down."

Mandy (15):   "His head goes like this (imitates nodding)."

Paul (16):   "He goes - 'and this chemical is called *Mercury*' (emphasising word)."

Ian (15):   "So remember that in future!"

Not only was this child-orientated language style irritating, it was also off-putting.

Paul (16):   "I didn't actually catch a lot of the first part when he was talking because I was too busy listening to the way he was speaking rather than what he said. But I did actually get the gist of what it was all about eventually."

In terms of how 'truthful' the item was perceived to be, again the presence of pictures sold its authenticity to many of the younger children.

Angelina (12):   "Very true - because we saw the pictures of the rivers."

For the older respondents, however, they felt that the lack of detail about the "facts" of pollution created uncertainty in knowing just how extensive or localised the problem was. However, this lack of factual data was explained by the group by assuming that *Newsround*, because it was made for young children, should not engage in too many facts and figures.

Paul (16):   "Perhaps a little kid wouldn't actually understand like if you told him about the percentages of what's happening and that anyway."

Allowing for this possible constraint imposed upon *Newsround* concerning the level of detail presented, all agreed that as an information source, *Newsround* was "easy to follow", "easy to learn from", basically "told the truth" and made good use of film. The presentational style was, however, an issue that older children were quite negative about - especially the speech styles of the presenters.

The third and last clip that was shown (ITN early evening news) involved the lead-up to the trial of the SAS for the shooting of IRA terrorists in Gibraltar, and especially the testimony of an eyewitness to the killings.

This was the most difficult of all the clips for all of our groups. All age groups found it a little difficult to follow and they all appreciated that previous knowledge was helpful and probably necessary for full understanding of the specific clip shown to them.

Mervyn (15):   "They were going on about how they've all been shot - I mean - if you didn't know there were IRA terrorists on the Rock or any of that sort of stuff you probably wouldn't have got the full impact of what they were planning to do - and you wouldn't have understood that (the clip they had just seen)."

This need for prior knowledge was shown by some of our second years.

Benitsha (12): "It was quite difficult - I kept getting mixed up between the IRA and SAS."

Zishaan (12): "It was a lot more complicated than the other clips."

Bradley (12): (the voice of advanced reason!) "It was a complicated thing they were on about!"

Benitsha (12): "Yeah - but you need to know all the details beforehand or else you get lost and get the wrong idea of what's happening."

While this item was generally rated as having "too much talk" this was argued to be necessary.

Roy (14): "In that case they had to talk a lot. They had to show us an example of how she was saying her story."

The content was especially difficult for some of the youngsters.

Samantha (11): "When they were talking about the court case they used words like 'guilty' - we don't really know what they mean."

Terry (13): "I found the part about the actual court case was difficult to follow."

But while the specific content proved problematic to certain children, the overall content (i.e. the topic of the news bulletin) was regarded by all as problematic, for different reasons.

Martin (11): "Shouldn't be on because it's a bad influence or - at least - it shouldn't have been on the early news (this was referring to the violent content)."

April (11): "It's also secret."

Christopher (11): "It could give the SAS a bad name."

Dipty (11): (interrupting) "It has already, actually."

Our oldest group of respondents was concerned with the impact of the way in which the news item had been put together, and the possible inherent bias in it.

Mervyn (15): "And they were repeating things - like her version of the story was obviously fabricated but they repeated that later again, and I remember seeing that similar item on BBC1 and it seemed a lot better than what that one actually did."

Ian (15): "I think the man at the start was biased."

Mandy (15): "He was on the side of the IRA."

This clip obviously struck a chord with our oldest respondents who treated is as a stimulus for discussion of the bias that they thought could be found in the media in certain areas of current affairs.

Ian (15): "If an IRA bomb - or killing - did actually go off I don't think the news would go on for so long ... but just because an SAS man shot the IRA terrorist before they managed to set the bomb off, it goes on for weeks."

Mandy (15): "I mean - if the IRA shoots a policeman, you just hear it - there's never any "Oh, it's one of them - they're going to carry on doing it anyway". But as soon as

155

| | the SAS shoots someone back - then everyone goes mad - well not everyone does, just the news readers." |
| Paul (16): | "Because they say everything they do (says this loudly) and the IRA did something like that (lowers his voice to a semi-whisper in an attempt to mimic a news reader minimizing the importance of a news item) - it's like if someone else does it they shout it out - but if it's them (meaning the IRA) they're covering it up." |

And from here this group's 'thinking aloud' broadens out.

Louise (15):	"She's (meaning Margaret Thatcher) always going on about it."
Int:	"So the Prime Minister influences the news?"
Mervyn (15):	"Yeah - "
Louise (15):	"Yeah - they censor it."
Paul (16):	"On the BBC more than they do on ITV - I think."
Int:	"Why?"
Paul (16):	"They've got more power over them."
Mervyn (15):	"ITV's more independent."
Natalia (15):	"The leader of the BBC - like when they get a new Chairman - he's always a good buddy of the Government (all laugh)."

This clip then seems to have touched a raw nerve, and the vociferous comments can leave the reader in no doubt that what they have been hearing is far from an example of passive youth unconcerned with values such as truth and fairness. If TV is a drug then it is a stimulating drug, one that feeds the developing political awareness of today's youth. It also suggests that with items such as this one, which runs and runs, teenagers turn to other sources of news such as radio and the newspapers to find out about it. Perhaps it can even become a talking point with friends and family. It is also interesting to note, as we did above, that at the beginning of our interviews our respondents tended to imply that while newspapers were a little untrustworthy, news on TV was a truthful style of programming. However, once probed in depth, and with specific clips to refer to, our respondents began to show that they perceived political bias in the latter, and also the social and political reasons as to why this might occur.

All the above responses to the three clips we showed serve to indicate that the categories we sought to explore earlier - in the abstract if you will - are in fact categories of evaluation and appreciation that the young viewers spontaneously use when they sit down to watch news and current affairs. These responses indicate that with factual programmes the viewer wants the facts and the details; that they want an even-handed treatment of issues; and that thy are aware of, and appreciate, good television production techniques. The children's comments also indicate that the news has to be well-read, in an interesting manner, that the presenter should neither dominate nor distract attention from the story being told, by the way he or she tells it. Their spontaneous recognition of the source of all three clips testifies to the fairly high rate of viewing espoused by our respondents in the earlier part of this chapter. If, then, the news bulletin really is the 'main source' of information about the world today, we can rest easy in the knowledge that the adults of tomorrow are actually looking through this 'window on the world' and seeing fairly clearly what lies out there.

Current Affairs

In broadcasters' minds news and current affairs programmes share many of the same characteristics. They are both concerned with presenting or conveying information about currently important issues. While the means and methods employed may be different the ends of the two types of programme are held to be the same: a better informed and educated audience. However, the formats are very different, with current affairs programmes being more in depth, focused and extended in time. The presence of comment and evaluation is a very noticeable difference, although the concepts of balance and fairness are held to be a guiding framework here just as they are in the news programmes. So, did our respondents know the difference between news and current affairs programmes? As we will see, there was confusion among some - especially the youngest children but with increasing age the distinction becomes clearer.

In our groups, knowledge of Current Affairs ranged from an incredulous "Pardon?", through a 'slang' association to knowledge more akin to the real thing:

April (11):   "Is that the programme where that man is having an affair with a lady, and his wife - you know - doesn't want to know about it?"

Natalia (15):   "About anything that is happening at the moment."
and
Louise (15):   "Usually discussion programmes - that go into more depth on a topic that is in the news."

Our first-year secondary groups (aged 11-years) could not name any such programme, and when given titles of Current Affairs programmes said they never watched them and gave as their chief reasons "boring" or "too many long words in them". The children went on to explain their non-viewing by arguing that

Dipty (11):   "They're on a bit too late for us really."
Samantha (11):   "They show more gory bits that I don't like."

The second year group (aged 12) however were beginning to show a glimmering of some understanding of such programme type.

Bradley (12):   "Do you mean - like political things?"

When given *Panorama* and *World in Action* as programme titles all said no they did not watch, because "they're boring".

Angelina (12):   "As soon as I hear the music (of *Panorama*) I just turn it over."

When asked what she would do if her mum and dad were watching the programme she said

"I'd go and help myself to some trifle."

By the age of 13 years (third year of secondary school) a fuller understanding of current affairs programmes had clearly developed.

Matthew (13):   "They tell you about things that have been happening in the world."
Hailey (13):   "They're on longer than the news."

Terry (13):   "They tell you about Europe."
The members of this group could name *Panorama*, *World in Action*, *Weekend World*. However all, save Roy (14), said they were boring programmes because:-
"They keep saying the same things over and over again."
Roy watched such programme if he found them interesting and not just because his mum or dad watched them, nor because of the programme's placing in the schedules. However, he did not remember any time when a Current Affairs programme had stimulated any discussion within the household.

Our group of 14-15s broke the steady indication of flowering political awareness by stating strongly - after a total silence greeted the question 'What is a Current Affairs programme?' - that such programmes were boring. They could not name any programmes nor could they say how such programmes were different from the news. They were however aware that current affairs was to do with "general things - what's happening generally" (Cheryl, 14).

They admitted to reading the programme previews in the paper or TV magazine, but if they happened to "come in on one" they would turn it over. No one in the group had ever found a current affairs programme that was interesting or "captivating".

By age 15, however, a change in both knowledge and attitude could be detected. For a start, all the popular Current Affairs programmes could be named, although there was still a residue of misunderstanding concerning the essence of such programme, even at this age, as demonstrated by Mandy's spirited defense of *Network 7* as a Current Affairs programme. When it was suggested that this was more of a magazine programme, the retort was:
Mandy (15):   "Well they have debates on that - and then advice about things."

This group found Current Affairs programme that debated several issues better than ones that went into great depth on only one issue - unless the latter was an "interesting" or "good" topic.

They exhibited active selection rather than passive reception of television offerings, by pointing out that they were guided to watch by reading the blurbs concerning the programmes, much as the fourth years had done. However, it became obvious in discussion that they were learning that viewers could really only judge a programme by watching it - not just by reading a summary about it.
Mervyn (15):   "Torture - I saw one about torture - I sort of sat down and accidentally watched it - I wasn't meaning to - I just sat down and I saw it and it was about torture in different countries - and some people might not have found it interesting and nor did I particularly - but after I watched it -well - then it interested me - so I don't suppose you can see what's coming on and then think "Oh, I'll find that interesting". I think you've got to watch it and then see if it's interesting (majority agree)."

During this group's discussion of this type of programme, it became clear that adolescents had some difficulty handling issues that could have mutually exclusive but still valid alternative points of view attached to them.

Paul (16):   (Discussing the coverage of Chernobyl) "You've got so many programmes about the different effects of it, you don't really know which one to believe."

Ian (15):   "Well you've got to have - um - like - um - all different views and opinions about what happened - but they should give - um - you know - I mean, you're not sure which one to believe, so it confuses you."

The catalytic effect of television in stimulating family discussion was also evident in this group. It appeared that the majority discussed current affairs programmes that they had watched, at least "sometimes".

Natalia (15):   "We start rowing."

They appeared to appreciate the value of family discussion, even rowing;

Louise (15):   "I think it's good to row - because then you see other people's sort of opinion - especially if it's about the government."

The criteria of a good current affairs programme (of a certain type) was clear in this group's mind.

Mervyn (15):   "You can tell if it's a good Current Affairs programme because if it's moving and it makes you think about it - then it's good."

When asked to indicate any programme that had done this, the group cited *'The Journey'* (a programme that followed the last few months of a convicted prisoner's life right up to 15 minutes before execution).

Louise (15):   "It was brilliant."

Mandy (15):   "Yeah - it really made you think - because it goes into depth - about whether you should have the death penalty or not, you know."

Mervyn (15):   "It definitely made you think."

Mandy (15):   "Yeah - you feel "Oh, don't get killed"."

Paul (16):   "Yeah - you do that don't you? Because even when you've already seen it, you're still tense, even though you know what's going to happen."

Mervyn (15):   "It makes you feel better though because seeing the way he went through it - it does make you feel that there are some good points in life."

These verbatim transcripts serve to show the power of television - it's power to evoke emotion, to generate values and to precipitate thought and reflection - and all in that supposed most recalcitrant group of couch potatoes, the adolescent modern-day youth!

In summarising our children's views of Current Affairs programming then, it is clear that younger age groups get very little from them. Such programmes are actively avoided or quickly zapped by the changer. Only with increasing age does the frequency of 'boring' as a ready response drop away. With increased age the respondents began to appreciate that current issues are complex and need to be discussed, with opposing views requiring to be presented. While the presentation of equally cogent but conflicting views is troublesome, not to mention confusing, in many cases, the thrashing out of an issue in some depth is appreciated.

If a programme makes contact with deep-seated emotions then it will be appreciated. Talk about talk is the least appreciated form of current affairs programming, but even here there was some evidence that our respondents were beginning to appreciate that certain concepts and ideas could not be rendered into visual form, and that nothing but "concentration and close listening" (Paul, 16) would suffice, or was possible.

Conclusion

The media can serve to alert, mobilize and activate predispositions in viewers that exist prior to actual news reports. This means that television has implications for the socialization of young people in society. But here we are faced with two, mutually exclusive, problems. If children do not choose to watch the news they will have no knowledge of world affairs upon which to cut their fledgling political teeth. On the other hand, if they do watch the news then they have direct access to world events, with television reporters (rather than parents or teachers) acting as immediate interpreters of news events. In this latter case, they are less dependent upon traditional elders and elites for their developing 'world view' interpretations. Rather, they are directly and persuasively reached by the way journalists report and frame the news. Any malevolent influences of these 'persuaders' are feared to be most strongly felt by those who are most television-dependent, those least open to counter information from their own experience, from alternative media or from interpersonal conversations - in a word, today's youth.

It was with these two problems that this chapter was concerned. We now have answers. We found that our respondents *did* watch news and current affairs programmes, especially as they grew older. What we did *not* find was gullibility, or credulousness. Nor did we find sullen non-interest in world affairs. Rather, we found an active, selective, critical audience who saw clearly bias, exaggeration and selective reporting for what it was. We found a youth that was concerned about fairness, representativeness, and even-handedness of treatment of individuals, groups and nations, whether in news or current affairs programmes. We found that they were critical of news bulletin compilation in terms of emphasis, pace, speech styles and item repetition. Certain format features they found conducive to understanding and comprehension; others they found antithetical. They appreciated that certain aspects of television presentation (such as the news and current affairs) required a different type of 'watching' from that required for other, non-informational, television. What was pleasing to us was that our respondents, especially the older ones, were willing to put in this effort. The attitudes revealed in these interviews leave us in little doubt that the youth of today are active watchers and good sense-makers of television news and current affairs.

References

1. Gunter, B. and Svennevig, M. *Attitudes to Broadcasting over the Years*. London: John Libbey and Company, 1988.

    Roper Organisation. *Trend in Attitudes Towards Television and the Media:* A Twenty-Year Review. New York: Television Information Office, 1983

    Tunstall, J. *The Media in Britain*. New York: Columbia University Press, 1983.

2. Gunter, B. News sources and news awareness: A British survey *Journal of Broadcasting and Electronic Media*, 1985, *29*, 397-406.

3. Robinson, J. P., and Sahin, H. *Audience Comprehension of Television News: Results from Some Explanatory Research*. London: British Broadcasting Corporation, 1984.

4. Atkin, C, and Gantz, W. Television news and political socialization. *Public Opinion Quarterly*. 1978, *42*, 183-197.

    Conway, M. M., Stevens, A. J., and Smith, R. G. The relations between media use and children's civic awareness. *Journalism Quarterly*, 1975, *8*, 240-247.

    Dominick, J. R. Television and political socialisation. *Educational Broadcasting Review*, 1972, *6*, 48-56.

5. Cairns, E. Television news as a source of knowledge about the violence for children in Ireland: A test of the knowledge-gap hypothesis. *Current Psychological Research and Reviews*, 1984, *3*, 32-38.

6. Rubin, A., and Rubin, R. Older persons' TV viewing patterns and motivations. *Communication Research*, 1982, *9*, 287-313.

7. Rubin, A. Rationalised and instrumental television viewing. *Journal of Communication*, 1984, *34*, 67-77.

8. Roper Organization, 1983, *op.cit*

9. Gunter, B. and Svennevig, M., 1988, *op.cit*

10. Gunter, B. and Svennevig, M., 1988, *op. cit*

161

9   General information programmes

While it is true that television is predominantly an entertainment medium, it has traditionally had as part of its raison d'etre, a mission to inform and to educate.

In this chapter we examine children's opinions about programmes that either incidentally or more deliberately impart information. Thus, we question them about programmes such as, the often hilarious, *That's Life*, about *Blue Peter* and *Splash*, but also about programmes that are more clearly orientated to conveying scientific knowledge, largely stripped of any sugar coating of entertainment paraphernalia, such as *Tomorrow's World*, *Know How* and *Wild Life on One*.

We will see that children, in general, like all these types of programmes but for subtly different reasons. We will also see that what is remembered is not always what programme-makers intended to impart. It will become clear that loyal viewership among children derives from a variety of features; the nature of the programme's subject matter, the way it is presented and the personalities of the presenters.

We began by asking the children what information programmes they thought were specifically designed for them. The older children (14/15 years of age) felt, at a general level, poorly catered for: nicely encapsulated by:

Kelly (15):   "There isn't any - we're not like - um -we're an in between age - so there isn't any."

On being probed further, however, when asked to "name any programmes that give information or from which you can learn things, but not school programmes", members of the groups came up with *Tomorrow's World*, *The News*, *Horizon*, *Nature Watch*, *Wildlife on One*, and, to a chorus of laughter, one respondent ventured *Blue Peter*.

When asked about medical and health programmes, *Jimmys*, *Hospital Watch*, *That's Life* and *Tomorrow's World* were spontaneously mentioned, with approval. From the above, then, it seems clear that children of all ages, after a faltering start, were aware of, and watched with a variety of intensity and dedication, a whole host of programmes that could be classed as 'informational'.

The scene was thus set to enquire more deeply into just what they watched; what they liked and disliked about specific programmes; and what, if anything, they were picking up from such programmes.

Subject Matter and Presentation

Looking across the many hours of discussion with our children, one thing kept cropping up in terms of subject matter; the extent of audience participation that a television programme invites and allows. While direct experience (such as writing or phoning in, and entering competitions) was most preferred, vicarious involvement via children seen participating in the programme was a second best option. This was a powerful, recurring, theme.

Keetan (11):   "There's this other programme called *Who's Next* and that's quite good because it gives the children a chance to say what they want - like about smoking, drugs, and stuff like that."

Splash was especially liked for this:

Kelly (15):   "They got the kids going out and interviewing people - like pop stars and things like that."

Wish You Were Here (a holiday guide programme) was also seen to make good use of children.

Emma (15):   "Well *Wish You Were Here* - they have children going out on holiday and that's sort of for our age."

All agreed that there should be more TV programmes with children in them and the more one could actually participate the better.

Keelie (11):   "With the *Really Wild Show* - I like it - its good, like Stuart says, they show you tropical things and you're allowed to write in and ask if you can hold something.

Baljit (11):   (Talking of *Blue Peter*) "They let you enter competitions."

Across all informational programmes there was a tendency for a complaint to arise concerning 'failure to describe things properly'. This was frequently caused by either the presenters the programme composition. Whatever the source, however, the presence of the complaint is a cause for concern given the nature of the programmes under consideration.

Keetan (11):   "They don't describe it (left undefined) properly."

Seema (11):   "They keep talking".

Stuart (11):   "They're all from different places and you cannot understand them."

Keetan (11):   "Just after they've shown - um - something they put

163

the camera on them quickly and they're talking about something ...."

Seema (11):   (interrupting) "Then they change the subject."

Brijesh (11):   "But they're still talking on something ..."

Seema: (interrupting) "Half way through it, they go on to another subject."

Interviewer: "So they don't keep to the point?"

Keetan (11):   "No - they don't actually carry on with it - and once there was this kind of cloth they said that's getting researched - about Jesus I think it was - all they showed you was how they do it - they didn't show you if it was really Jesus - they should show you if it was or not."

This criticism is not so much about keeping to the point as making the point; children like to know about outcomes, and fairly immediately.

However, while critical of specific presenter's styles and programme content, the children were aware of the time constraints placed upon programme makers.

Kellie (11):   "What they do is - they try to fit in a load but in the time they have they have to say only a little about it if they ant to get it all in."

This awareness however, did not prevent the children disliking programmes that were 'too cluttered' or 'racey'. When discussing *Network 7*, it all became too much for Paul.

Paul (15):   "It's all crammed in. Its a bit weird actually because you don't know who's presenting what."

Our younger age group, while discussing many programmes, were specifically asked about the well established programmes, *Blue Peter*, and a newer, but shorter lived programme, *Splash*. A common feature of both *Blue Peter* and *Splash* is that they offer children the opportunity to make things rather than just learn facts and information. Our children especially wished to talk about this aspect of programme content, and to express their disappointment with it. It soon became clear that in this respect the *Blue Peter* programme is poorly planned and executed, and as a consequence dispiriting to the children, despite their resilience!

Stuart (11):   "Well, on *Blue Peter* when they make things - they don't actually show you how to make it - they show you a bit and then they bring another thing round from somewhere and then they show you the rest of it."

Chorus: "Here's one we made earlier."

Stuart had tried to make a jewellery box "but it fell apart". Sheema (11) had tried once but "it didn't work", Keelie (11) had tried to make one of the cakes they were making but it turned out "flat as a pancake".

All agreed that the programme did not give enough warning as to what was needed or what was to be done. The children bemoaned the fact that it was difficult to remember all the steps and that to go away and get a paper and pencil inevitably resulted in them missing information. They also complained that some of the material suggested for construction was either not readily available, or "quite expensive". The 'making' aspect of *Splash* was felt to be even less well organised than *Blue Peter*.

What was tepid criticism of the 'making' aspect of *Blue Peter* by our younger viewers became white hot with our older children.

Emma (15):	"I've never managed to make anything from *Blue Peter*."
Kevin (15):	"I tried one of them sledge things."
Sarah (15):	"They were making this periscope and they go from one step to another so quickly you think "Oh God - how did they do that?"
Kevin (15):	"Yeah, they always pull out one that they done earlier."
Kelly (15):	"It takes about an hour to do it properly and they go through it in about 5 minutes."
Int:	"So you've tried to do those things, and ....?"
Kelly:	(interrupts) "No - I've never tried it."
Sarah (15):	"I have! (laughs) - it never works."
Int: (to Sarah):	"What happened when you tried it."
Sarah (15):	"It just fell to pieces as soon as I picked it up."
Int:	"So you weren't happy with the finished result?"
Sarah:	"No!"
Int:	Were you doing it yourself, or did you try asking your Mum for help?"
Sarah:	"Yeah, I asked my Mum but - um - I don't know - she just looked and said 'Huh! interesting' (sarcastically).
Int:	"How easy was it then to follow the instructions?"
Sarah:	"Hopeless."

In terms of specific content, children were able to categorise the type of material that was likely to appear in specific programmes. Thus *Splash* was rated highly compared to *Blue Peter* by some of our respondents because of its sports content and its preoccupations with "modern things". *Blue Peter* was seen as "showing you history and that" (Baljit, 11 years). Contrary to our stereotypes of children as music-loving, history-hating, many children liked this *Blue Peter* emphasis.

Keetan (11):	*"Splash* shows you more like - um - pop - and some people don't really like pop - they want to learn about famous cities - if they show history, you can find out more. In the competitions they ask you questions like the history - um - of Tutankhamun and the World Wars."

Some of our oldest discussants thought that *Blue Peter* was still appropriate for their age group, and several thought they could learn from it "but only in certain ways". Others, however, had never liked its content on format and had always found it boring and there were other aspects that were also frowned upon.

Sarah (15):	"They're always having appeals for everything aren't they?" (scornfully).

Across programmes, 'live audience participation' and 'relevant people' were liked.

Kevin (15):	"Well its got a live audience (*Where There's Life*) and

some of them have the problem and some of them just talk about it."

Emma (15):   "That's like - um - *The Time and The Place*."

Our respondents could remember UFO's and exam pressure being discussed in this latter programme.

While "boring" was a word that appeared frequently in our transcripts, offset mostly be programming that had several topics in the one programme, the above types of programme escaped this accolade. Here the children were happy with the particular programme having only one topic or focus, because:

Emma (15):   "If they didn't have the person telling what they've been through - um - it's that that's interesting (talking of *Where There's Life*, which focuses upon one topic per programme)."

The one programme that came 'bottom of the pops' was a programme designed specifically for children during the long school vacations, intended to stimulate interest and to suggest ways of occupying their time: *Why Don't You?* However, they didn't like the way it was presented.

Sarah (15):   "It's got a bit formal now."

They didn't like the presenters themselves.

Kevin (15):   "(regretting the introduction of new presenters) "Yeah, you can't understand what they're saying - its pathetic."

They did not like the videos or the material contained in the videos because "they were boring" or showed "unattractive material such as spiders".

The making/cooking parts were seen as hilariously inappropriate and poorly presented (shades of *Blue Peter*?).

As has been said a chief attraction of children's information programmes, for youngsters themselves, is the possibility of participation, either directly or indirectly. This reflects a perception by the child that television is just another aspect of their world, not something apart from it. However, this desire to "get involved" on the part of the children can have amusing consequences when it bumps up against the adult world, especially when phone-in programmes are involved.

Sarah (15):   "Yeah - I tried to get the number once for Roland Rat but ..." (falls into fits of laughter).

Int: What happened?

Sarah (15):   "Well, I rang up the operator for the number (continuous laughter throughout) but she put the 'phone down on me."

Int: "What did you ask?"

Sarah (15):   [who cannot stop laughing]: "Just - do you know Roland Rat? - but she put the 'phone down on me, she must have thought I was joking."

The Presenters

It appears that presenters are very important in information programmes.

Our respondents exhibited strong likes and dislikes of particular presenters, of their demeanours, and, in certain cases, their dress sense. The children were also very sensitive to the attitudes and approaches of the presenters to those they were interviewing or questioning.

So, for our younger viewers, *Splash* presenters were more "exciting" and "lively" than *Blue Peter* presenters.

Kelly (15): "On *Blue Peter* they just talk and - um - they just don't do anything."

Sarah (15): [laughing]: "Yeah - they just sit on a couch and stroke cats."

In *Blue Peter* discussions, children's liking for regularity and familiarity was to the fore.

Keetan (11): "I used to like the presenters before - these people are not so good."

(having just seen a current clip of *Blue Peter*).

Keelie (11): "They're too posh - they should have someone like Andy Crane or Paul Scofield or - um - some superstar on it."

This connotation of 'posh' cropped up repeatedly with *Blue Peter* discussions, despite the fact that current presenters speak with regional accents.

Seema (11): "Yeah - they keep saying 'OK - um' when they talk about something". Like they go 'Oh, yes - 1984 - something happened' and then four minutes later 'Oh, 1986, that happened' - they don't tell you the whole thing, do they?"

The presenters of *Blue Peter* and *Splash* were also spontaneously compared and contrasted on clothes sense! The *Splash* presenters were seen as more fashionable and thus gave children "clues to what is fashionable at the moment", while *Blue Peter* presenters were "too posh".

Keelie (11): "*Blue Peter*'s clothes are tight fitting and they can't hardly walk - like they stand up and they're like that (demonstrates). In *Splash* they're comfortable clothes."

At this point the girls in one group got into a rarefied discussion about the relative merits of *Blue Peter*'s presenters wearing high heels, while *Splash* presenters wear flat shoes!

The older children did not seem to be aware of the fact that *Blue Peter* presenters now talk with regional accents and wear casual clothes, and thus it could be that their responses were reflecting reliance on old images of *Blue Peter*. Notwithstanding, however, this level of discourse clearly indicates that children can become attentive viewers and active evaluators of some programmes to a level of very fine detail.

But most interesting of all was the social skills ratings that the children were able to give to the various presenters they were familiar with.

Danny Baker of the *6 O'Clock Show* was acutely perceived by a fan:

Kevin (15): "A good personality - he jokes about a lot of things but he has his serious side."

Michael Aspel (of the same show) was given a bit of ambivalent stick:

Sarah (15):	"Yeah - he's boring."
Emma (15):	"Well, he's good but he doesn't make you laugh as much as the others."
Sarah (15):	"He's not too serious but he's not very funny either".
Emma (15):	"I think he fits the part, because I don't think someone like him, because he presents it, should be too funny or too serious - I think he's just right."

Insightful perceptions were also observed when discussing Miriam Stoppard of *Where There's Life.*

Kevin (15):	"She's alright."
Emma (15):	"She's not sympathetic to what people have been through."
Int:	"She is *not* sympathetic, do you think she should be more sympathetic?"
Emma (15):	"Well, I suppose not on television, although you feel they should be, maybe they shouldn't."

This equivocation indicates that children are aware that no matter how personal the topic, television calls for some sort of "performance" that maximizes the 'televisibility' of the programme.

But the most outraged indignation was reserved for a presenter on *Watchdog*, especially by an articulate, but irate 15-year-old.

| Sarah (15): | "They tend to put the companies down - but they tend to go over the top." |

She went on to discuss a particular programme she had seen where a *Watchdog* presenter had brow-beaten a time-share operator concerning a 'waste-tip', but concluded:

"... it was terrible - it was really bad."

Children have an acute sense of fairness and fair play. Confrontation and heavy-handedness are no more seductive to children than they are to adults. Abrasive interviewers are quickly spotted and instantly disliked.

Kelly (15):	"Well, there was this lady (on *Network 7*) who was interviewing Kylie Minogue and I didn't like her at all because she was just being so hard."
Int:	"So you think they are a bit harsh in their line of questioning?"
Kelly (15):	"Definitely!"

But all consumer programmes were not tarred with the *Watchdog* brush. As a group, our respondents believed such programmes could be fair and even-handed, and that *That's Life* definitely *was* fair. This programme had another big thing going for it - it was entertaining. Individual members of our groups could recall, with full animation and sound effects, the *That's Life* "dog that walked on two legs (Emma); the "croaking dalmation" (Jonathan) and:

| Emma (15): | "Oh yes - the Persian cat who died and this lady sent it away to be stuffed and when it came back it was totally destroyed - it was so funny - the way they put it across." |

However, to the question of whether they liked *That's Life* because of the fun or the consumer side, all agreed "a bit of both". One respondent affirmed with not a little knowledge of dramaturgical techniques:-

Sarah (15): "No - I think the serious side is good because they go from one extreme to another - like from - um - say it is like - um - something really funny, well the next item is more serious, like - um - a girl who is disabled, or something. I think its good that they do have a serious side as well."

Over and above the injection of entertainment *That's Life* scores with the children again because of the interactive, responsive, nature of its offering.

Emma (15): "They help people as well because when like people - um - have got a problem they write in and help them - with business problems and that."

Can Children Learn from such Programmes?

To our question of whether they could learn anything from the types of programme that we had been discussing, the children agreed that they could and had. When pressed further, it became clear that describing different jobs (as for example *Blue Peter* does) can give the children insight into occupational roles. Such programmes also offer help in how to go about achieving these occupations.

Another aspect mentioned by several respondents was that informational programmes could give leads and guidance on how to make things happen, or how to further an interest, or stimulate a new one.

Keetan (11): " ... and they tell you where to ask - at the Town Hall - so you can find out more

Brijesh (11): "And they show you new places that have just opened - like museums."

This guidance aspect of informational programmes was most clearly articulated when discussion centred on Travel programmes, which children found very enjoyable. *Wish You Were Here* was variously seen as giving information on:

Keetan (11): "Food."

Keelie (11): " ... the type of people - it gives you a good idea of what it would be like."

Stuart (11): "Because it shows you where it is - and sometimes they show you a map".

Sarah (15): "You can learn the traditions of the country."

Clearly then the children were picking up exactly what this type of programme is designed to impart. However, the children issued a warning because, when asked if they or their families ever acted on the information given out they all said "No". They had never been on a holiday recommended by such a show and they always used brochures. They all seemed to agree that such programmes feed fantasy, stimulate interest and desire, but rarely precipitate purposeful activity.

Sarah (15): "After my mum's watched it, she always says 'roll on summer' or whatever - and 'go and get a brochure" - but we've got hundreds at home!"

Comparing travel programmes, our respondents felt that *Wish You Were Here* and *Holiday* were addressing different audiences. *Wish You Were*

Here is "classy" and concerned with foreign-based holidays, while *Holiday* was for "normal, local, people e.g., camping, adventure holidays and UK-based". There were some shows where the children were convinced that fun rather than fact was what was of interest. *The Six O'clock Show* was perceived as such a programme.

Sarah (15):   "Well they do give you some information but 'not a lot'."

Emma (15):   "Not useful things; stupid things".

Sarah (15):   "Yeah - stupid things but they're good".

While the children could recall nothing specific from any of the *Six O'clock Shows* they had seen, they did know it was about weekend matters, and they did have a clear recollection of the format of the programme.

Paul (15):   "It doesn't stay waiting for something - like they went to a hospital and then went back to the studio and kept going back to the hospital ... this happens every week."

It is interesting to note that the children could remember nothing about what the hospital item was actually concerned with.

Emma (15):   "It makes you watch the programme until the subject is over."

Here than was evidence that a fairly novel programming format had the power to attract and hold viewers, but in and of itself served to fixate very little information or knowledge.

Science Programmes

So far we have discussed what children liked or disliked, appreciated or abhorred, and were attracted to or repelled by in TV programmes that could be seen as giving out social or personal information that referred to their everyday world of school, home and leisure. We now turn to programmes that specifically set out to inform the viewer of advances in structured disciplines and bodies of knowledge which, while still touching areas of their life, do so more tangentially and remotely - science programmes.

While the nature of the information conveyed in science programmes, its underpinning by disciplined thought, and its non-immediate practical benefits, all differ from the type of information we have looked at earlier in this chapter, none-the-less there is one common element which binds the two strands together - they are both designed to be conveyed by television. Thus our discussion of science programmes followed similar lines to that of the more personal information type of programme we have already examined.

Because science as such is not taught as a separate discipline in most primary schools, it was felt that requiring younger age-groups to discuss those kinds of programmes, on an individual basis, was possibly asking too much of them, given their limited prior knowledge of the subject. Although primary children were encouraged to comment freely on the topic during their discussion of more general information programmes, more precise questioning for this part of the research was reserved for secondary aged pupils - boys and girls aged 12 to 14 years of age. The format was similar however to that indicated earlier: a general discussion about science and science programmes, then specific discussions of specific programmes aided by clips from *Tomorrow's World*, *Know How* and *Erasmus Microman* to focus their opinions on science programme offerings.

We began by seeking to find out how children conceived of science. Their views proved broad and eclectic.

Samantha (13):	"Its to do with your body."
Mark[1] (13):	"It's to do with experiments."
Mark[2] (12):	"Finding out things."
Samantha (13):	"Different chemicals."
Mark[1] (13):	"Biology."
Anne (14):	"New inventions."
Sonia (14):	"Technology."
Sarah (13):	"Everything that is around us."
Michael (12):	"Things like machines."
Amanda (14):	"To stereotype it, people will think of chemicals and that sort of thing - but how I would think would be plants."

And as if to prove Amanda's point:

Mark (12):	"Physics, Chemistry, Biology."

On the whole all the children liked at least some aspects of science, with respondents suggesting the bases for liking being "the experiments", "the teacher" or "the human body, its really good" (Samantha). One respondent however seemed to be on a different wave-length altogether and would have been a joy to teach.

Cassy (13):	"No I just like all the activities, because its like you're going into another sort of phase, you can see all these, like different things and, like you don't know about and its really just making them clearer - say that you know that a machine is a machine and it moves or something but you go right into the actual thing of it - like you go right from the beginning of the actual thing."

Despite not *one* respondent confirming that they had been directed by any teacher to watch any science programme on TV out of school time, it was clear that the children did view such programmes of their own volition. When asked which TV science programme they could name they spontaneously offered *The Living Body*, *Open University*, *Q.E.D.*, *Tomorrows World*, *Body Matters*, *Know How*, *Think Again*, *Think of a Number*, *Wild Life on One*, *Panorama*.

However, very few children said they video-taped any science programmes - perhaps the acid test of true involvement in television programmes in todays high-tech society. Where taping of science programmes did occur it was under the influence of parental involvement - usually fathers who were teachers.

Subject Matter and Presentation

Tomorrows World was perhaps the best-liked science programme, and the reasons for this are instructive.

Mark[2] (12):	"*Tomorrows World's* a bit like science."
Sarah (12):	"That's good actually."

171

Cassy (13):	"*Tomorrows World* is good - yeah."
Int:	"Why?"
Mark[2] (12):	"Because its interesting."
Cassy (13):	"Its not boring."
Sarah (12):	"They show you all different experiments."
Cassy (13)	"Its not like a person sitting there with all chemicals."
Sarah (12):	"And they explain things - like they show you what you may have in the future - like once there was a plant and when you touched it it put a light on."
Mark[1] (13):	"They show you loads of things, and they explain it well."
Cassy (13):	"They show that - um - they show the way how different technologies today improve in science."
Sarah (12):	"And it doesn't treat you like children - it treats you as if you know things because you are at school."

This last point (a recurring complaint throughout *all* our research) formed one of the few negative statements made about *The Living Body* programme which otherwise was well received.

Michael (12):	"I mean this *Living Body* programme."
Sarah (13):	"(interrupting) "Yes it treats you like children with great big diagrams of - um - not molecules or anything like it does in *Tomorrows World* - but - um - you know what I mean - it has - um - cartoons and things - it just makes you feel like a baby."

Insensitivity to the childrens' perceptions of the level of content was also raised as a criticism with *Erasmus Microman*.

Amanda (14):	"Well there's this programme - I think it's meant for our age group, but it treats - um - well, I watched it and I felt insulted because it was as if they were - I don't know - it's as if they were treating us very young and we didn't know anything."

In terms of presentational style, then, several science programmes, while liked in many respects, were clearly seen as wrongly pitched by certain age groups that watched them, although it should be noted that in the particular case of *Erasmus Microman* this was produced as a junior science programme. While graphics can add insight and understanding it is clear that they must be very carefully handled and put in proper context, in order not to alienate potential older viewers of the programme.

We asked our children whether they preferred "straight information" or "information embedded in entertainment". The majority said that for science programmes they preferred straight information. However there were differences both within and across groups, with those who favoured entertainment suggesting that this could keep up interest.

Sonia (14):	"I suppose it's one that tries to be entertaining" (girls in the group agree).
Int:	"Why?"
Joanna (14):	"It keeps you watching it - its as if you don't want to get up and walk away."

Interestingly, it was our youngest respondents who preferred the straight information format most.

We than asked the children if they preferred science programmes that covered a single topic or programmes that covered several. Once again, the children were split on this issue.

Cassy (13): "Ones that concentrate on one particular item, because its too much to take in when you've got lots of different things."

Samantha (13): "Yeah - even if it drags on its still better."

Billy (14): "I like it best when they have a variety of things instead of just one thing."

Int: "Why."

Billy: "Well, you get bored with just one thing so you turn over or something."

The alternative perspective was provided by Amanda (14) who believed "If there's too many you just get confused".

To our question of whether the children ever took notes, all responded that they never had, and many saw this as something you only did, reluctantly, in school.

On the issue of what content appealed to the children all agreed that nature programmes were good, especially if conveyed with high technology footage - like "going down a mole hole" (Michael). There were, however, gender differences in liking for technology, with boys liking things to do with cars and machines, which they talked about with their friends, but the girls adamant that there was "too much" of that kind of thing in science programmes" (Samantha).

The desire (and perhaps the need) of children to move from the known to the unknown was exhibited in the near-universal interest shown in programmes that related to the human body, such as *Body Matters* and, despite the negative criticisms voiced above about the use of uniquely - TV technology, *The Living Body*. These programmes were seen as informative, lively and interesting.

Again, information that either related to, fed into, or built upon school work was also well received. The children constantly and consistently referred to programmes such as *Tomorrows World* being of interest because they related to school work. However, the difficulty of meeting most of the children's needs most of the time was indicated by

Cassy (13): "They're either too advanced or you've done it already."

A major factor in the liking of a programme was the perceived level of content and appropriateness of television techniques, taken together. Talking of *Erasmus Microman* this became obvious.

Amanda (14): "Its boring, I just turn it over."

Stephen (13): "Yes every programme is so boring the way they keep taking you back in time."

Amanda (14) "Well I don't know if it was for our age group but it was treating people my age as if they were very young and didn't know anything - I though it was quite insulting actually."

We did ask our children to device the 'ideal' science programme and while this proved very difficult, their straining towards a solution reveals certain key elements. By referring to *Body Matter* these elements become clear.

Michelle (14):	"Its not easy, well - it is - its just because they put it in a - um - ... "
Amanda (14):	"They go into detail."
Michele (14):	(interrupting) "Well they go into detail but not too much detail."
Amanda (14):	"Yes the subjects are good but it is not only that, it's that they act seriously but they have a laugh at the same time."
Stephen (13):	"And they don't talk down to you, at all."

So, the ideal science programme would have a certain amount of detail, but not too much; that detail would be explained and illustrated well, with a degree of light-heartedness where appropriate. The presenter would be serious, but not over-serious, and above all would not talk down to the viewer. Once again then, the proposition is substantiated that subject matter, presentational format and presenters, as a trilogy, is essential.

We have looked at the first two in terms of science programmes, now let us look at the third essential element - the presenters.

The Presenters

As with programmes discussed by our children that conveyed social and personal knowledge, so with scientific programmes - this area of questioning produced the most vociferous and animated comments.

When asked how programmes could be improved and/or made more interesting, several respondents agreed with Michael:

Michael (12):	"They could get some better presenters for a start!"

When asked to name any presenters of science programmes that they knew, the children offered Maggie Philben (*Tomorrow's World*), David Attenborough (nature programmes/*Living World*), David Bellamy (*Bellamy's Bugle*), Johnny Ball (*Know How*), Bill Oddie (*Fax*), and several more.

When asked why they liked or disliked particular presenters many reasons were given but they resonated with previous findings.

Sarah (13):	"I like - um - there's that woman on *Tomorrow's World* - Judith someone. I think that she's good, and - um - she explains things and she doesn't - um - although she tries to explain it to make you understand, and she knows that you may have trouble understanding it, at least it seems like that, so she tries to make it sink in - whereas a lot of other science programmes - its just all sort of talking in the same tone. It doesn't interest you if they say something surprising because its just like saying "there's another person dropped dead" and saying all of a sudden "the person has come alive again", and they don't change tone, whereas she does."

This level of perceived detail concerning tone of voice was repeated several times. Talking of another presenter:

174

Michael (12):	"She just sounded sort of flat - and didn't make it interesting."
Sarah (13):	"Everything was la-la-la." (mimicking monotone)

Certain presenters were seen as patronizing and several were seen as inexperienced. A few were seen a both!

Michael (12):	(talking about *Know How*) "I hate the lady presenter, she's always there first and she sort of - um - like - um - (he mimics) 'Oh wow! - this is an air-ship and its pumped up by helium' and you think 'Oh wow - I know that.' She thinks you're all children or all babies, but Johnny Ball - I've seen him in various programmes before, and well, he's sort of - um - for all age groups in a way - he makes it more interesting and you laugh at him like - um - he throws a record away or suddenly pops up laughing - he's jolly! ... he adds a bit more characters to the programme (*Know How*)."

Johnny Ball appeared to be consistently well liked by all the children.

Joanna (14):	"He uses different tones."
Billy (14):	"He makes you look at it more - you want to see what he does next, don't you."
Amanda (14):	"Yes he is good because he presents in a way as if he doesn't know."
Sonia (14):	"Yes, its as though he's asking the questions himself."

Alas not everyone presenting science programmes is a Johnny Ball. Certain presenters were seen as a little over the top - such as Bill Oddie who was over-enthusiastic (in *Fax*), and David Bellamy whose arm waving was regarded as "stupid and boring" by many. Presenters who were seen as reading form 'cue cards' and thus not interested in or knowledgeable about the subject matter, and by implication, the children receiving the information, were universally disliked. One presenter on the clip we showed of *Tomorrow's World* (a very well regarded programme overall) came in for a roasting.

Sarah (12):	"I could tell that what she was saying she was reading. She wasn't making it interesting."
Cassy (13):	"It sounded like she didn't know what she was talking about herself ... it was just like off a script."

All children agreed that programmes should have more than one presenter

Cassy (13):	"Because you get sick of seeing the same person's face all the time."
Sonia (14):	"Its nice to have a change."

and that presenters should be of both sexes, for no other reason than it would be "sexist" to have only males or only females as presenters. Interestingly, over half our sample actually used the word "sexist".

And once more, as with the non-science information programmes, our children wanted more child presenters.

Cassy (13):	"I think that younger children should be able to present things like that (science material) because its mainly

	younger people that watch it (talking of *Erasmus Microman*)."
Sarah (12):	"I think it makes it more interesting when your own age group is presenting something, they sort of know what you like."
Cassy (13):	"And you sort of pay attention to them and you say 'Oh this is good'."

Erasmus Microman, disliked for many reasons by many children, none the less was praised for this aspect.

Mark (12):	"It makes it more exciting because its got children in it."

Can and Do Children Learn from Science Programmes?

We asked our children whether they could and had learned from science programmes seen at home. There were obviously very different interpretations of learning being used in the answers we received.

Mark[1] (13):	"Well you can watch them (TV programmes) and then go and ask the teacher questions about them."
Cassy (13):	"I don't think I could actually sit down there (at home) and watch a science programme for half an hour and take everything in."
Mark[1] (13):	"Sometimes you can take a bit in."
Samantha (13):	"I don't think you really learn anything because its not what we're doing at school at the moment, its all in the future." (talking about *Tomorrow's World*)
Cassy (13):	"It gives you hopes actually (again talking about *Tomorrow's World*). It gives you a new sensation in the brain - it sort of says - yeah, well I could have that or I could try to get that."

But Gurcharn (12) was more pragmatic and utilitarian:

"Well we had it for homework (Compact Discs) and then it was on (the TV programme) and it explained it to you and that helped."

We then asked about their preferred mode of learning about science topics - books, teachers or TV. The majority agreed that TV was their preferred mode - but they were also aware of the possible negative aspects of TV presentation of information.

Michael (12):	"TV, because it makes it more interesting, its like its directly talking to a radio or tape you can't see the person."
Michael (again):	"TV - I like their sort of computer graphics - um - sometimes the cartoons are OK - sometimes because its just like a simple diagram and you get so indulged (sic) in it - I mean with a book, there's just pages and pages of writing and you can just doze off at any moment ... but if they have these spectacular images - like muscles working - it sort of - um - draws you into the programme and gives it a bit of interest."
Amanda (14):	(of books) "It's just dead, there is no one telling you

176

	anything."
Sarah (13):	"Well the one thing about some (TV) programmes is that sometimes the visual image sort of sidetracks your mind and your watching what is happening on the screen instead of what's coming out of it really - um - what you're listening to."
Cassy (13):	(While agreeing that TV would be her preferred mode of learning science) "When you read you can sort of go back to it - when you watch it, you've just got to take it all in now ... If you're watching something interesting you may be thinking 'well what about this and that' and you can't really answer questions about it because your just in front of a TV."

These comments serve to give the lie to the belief that children are 'couch potatoes.' Clearly they like TV but they appreciate its multi modal channels as possible sources of conflicting or distracting stimulation and its non-interactive dimensions.

While we have indicated above that certain children felt that specific TV 'tricks' were sometimes used inappropriately, the majority felt strongly that - especially in science - the use of models, diagrams, video and computer graphics, and 'trick photography' (e.g. miniaturization) made learning more enjoyable, interesting and possible. The appropriate employment of this technology greatly expands the comprehensibility and understandably of such things as video and compact disc operation, animal behaviour, physical and chemical laws, and the internal workings of the human body.

Cassy (13):	"In the *Living Body* programme it showed you all the joints and all the ribs and cartilage, and we didn't know them off by heart but now you're getting sort of familiar with it."
Sarah (12):	(talking of *Tomorrows World*) "Because they explain it well, everything's sort of pictures and diagrams, and how things work."
Sonia (14):	(talking of *Know How*) "Yes, they show things working and not just describe them - they take them apart."

When asked directly what things they remembered from any science programme that they had watched at home over the last few months, the childrens' recollections were satisfyingly kaleidoscopic - sleep, dreams, cancer, bone growth and breakage, muscle and nerve transplantation, magnetism, electricity, car technology, whales, seals, memory, perception, cognitive dysfunction (amnesia). Having shown them clips from three television science programmes we were pleased to see that they had abstracted the essence of often quite difficult message that was being conveyed. Here then is evidence that children can learn about scientific matters from TV.

From their recounting of previously seen programmes and their comprehension of the wider issues raised by the programmes presented by us, there is cause for optimism that TV may be a very suitable medium for the enhancement of deep understanding of elemental forces and developing technology that touch all our lives.

Conclusion
Whether viewing of information-type programmes takes place or not seems to depend upon the nature of the programme's subject matter, the way it is presented and the personalities of the presenters. In this, then, viewing motivations concerning information-based programmes differ little from the motivating factors present with other television genres we have looked at previously.

If one accepts a fairly catholic definition of information-based programmes, then we find that children, especially as they get older, tend to avail themselves of these programmes. However, it must be accepted that such programmes are not their first choice of viewing.

A major problem children raised about informational programmes was the degree to which they 'made their point' and 'kept to the point' of their discourse. Several children felt that these programmes were often too fast=-paced and, as a result, it was often quite difficult to be clear when one item had finished and another had begun. The children did appreciate that there was limited air-time in a programme but the point they were making was more about how that time was organised and planned for.

While many of our children had attempted to make things demonstrated in various programmes, they seemed to have experienced universal failure. Once again the children felt this could have been better handled by the programmes themselves - for example, by giving warning the week before of materials that may be required on the day.

When children do watch information-based programmes they can become attentive and active evaluators of such programmes. This can be clearly seen by the way they pick up on the social skills of the various presenters. For a presenter to be liked and capable of cultivating programme loyalty in our children they had to be seen to be professional, lively, respectful of guests and non-patronising of their audience. Our children were very sensitive to being "talked down to".

There is evidence in the above interviews that children can learn both the social and personal and the more academic-based information conveyed by the various programmes we asked them about. In terms of science programmes, the older children were also able to make sensible statements about the relative merits of audio-visual versus verbal media as a source of learning. They clearly appreciated that the use of camera techniques and 'special effects' could enliven a programme and make learning more enjoyable, interesting and possible.

There was no clear view, one way or another, as to whether informational programmes could benefit from an injection of 'entertainment', or whether covering one topic in depth or covering several topics at a more superficial level in a programme was better. The children themselves suggested that there may be no simple answer: entertainment could be useful - if used appropriately; a single topic approach is good - but only if the subject matter merits it.

178

10 Discerning young viewers

Television is a persuasive presence in children's lives. They spend many hours every week watching it, although patterns of viewing and programme tastes change as children grow older. As we pointed out, amount of viewing increases up to around age 10-12 and then drops away during teen years. Throughout childhood, however, youngsters in this country spend some 20 or so hours a week in front of the television set.

As the most prominent mass entertainment medium, television is familiar to most people. Most of us have opinions to offer about television in general and about many of the individual programmes we watch - and sometimes even about those we don't watch. Children are no exception. They have things to say about television. It is rare, however, that young viewers are given an opportunity to express their opinions fully and openly. This book reports research which gave groups of children of primary and secondary age just that sort of opportunity. What emerged from this work was that children, even down to age eight, are able to express often lengthy and well-articulated views about television programmes.

The focus of this book has been on programmes rather than issues. Issues, such as the effects of television on children's intellectual, moral and social development, have been adequately covered elsewhere.[1] So too, has the debate about how children watch television.[2] In other words, do youngsters simply sit impassively in front of the screen watching with a lazy eye anything that comes on, or do they deliberate over and select what to watch, paying careful, even critical, attention to programmes?

Although we do not tackle the active-passive issue directly, implicit in the findings we present is support for the "active" view. Children are able to express a variety of opinions about television programmes, some of which are favourable and others less so. They could distinguish the realism and far-fetched qualities of programmes. Furthermore, they were able to articulate insightful criticism of many programmes which displeased them in one way or another.

The qualitative research reported in this book involved semi-structured interviews which guided children through a series of questions, dealing with their experience of different programme areas, becoming progressively more detailed as the interview went on. Using this technique we tried to give the children as much opportunity as possible to express their own views about the programmes with which they were personally familiar.

We felt that it was important to retain some control over the direction of all interviews, because children are prone to go off at tangents and talk about the things which most interest them. While this was allowed to a limited extent, we were always careful not to let the conversation stray too far from the designated theme of each interview. In this way we hoped to be able to obtain freely articulated opinions about programmes which were pertinent to the particular programme area under discussion.

It became clear that children vary in their willingness and their ability to talk about television programmes. Most of the children we interviewed were enthusiastic participants and ready to share with us their views about programmes. Understandably, this ability improved with age, as their use of language got better, but even pre-teenage children had plenty to say.

In this book, we have examined children's opinions about eight broad programme categories which covered drama, entertainment and information programming. In all programme categories we explored children's views about programmes made specifically for their age group as well as about adult programmes. All the programmes about which the children were interviewed were, however, broadcast during what broadcasters designate as *family viewing time*, and went out before the 9 o'clock watershed. After this time, programmes may be broadcast which are not necessarily suitable for young viewers and broadcasters expect parents to share with them the responsibility for what children watch.

During the course of the group interviews the children were asked initially for their spontaneous opinions about the programme area under consideration. Then the interviewer prompted them for more specific opinions about certain programmes or aspects of programmes. At various stages during the hour-long discussion, two or three clips were shown to the children to focus their attention on particular programmes.

We want now to review the major insights into children's experience of television that can be gleaned from their comments and remarks about the programmes they know and watch.

Drama

Drama is a principal component of the television schedules. Drama programmes tend to be among the most expensive items to produce and major drama series occupy prime positions during television's peak-time schedules. Drama series are also made for children and shown in the late afternoon or early evening, during that period traditionally designated as children's viewing time.

We found that children had varied opinions about this type of television. Customary concerns about the influence of contemporary drama on young viewers were not strongly confirmed here. Usual fears stem from the belief that fictional television portrayals may affect children's social behaviour in undesirable ways.[3] Violence on television has been a prime concern throughout the history of the medium.[4] There are additional worries about depictions in adult programmes which expose children to issues and behaviour they are not ready for or do not have the maturity to understand. These are legitimate concerns about the effects of television, which need to be continually monitored. Although this book is not about the effects of television on young viewers, in considering in detail children's opinions about programmes, it does shed some light on how children interpret television content.

What we found was that children held open, and occasionally critical, attitudes towards television drama. There was no doubt that drama programmes were popular as a form of entertainment among young viewers. Individual tastes, of course, did vary. In particular, adult-orientated drama became more popular as children grew older, while children's dramas lost some of their appeal. From what the children said, however, it became clear that television drama is not simply a form of entertainment, it fulfils other functions and has other purposes for the young audience. Contemporary drama especially can teach children a variety of things. Such programmes can impart knowledge about life, show youngsters images from different parts of the world, provide insights into personal and social problems and possible ways to resolve them.

Children comment readily on the realism of television drama. As they grow older, they are able to express more sophisticated opinions, show a better understanding of storylines and so on. With increased age, young viewers are also able to relate events in drama programmes to their own experiences. Children perceive the social lessons of television drama as an important function of such programming, but believe that this kind of subject matter should be handled responsibly. Any drama programme which labels itself as realism is likely to come under close scrutiny by children, who become more critical in their appraisal of it.

Soap Opera

Among the most popular programmes on television are serialised dramas, also known as soap operas. Some of these serials run for years and become associated with specific points in the television schedules. Furthermore, the fictional lives of their characters, as well as the private lives of the actors who play them, regularly feature as news in the daily press. Thus, this form of popular fiction becomes intimately entwined with a subtle, yet pervasive media-hyped 'reality'. After they have been around long enough soap characters become almost like real people.

To what extent are children fooled by all this hype - do they believe that soap operas come from real places and feature the lives of real people? Or are these programmes seen as nothing more than one form of fictional drama, though having occasional lessons for real life?

Soap operas are perceived by children as enduring elements in the television schedules, characterised by cliff-hanger endings and characters who often take on realistic personas. Some soaps are undoubtedly more popular than others. The Australian serial, *Neighbours* was easily the best liked soap at the time of our research. It is important that soaps offer some opportunity for escape and for identification with the characters and settings if they are to involve their audiences. This seems to be especially true with children.

The popularity of *Neighbours* was underlain by all the reasons which typified liking for soaps. Cliff-hangers at the end of each episode together with the realism of the setting and characters were the most mentioned ingredients. The characters were like real people and had real problems with which young viewers could readily identify.

Analysis of soap opera performances in the past have highlighted the clear divide in sex roles.[5] Soaps tend to stereotype the sexes. Of late, some of the glossy US soaps (e.g. *Dynasty*, *Falcon Crest*) have portrayed central female characters in powerful, domineering, matriarchal roles, thus cutting across the traditional soap grain. *Neighbours* has attempted to redress the balance by depicting one leading female character pursuing a career normally seen as the preserve of males - a motor mechanic. This was a source of inspiration and admiration for some of the teenage girls we interviewed. While girls still liked and valued feminine qualities in soap female characters, a little added ambition was welcomed as well.

Boys were generally less willing to reveal an identification with soap characters. Their reluctance seemed to stem partly from a fear of being ridiculed by others for doing so. One exception was an identification with a sibling relationship in *Neighbours*. Here, young male viewers were able to empathise with one character who was seen as being unfairly dominated by his elder brother in the serial.

Learning from soaps. This was a difficult idea for some children to grasp. It never occurred to many of them that they might learn something from a soap opera. Learning was associated more with factual programming such as documentaries, the news and magazine shows. It required further probing and explanation before they began to understand the question being asked. Once they had clicked, a few insights emerged. The children began to recall storylines that had dealt with teenage problems such as drinking, taking drugs and stealing. Furthermore, they were aware that problems in family relationships were also explored in soap operas and could help them to understand similar problems in their own lives a little bit better.

Realism

Neighbours fed impressions of Australia. Older children were less taken in by this serial's portrayal of "down-under" than were younger children. The serial was generally perceived to offer escapism. Turning to a British serial, *Eastenders* was closer to home for these children. They had more reference sources against which to judge the programme. As a consequence they were more critical of the characters and events portrayed in it. Only a few of the characters were identified as being like real people.

Eastenders has covered its fair share of social issues and problems over the years. These have included alcoholism, drug dependency, homosexuality, unemployment, single parenthood and school girl pregnancy. The children had mixed opinions about these portrayals. Some felt that certain storylines could set a bad example for other children. Others felt that there was probably some benefit to young viewers who saw these social problems dramatically played out on screen.

In contrast with *Neighbours*, however, the Albert Square environment of *Eastenders* was seen as drab, unattractive and uninviting. In *Neighbours*, the sun seemed to shine, people were generally happier, and the quality of life was perceived to be far superior to that portrayed in the east end of London. *Eastenders* was, for many of the children we interviewed, often a depressing programme, while they could turn to *Neighbours* to be cheered up.

One significant finding to emerge from our interviews with children about soaps was that television serials are a major source of conversation. Many of the children admitted that they regularly discussed the events of last night's episode of *Neighbours* or *Eastenders*, swapped opinions about how different characters behaved and tried to guess what would happen next in the storyline. Clearly, those children who fail to keep up with what is happening in the most popular television serials are likely to find themselves excluded from the "in-crowd" who do.

Situation Comedy
Sit-coms represent another popular television entertainment genre. Children's understanding of what the genre is, however, was somewhat fuzzy. Some youngsters made reference to stand-up comedians. Others were able to name actual comedy series, thus showing that they had grasped what was being asked about.

Sit-coms have changed in certain respects over the years, though there are still series which stick to the old, cliched formats. The essence of success in sit-coms is that the audience should be able to identify with characters and events. The children we interviewed revealed some of this. But children also like something different. The new breed of "alternative" comedians who emerged during the 1980s were greatly liked. The subtle humour of this form of comedy was appreciated because, as one child put it, much of the humour is so unfunny it's hilarious. The sarcasm and wit of people such as Rowan Atkinson of *Blackadder* were favourite ingredients.

Among the more traditional forms of this genre, liking by children seemed partly to depend on how realistic or 'sugary' were the characters and events portrayed in the shows. The UK sit-com, *No Place Like Home* has a family setting, traditional but nonetheless very funny for children. US shows such as *Family Ties* and *The Cosby Show* were liked, but were perceived to be a bit too good to be true by some children. The UK series just mentioned depicted conflicts and tensions between parents, and their grown-up children who having at various stages flown the nest, had eventually, for different reasons, returned to the family home, much to the chagrin of the father, who believed he had finally got them off his hands.

The US shows depicted two middle-class American families - one white and one black - with both young children and almost grown-up teenagers still in full-time education. While family conflicts and social problems were displayed, prosocial solutions were inevitably found in the end. Both shows emphasized family solidarity and the ultimate dependency of the children on their parents and, moreover, parents' willingness to continue to assume that role. For some of the children we spoke to, these American parents may just have been a little too understanding and 'nice' at times.

In focusing the discussion about situation comedies, we had children make comparisons between three shows: *Me and My Girl* and *Bread* from the UK and *Family Ties* from the US. Clips were shown from these shows as prompts. Differences between children emerged in what aspects of these shows affected their enjoyment. In particular, tastes and preferences changed notably with age.

Enjoyment of sit-coms is partly tied to identification with a character in the show. Identification with leading characters, for instance, can work in different ways. Youngsters become more critical of a leading character's behaviour if they think he is just being plain silly. Obviously, certain tomfoolery is expected in a comedy context, but there is an optimum point beyond which the character will lose credibility. Real silliness is accepted only if the comedy is classified as alternative or zany. Sub-genres of comedy are identified by children and in some cases allowances are made for extremes of characterisation in certain respects. However, the subtle comedy of alternative comedy shows, where such allowances were made, was really only appreciated by the older children (13+) whom we interviewed. For younger, pre-teen children, such humour was mostly beyond their comprehension.

Youngsters would sometimes judge the realism of family interaction in a comedy show against their own experiences at home. This accounted for appreciation of certain aspects of shows, for example, the common sibling rivalry in *Family Ties*. For a simple good laugh, however, today's youngsters seem to settle for cartoons and stand-up comedy in preference to sit-coms. From sit-coms they expect more; here they look to be emotionally stirred up and to experience sadness as well as joy.

Quiz Shows
Television quiz and game shows are widely viewed and enjoyed by children. From the youngsters we interviewed, it emerged that children are familiar with the major quiz shows on television. They have definite likes and dislikes, and these often relate to specific attributes which affect enjoyment of these shows by young viewers. Children watch quizzes and game shows made especially for their age group as well as ones made for family audiences. Children can be fussy about what they like in respect of any of these shows.

In probing further for significant ingredients, we found that game shows in which children themselves can take part is important. This, incidentally, is also true of adults.[6] An important requisite of viewers' enjoyment of quiz shows is that they must be able to test their own general knowledge against that of contestants, or compete with others watching with them at home.

Young viewers also like quizzes and games requiring an element of skill. The contestants must be seen to have to work to win. Luck or chance alone are not enough to maintain the appeal of television quiz and game shows. While young viewers like to see contestants stretched and enjoy being mentally challenged themselves, nevertheless, the game must be relatively easy to follow. In particular, the language must not be beyond their comprehension.

Watching contestants with whom they can identify or have an affinity is also important. Thus, children identify with others in their own age group or who are a little bit older than themselves. Some children reported that they pick sides at the start of the show and root for one contestant or one team throughout. Others were more fickle and claimed to switch their allegiance during the show to whoever was winning.

When asked to say what was meant by a quiz show, children named a number of examples. Making the distinction between a quiz and a game show is more subtle, however, and posed problems for them. Some children had a stab at it. In quizzes, they said, contestants have to answer questions. In game shows, a game element is either central or is added to the quiz part of the show.

Active versus Passive Participation

Passivity was not characteristic of quiz show viewing among children. Children are readily able to identify the features of quiz and game shows which appeal to them. They generally enjoyed the challenge such shows posed to their own general knowledge. As mentioned above, young viewers like to see a proper contest in which contestants are made to work and compete for prizes. They also favour shows in which they can participate themselves. Special effects and gimmicks (moving computer generated graphics) were liked, especially by the youngest children. Prizes offered an important ingredient, giving the show an edge, but they were not more important than the quality of the quiz itself.

Sports Programmes

Sports programmes consume a fairly substantial part of television air time. While the nature and quantity of this coverage is changing we were interested to find out what our young viewers thought of the current and possible future coverage of sport on television.

It was clear that, at least for the boys, they wanted even more, and more varied, coverage. The story was different for the girls. With increase in age, girls appeared to become progressively more disenchanted with televised sport, being attracted, if at all, only by major events - such as Wimbledon or the Olympics.

However, both sexes seemed to appreciate the exposure to *new* sports that the television afforded them. Their only major complaint here was the time at which these 'new' sports were broadcast, in most cases it was much too late at night. As an indication of the favourableness shown to these new, and often minority, sports, several children argued that older, more traditional sports, such as football or horse racing could be cut back to make room for these new activities.

In terms of current viewing patterns, our children preferred to view live extended coverage of events, with edited highlights being a very poor second-best. Where possible, video-recordings were made to allow the children to 'relive' the events of their choice.

In terms of how the events were presented, protracted build-ups and extended in-depth discussion by 'experts' was not particularly favoured. However, discussion with the players or competitors, close to the end of an event was liked by most. It was felt that this allowed the children to get an insight into the player's innermost feelings. This emotional aspect of sport frequently appeared in the children's conversation, and clearly relates to the involvement they feel when a favourite item or player is involved.

Over and above their actual viewing of sport, we were interested to probe the children's views on issues that surrounded sport and sports coverage. Thus, we took the opportunity to ask them about sponsorship, televising of violent sport and of showing violence surrounding sporting events. Here it was clear that, with increasing age, maturity and insight were being gained. Thus, while our younger viewers tended to argue, quite starkly, that neither violent sports, nor violence occurring on the terraces, should be shown (because they could be imitated), our older groups took a more balanced view. On the tricky question of sponsorship of both events and specific teams or individuals, our older viewers appreciated the ambivalence that existed between more money for the sport concerned, and the fact that the money was coming from sources essentially antithetical to health and fitness. Our younger viewers, while they could name numerous sponsors, did not see (or at least could not articulate) this anomaly.

We also questioned the children about satellite and cable television and the implications they thought this had for sports viewing. For those who liked sport on television they welcomed such new developments, seeing in them the promise of more novel sports and more sport overall. For those children not motivated to watch sport on television, their hope was that such dedicated channels would mean that much less sport would appear on the BBC and ITV.

Over and above discussion of sports programmes such as *Sportsnight* and *Midweek Sports Special*, we also found that out children were ready consumers of new television programmes where sporting-type events were the main ingredients. Thus, *Run the Gauntlet* and *Survival of the Fittest* were greatly appreciated, especially the hi-tech vehicles and the daring activities, such as parachuting. These activities were clearly seen to be stimulating interest in our children and thus possibly increasing their future participation in a wider range of sports.

Information Programmes
So far we have looked at children's opinions about TV's entertainment-orientated fare. Television, however, is not simply about entertainment. In addition we asked children about television's information programming. In doing so, we questioned children about their opinions of informational programmes made for their own age group and about those made for wider family audiences.

Children's attraction to factual programmes derived from a number of features: the nature of the programme's subject matter, the way it is presented, and the personalities of the presenters. Audience participation in the programme emerged as another important factor. Among children's programmes, those which included invitations to write or phone in or to enter competitions were highly preferred, while in the absence of that sort of involvement, vicarious participation via seeing children of their own age taking part in the programme was the next best thing.

Awareness of Production Constraints

Children objected to programmes which tried to cram in too much information. At the same time though they realised that programmes had limited airtime. There was some indication that certain programmes were seen as badly planned as far as children were concerned. Children's programmes which tried to show children how to make things, for instance, often did not allow enough time or forewarning for young viewers at home to get the items together that were required.

The style of presenters was important too. Children we interviewed liked professional, lively presenters. Presenters must be respectful and not patronising, and yet they must also be sympathetic to the needs of the young audience.

Learning from Information Programmes

Children themselves thought that they could learn from information programmes. For instance, a programme which told them about different jobs could provide insights into working in particular occupations. These programmes could also provide insights into how to achieve certain occupational goals. The guidance aspect of informational programmes came out specially well in discussion of holiday programmes. According to a few children these programmes can tell you about people and traditions overseas, and show you what it is like in other countries, food that is eaten and so on. Children thus felt that there were additional side-benefits to be obtained from consumer information programmes of this sort, over and above the subject matter on which they were centrally focused.

Science Programmes

As well as information programmes which tell the viewer about social, leisure and consumer matters, there are other programmes on television which deal with science and technology. The former groups of programmes can be linked together through their tendency to deal with practical matters and problems to which viewers need answers. The latter, however, often deal with more abstract matters divorced from or with only an indirect bearing on viewers' own lives.

Among the children we interviewed, many claimed to watch science programmes on television of their own choice and apparently enjoyed them. The programmes they watched included both children's and adult's programmes. Presentation style and the level of the content were critical factors underlying enjoyment. Children did not like being talked down to, nor did they enjoy overly simplistic material. In addition, they seemed to prefer straight information over information embedded in entertainment. There were mixed opinions about whether a programme should have a variety of items or concentrate on a single subject for its entire duration.

Children have curious minds and like to be shown new things in a form that they can appreciate and understand. If the content of a programme is related to things they have done at school, this also tends to be well-received.

In summing up the comments we obtained, the ideal science programme would have a certain amount of detail, though not too much. The detail should be explained clearly and be well-illustrated with good concrete, visible examples. A degree of light-heartedness, where appropriate, can serve to enhance the overall appeal and interest of the programme. The presenters, however, should be serious, though not too serious and they should not talk down to the young audience.

On the question of learning from television science programmes, subjectively the children felt that they could and did learn from television. The visual nature of television certainly enhances its appeal and perceived impact. There were certain shortcomings which some children associated with the medium, however. For instance, when reading you can go back over the material again and go at your own pace. With television the material is presented once and at a pace determined by the producer. Children also felt that on occasions certain tricks were used inappropriately by television. Thus, while the children felt that the use of models, graphics, diagrams, video, etc, in science programmes could enhance learning, they needed to be used properly and in a way that was relevant to the content.

News and Current Affairs

Another ever present feature of the television schedules is news and current affairs programmes. News programmes are probably (together with certain long-running soaps) the most regular feature of television. Occurring mostly at the same times every day, they serve as reliable punctuation marks in the schedules. Television news programmes' regularity add a certain constancy and reassurance to an otherwise turbulent world, full of change.[7]

Television news is widely recognised among adults as the most important news source - for all except the most local of news.[8] The news is not the most popular form of television programming among children, however. It is really not until youngsters begin to develop political awareness and interest, usually in their teens, that they start to pay attention to the news.[9] There are, of course, special news programmes made for the child audience, designed to stimulate interest in current affairs. These have been found to generate some news interest among children, though this still tends to be limited until real political awakening occurs as they approach adulthood.

News programmes, taken at face value, are seen as a series of news items. However, there is much more to the news than that. The programmes have an underlying structure and are characterised by stereotyped modes of production. These are designed both to enhance the entertainment value of bulletins as well as their comprehensibility.[10] The reasons for this include the fact that news programmes must compete for audiences with entertainment-orientated shows and at the same time serve as vehicles carrying to their audiences information about what is happening in the world.[11]

How do children respond to television news programmes? Do they watch them? Do they like them? Can they understand and learn from them? Among those we interviewed, children across all age groups from eight onwards claim to watch at least some news bulletins on television. Only the oldest ones claimed to be regular viewers, however. Some children preferred to get news from newspapers.

There was, among teenagers, a growing interest in surveillance - in other words, monitoring what is going on out there. Some primary-age children also said they were interested in news for this reason. For most of the children we spoke to, watching the news was not determined by any specific interests in news topics, but more by a general concern about what is going on in the world.

News about politics and economic affairs was not liked. Industrial disputes were found somewhat more entertaining, partly because of parental reaction to them. The continuity or serial nature of some news stories drew children back to the news in some instances. Like the continuing storyline of a soap opera, young viewers didn't want to miss the latest developments.

Television news was not the only source of information valued by children. Many liked the depth of newspapers and the fact that absorbing information from papers could be self-paced. Many children were also avid radio listeners and liked to pick up the news on radio.

Biased News?
Children, by and large, thought that the news on television was truthful, but a few thought that it sometimes exaggerated stories unnecessarily, or held back on some details. Mild and subtle distortions were perceived to occur on occasions, especially by teenagers.

Children believed that the news *should* be truthful and should not show things which are untrue. They were also concerned about showing violence or reports about violent events. Younger children were more concerned about this than older ones. Teenagers began to accept that scenes from disasters or wars should be shown "to let you see what happened". The overriding belief was, however, that this should not be done gratuitously, but in the service of providing the public with a realistic picture of events.

Children liked *Newsround* the BBC bulletin made especially for young viewers. They appreciated that it attempted to tell the news in simpler terms, while using standard news presentation techniques to good effect. As they grew older, however, some children began to turn against *Newsround* and criticised it for talking down to them.

Children were shown clips from some news bulletins and were then questioned about the clips afterwards. Recall of information was quite good, in addition to which they also claimed to be able to understand the items. The clips were taken respectively from early evening news programmes on BBC1 and ITV and from *Newsround*.

The need for prior knowledge emerged for some children. Unfamiliar content or subject matter, with unfamiliar terms, inhibited understanding and recall. Background knowledge about an issue has been found to act as one of the most powerful determinants of news comprehension among adults too.[12]

Summing up, children exhibit an active, selective and critical view of the news. Their interest in news grows with age. As they become more active seekers after news, young people become concerned about fairness and truthfulness in news reporting, and also become more perceptive about the way the news is produced and presented.

References

1. Bryant, J. and Anderson, D.R. *Children's Understanding of Television Research in Attention and Comprehension* New York: Academic Press, 1983

    Davies, M.M. *Television is Good for Your Kids.* London: Hilary Shipman, 1989

2. Anderson, D.R. and Loch, E.P. Looking at television: Action or Reaction. In J Bryant and D.R. Anderson (Eds) *Children's Understanding of Television: Research in Attention and Comprehension* New York: Academic Press, 1983

3. Himmelweit, H.T. Oppenheim, A.N. and Vince, P. *Television and the Child: An Empirical Study of the Effects of Television on the Young,* London: Oxford University Press, 1988

    Schramm, W., Lyle, J. and Parker, R, *Television in the Lives of Our Children.* Stanford: Stanford University Press, 1961

4. Gunter, B. *Violence on Television*: Special Issue: *Current Psychology: Research and Reviews.* Transactional Periodicals Consortium, Rutgers University, 1988 (Spring).

5. Durkin, K. Television and sex-role acquisition 1: Content *British Journal of Social Psychology*, 1985, *24*, 101-113

    Durkin, K. *Television, Sex Roles and Children.* Milton Keynes: Open University Press, 1985

    Gunter, B. *Television and Sex Role Stereotyping* London: John Libbey & Co. 1986

6. Gunter, B. Come on Down: A Report on the Popular Appeal of TV Quiz and Game Shows. *Airwaves: Quarterly Journal of the IBA*, 1986, Spring, p9

7. Gunter, B. *Poor Reception: Misunderstanding and Forgetting Broadcast News.* Hillsdale, NJ: Lawrence Erlbraum Associates, 1987

8. Svennevig, M. and McLaughlin, C. *Attitudes to Television in 1989.* London: Independent Broadcasting Authority, Research Report

9. Gunter, B. 1987 *op.cit*

10. Glasgow University Media Group. *Bad News* London. Routledge & Kegan Paul, 1986

    Altheide, D.E. *Creating Reality: How TV News Distorts News Events.* Beverely Hills, CA: Sage, 1976

    Schlesinger, P. *Putting 'Reality' Together:* BBC News London: Constable, 1978

11. Gunter, B, 1987 *op.cit*

12. Gunter, B. 1987, *op.cit*